A.F. Al-Assaf, M.D.

Managed Care Quality

A Practical Guide

CRC Press
Boca Raton   Boston   New York   Washington   London

Acquiring Editor:	Dennis McClellan
Project Editor:	Albert W. Starkweather, Jr.
Cover design:	Denise Craig

Library of Congress Cataloging-in-Publication Data

Catalog record is available from the Library of Congress

Dedication

_____

To my mother for her efficiency
and effectiveness in raising her children;
To my father, the General,
for his sincere pride of my mother;
to Rehab, Ali, and Alia,
the reasons for making this project happen!

Contributors

A. F. Al-Assaf, M.D.. M.S., M.P.H.
College of Public Health
University of Oklahoma
  Health Sciences Center
Oklahoma City, OK

James C. Benneyan, Ph.D.
Department of Mechanical
  and Industrial Engineering
University of Massachusetts
Amherst, MA

Dale O. Bratzler, D.O., M.P.H.
Oklahoma Foundation
  for Medical Quality
Oklahoma City, OK

Tammy Brown, B.A., M.P.H
Tulsa, OK

Ramona Edwards, R.N., M.P.H.
Health Care Consultant
Oklahoma City, OK

Anita Ghosh, M.P.H.
Oklahoma Health Authority
Oklhahoma City, OK

William P. Gideon, M.D., M.P.H.
Health Care Consultant
Norman, OK

Sabra Hopkins, R.N., M.P.H.
Pacificare SecureHorizons
Tulsa, OK

Philip Mosca, M.D., Ph.D.
Welcor America, Inc.
Oklahoma City, OK

Jolee M. Reinke, M.S.N.
University Research Corp.
Bethesda, MD

Douglas Stewart, D.O., M.P.H
College of Medicine – Tulsa
University of Oklahoma Health Sciences
  Center
Tulsa, OK

Vivian Valdmanis, Ph.D.
College of Public Health
University of Oklahoma
  Health Sciences Center
Oklahoma City, OK

Dennis Zaenger, M.P.H.
Washington Hospital
Washington, DC

Preface

Managed care, without a doubt, is the care of the future. It is widely believed some form of managed care will be formulated further, and will dominate the care provided by U.S. health organizations. A few years ago there was a heated debate over whether Canadian health care could be applied in the United States. Voices from both sides of the fence emerged and the proposal, although diminished substantially, led to exactly the outcome the "forces" wanted: a managed care system. Managed care as a system is quite similar to those in Canada and the United Kingdom. Managed care principles are based on the idea that quality care should be provided in the most efficient and effective manner possible. Managed care as a concept theorizes that in the health care delivery system in the United States there always have been costs associated with waste, duplication, and rework. It further postulates that providing appropriate and necessary care will diminish and eventually eliminate those costs, thus rendering a system that is more efficient. In practice this concept is far from flawless, as different interpretations and influences of economic factors have made this concept unacceptable to a considerable number of citizens. Both fee-for-service providers and the misinformed general public stand on the opposite sides of managed care and have sentenced it to be a system that limits access and utilization of services, thus reducing its quality.

Certainly there are flaws. Managed care organizations still are in the learning mode and a number of them closed their doors soon after opening it due to their inability to sustain market pressures. Others, however, are thriving and making considerable achievements in the quality of care and services provided. Collective national health indices are improving continuously. The annual growth rate in health care expenditures is at an all time low compared to double digit inflation rates for most of years before 1992. Health care outcome indicators also show improvements during the past few years. Nonetheless, one should not attribute all of these accomplishments to managed care, but should give some of the credit to those managed care organizations that are "practicing what they preach" — emphasis on health promotion, disease prevention, and coordinated care. These organizations are paving the way to the future of health care delivery in the United States. Future health care will be appropriate care based on need, necessity, and availability of resources.

This book, however, is not on managed care, nor is it written to critique or praise managed care, but rather on how to ensure and manage the quality of services and care coordinated by managed care organizations. Several themes have emerged in relation to quality management, quality improvement, quality assurance, and monitoring. These and several other concepts and methods are defined, outlined, and discussed. It is a book of practical applications and experiences gathered from practicing and experienced health professionals from the field of managed care. They all had a common objective — to bring their experiences to the target audience: practicing health care professionals in the United States and abroad.

What can one accomplish by reading this book?

The chapters are arranged as gradual successive steps based on the practical application of the concept of quality in health care organizations. By following these steps, the reader is able to predict a positive outcome in the implementation strategy of health care quality. This process is augmented with other chapters that support such a strategy for sequencing of the process of implementation. Therefore, there are chapters on cost and quality, accreditation, alternative management strategies, and one on awards for excellence.

- Chapter 1 introduces the concept of managed care and the practices associated with it. It is intended as a true introduction to managed care and by no means is intended to be a comprehensive review. The chapter provides the reader with an overview of managed care, and defines most common terms. The concept is further presented with all its applications. The components of a managed care organization are outlined, including a description of the main positions and services. In particular, there is emphasis on the role of the physician in managed care delivery and administration. The chapter also presents a general outline of the current status of managed care organizations. It concludes with speculation on the expected outcomes of managed care and the future of managed care organizations.
- Chapter 2 is an historical overview of health care quality, starting with the first formal study in the mid 19th century by Florence Nightingale on the effects of nursing care quality during the Crimean War. The chapter takes the reader through time to the present, and shows how managed care has evolved to its present status, where quality is constantly scrutinized by both the public and interest groups.
- Chapters 3 and 4 present the concept of health care quality. One offers definitions and ideas about what is quality, who is a quality professional, and what is the effect of quality on an organization such as a managed care organization. The other presents quality and its meanings from the perspective of a physician and a medical director of a managed care plan. In this chapter, such issues as the role and responsibilities of the medical director are outlined, and a discussion of the issues of data management and communication is presented. These issues are described as paramount to effective medical management and to the quality of managed care organization.
- Chapter 5 presents a step-by-step methodology of implementing quality in a health care organization, with special emphasis on managed care plans. It begins with an introduction of methods of implementing quality, stressing the fact that customizing the process of quality implementation is necessary to achieve the desired objectives and to ensure success of the process. A fair amount of discussion is devoted to the processes of planning at the strategic and operational levels of the organization. Planning, if done correctly and successfully as the chapter outlines, has the potential of achieving positive results to the implementation process and has a

higher chance of succeeding to institutionalize quality in that setting. Once planning is completed, actual activities will take place and the chapter provides a step-by-step discussion of the method of quality implementation at both the strategic and operational levels.

- According to the model outlined in Chapter 3, the three major components of a quality process are quality assurance, monitoring, and improvement. These components are the topics of the next four chapters. Chapter 6 begins to illustrate the relationship between quality planning, the setting of standards, and the active communication of standards under the heading of quality assurance activities. Planning is further emphasized as an important process of introducing quality in a health care organization. This process is followed by a number of activities and tasks that may affect a wide range of disciplines and personnel to set and communicate the standards of care or services of that organization. Active communication is stressed, where personnel actively are soliciting input and participation from the target audience in complying with those standards. This discussion leads to Chapter 7 on monitoring, where the methodology and application of monitoring and quality control is outlined. The chapter presents several scenarios and examples on how to apply specific monitoring principles to real-life situations. What makes this chapter a strong one is that it is written by the medical director of a state peer review organization whose the main job has been to monitor the care provided by providers. His experience in the areas of monitoring, care review, and quality control is of high caliber and extremely valid.

- Chapters 8 and 9 concentrate on quality improvement. The first, written by an international health care quality consultant, presents comprehensive guidelines on the tools, skills, and methods used by health care organizations to improve quality. Each tool is described and an example provided to show its use and construction. Team-building skills and steps of forming effective teams are highlighted, and a comprehensive presentation of the roles of team members also is provided. Chapter 9 continues the discussion on quality improvement using the U.S. Preventive Medicine Task Force Guidelines as an example of the application of quality improvement tools in a managed care setting. Validity of the chapter is authenticated as it is written by a pediatrician and a preventive medicine specialist.

- Chapter 10 is on "lessons learned." It combines years of experiences in the implementation of health care quality in different settings and different countries. The chapter discusses the concept of institutionalization and sustainability of quality processes in health care organizations. It suggests that to sustain quality the organization must follow all the steps of implementation, including the processes of planning, quality assurance, monitoring, and quality improvement. All of these processes must be coordinated by a qualified system of participatory management and efficient operation. A number of lessons are presented to caution the health care organization about failure as processes are introduced and completed without due attention to details.

- The relationship of cost and quality is outlined in Chapter 11. The three types of quality costs; failure, appraisal, and prevention are described. The economics of health care quality also is presented and reference is made to the practice of total quality management (TQM), and its involvement in efficiency and effectiveness in organizations. The chapter provides an analysis of the economics of managed care and the effect that it might have on cost reduction.
- Chapters 12, 13, and 14 present three main issues important to health care organizations in general and to managed care in particular — accreditation, certification, and alternative management strategies, all of which contribute to the competitive nature of managed care, particularly non-price competition. The issue of setting standards and complying with them is paramount to achieving accreditation or a national award. Such organizations as the National Committee on Quality Assurance, the Joint Commission, the Malcolm Baldridge Awards, as well as the ISO-9000 series certifications, are highlighted in these chapters. Alternatives quality management strategies to the traditional approaches are discussed in Chapter 13. Here, such issues as demand management, risk-sharing arrangements, business coalitions, patient-focused care, report cards, and re-engineering are described briefly to give the reader a short introduction to these strategies, thus sharing the other perspectives of management that can be applied and are applied in some managed care organizations.

The purpose of this book is to introduce the reader to the methods, desired skills, and the practices of health care quality and its application in managed care organizations. Even though managed care organizations are focused on, the book can be used as effectively in learning the different techniques and tasks associated with health care quality as applied to other health care organizations. Several examples are applicable to hospitals, as well as ambulatory care organizations. In all cases, the book is been intended to present practical applications and practical solutions to questions related to health care quality. It is written for the health professional, current and future, by well experienced and highly credentialed health care professionals.

Therefore, the book deliberately is written for both practitioners and learners. Although its objectives are obvious to the practitioner, it should be as clear to the student of health care administration, nursing, medicine, allied health, pharmacy, and quality of all levels. For all these individuals, this book is equally helpful in learning the concept and the application of health care quality. This book has been supplemented with a number of practical examples and tools that should be beneficial to the average learner of these fields. Instructors are encouraged to use it as the main textbook in such courses as quality management, managed care, and principles of health care leadership and management. The principles and the concepts discussed in this book are highly applicable to general as well as specialized management techniques.

A. F. Al-Assaf, M.D.
Oklahoma City, OK, 1997

Contents

1 Managed Care: An Introduction

Ramona Edwards

CONTENTS

Managed care is a term commonly used to describe an array of health care delivery and payment systems, including health maintenance organizations (HMOs), preferred provider organizations (PPOs), and point-of-service plans (gatekeeper PPOs). Included in this range are a number of variants and hybrids of these plans. The term managed care has produced an expectation of cost containment by limitations imposed on access and exertion of external controls, and theoretically can include any medical expense plan that attempts to contain costs by controlling the behavior of participants (Beam, 1995). The behavior of both the provider and the health care recipient is influenced and controlled to some extent by the health plan itself. It is the control of behavior that makes managed care unique and sets these plans apart from those plans which merely serve as discount care brokers.

Elements of managed care can be seen in many traditional medical expense programs. Methods employed by these plans usually discount payment, restrict choice to those providers who agree to accept discounted fees, and may have some rudimentary forms of utilization management. The evolution into a true managed care plan combines the elements of restriction of choice through use of contracted providers, control of behavior of both participants and providers through external systems, the control of benefits and payment mechanisms, and a continuous effort to assure and improve the quality and types of care delivered.

Payment methods also will separate a true managed care plan from a managed care lookalike. Traditional medical expense plans, service plans, such as Blue Cross and Blue Shield and major medical plans written by both stock and mutual insurance companies (life insurance and some property-casualty companies), *indemnify*, or compensate for medical expenses after they are incurred. Health maintenance organizations often prepay for high volume services, empowering the practitioner to deliver services which are preventive in nature, allowing a practitioner the freedom to do testing that is needed, rather than worrying about costs. An example of this is a prepaid laboratory services contract, where a reference laboratory is paid on a capitated basis — a fixed monetary amount paid monthly for each member whether the service is used or not. This frees the practitioner to order necessary lab work instead of having to consider the cost of each test on a fee for service basis. Thus, plans which have the appearance of being restrictive, actually may allow greater freedom of application of health practice by allowing a wider range of services than the traditional medical expense plan.

It is the restrictive nature of these plans which leads one to question whether people covered by managed care plans receive the same quality of care as those covered under unrestricted traditional medical expense plans. Does loss of freedom of choice in itself reduce quality of care? Conversely, does freedom of choice, which includes patient self-diagnosis and self-referral, allow the patient greater quality of care?

These are difficult questions to answer, for quality depends upon the purpose of the managed care entity. If the purpose of the plan is solely to save money, then quality will suffer. If the purpose of the managed care plan is to provide appropriate care in a cost-effective environment, then quality of care will increase. This assumption is based on the adage: "Poor quality medicine is expensive medicine." The inference that uncontrolled systems are fraught with waste, and are expensive, lead many employers to seek "managed care plans" in attempts to save premium money. Employers may be lured into those plans which save money without the other components which make a true managed care plan effective: that of delivering appropriate, quality care in a cost-effective manner.

To be identified as a true managed care plan, a plan must have the following components:

- restricted networks which involve control of payment for services,
- benefits designed to maximize intervention,
- aggressive care management, the goal being to do what is appropriate for the patient as quickly as possible to achieve the maximum quality of outcome (NAMCP, 1995),
- a quality improvement program which strives to increase quality of care processes and outcomes, and
- data gathering and dissemination of information regarding the state of health and health activities of the population served.

HMOs have these components more often than PPOs or other organizations. The primary characteristic which differentiates a true managed care plan from an insurance plan is that insurance is a payer of claims, wile a managed care plan is a provider of health services. Because HMOs most often have that characteristic, it is the HMO that will be used as the managed care paradigm for the remainder of this discussion.

DEFINITIONS AND TYPES OF HMOS

In order to understand managed care concepts, it is important that one understand the many acronyms and definitions which have developed with the industry. This list is basic, and will certainly be lengthened as new acronyms and definitions are added in this rapidly changing industry.

Capitation A prospective payment to a provider paid on a per capita basis. Rates usually are adjusted based on demographics, such as age/sex, for primary care services, or based on the type of service provided, such a clinical laboratory, mental health or medical subspecialty services.

Case management A process by which individual patient care is managed by a plan to assure appropriate, cost-effective treatment in a timely manner. Case management an element of the utilization management process.

Closed-panel plan A plan in which members must obtain services from practitioners within the plan network if benefits are to be paid. There are no out-of-plan benefits.

Cost containment Restrictions applied to control benefit costs by reducing claims amounts, reducing the volume of claims through capitation, and minimizing administrative costs associated with administering benefit plans (subcontracting to provider organizations through risk sharing arrangements).

Fee schedule A list of procedures and benefits which specifies the maximum fee that will be paid to a provider of benefits. Fee schedules may be based on "usual and customary" fees in a community, may be relative value based, may be based on per diem rates, or case/procedure rates.

Gatekeeper PPO (Point of Service PPO) A preferred-provider organization that requires a participant to select a primary care physician if in-network benefits are desired. The participant may self refer within or out of the network, for a lesser benefit and higher copayment or deductible.

Group model HMO (group practice model) A closed-panel HMO under which a group of physicians provide services to HMO members. The physicians are employees of the group and not the HMO. The group may have centralized administrative offices. The group, and not the individual physicians, have the contractual relationship with the HMO to provide services for its members.

Health maintenance organization (HMO) A health care system that provides comprehensive health services to enrolled persons living within a specific geographic region. HMO is responsible for both delivering and financing health services.

Health Maintenance Organization Act A federal act passed in 1973 which defined the federally qualified HMO. The act required some employers to offer the HMO option, and it mandated benefits, many of which were preventive in nature. These preventive health benefits represented a shifting of traditional public health services into the private sector.

Independent Practice Association (IPA) An HMO under which individual physicians form a legal and management entity. The IPA may or may not include small group practices. The physicians maintain their own offices, and use the

IPA to bargain, contact, and control practice patterns of the individual physicians. These physicians may see both HMO and traditional medical expense patients.

Major medical insurance   A traditional medical expense plan designed to provide protection against catastrophic medical expenses. Participant expenses usually are in the form of deductibles and coinsurance.

Managed care   A process used to deliver cost-effective care without limiting quality or access. This is achieved by controlled access to providers, comprehensive regulatory controls, emphasis on preventive care, risk-sharing, quality, and behavior modification of both the participants and providers.

Maternity management   Formalized programs of maternity management by which potential high risk mothers are identified through use of intensive risk appraisal, and early intervention of problems associated with those risk factors is implemented.

Medical loss ratio   The amount of expenditure for medical claims divided by the total premium income.

Medical screening programs   Wellness programs designed to identify risk factors and medical conditions before they become severe and result in large medical expense claims. The health risk appraisal is a tool commonly used for this purpose. Issues addressed include lifestyle habits, cholesterol screening, hypertension screening, past symptoms and treatment, and review of medications.

Member   A covered insured who is enrolled in a managed care plan.

Mixed model HMO   An HMO which has characteristics of two or more of the basic HMO types. An HMO may have both group model and IPA or network model contracts. This occurs most frequently when an HMO is forced to change model types to meet market demands.

National Committee for Quality Assurance (NCQA)   A nonprofit organization that accredits managed care organizations. NCQA has established standards and a quality measurement program to help consumers evaluate the quality of care provided by managed care plans.

Network Model HMO   An HMO that contracts with independent physicians or groups of physicians to provide medical services to members.

Open-ended HMO   An HMO option which allows members to go outside the HMO provider network. Payment of services often is less than that paid for in-network services and involves higher copayments and may invoke deductible.

Plan   Refers to any managed health care plan regardless of type or organization structure.

Preferred Provider Organization   An organization sponsored by an insurance company or by providers themselves in which agreement is made to provide medical care services at a reduced rate.

Reasonable and customary (*also* **Usual and Customary**)   Provider charges that fall within a range of fees normally charged for a procedure within a geographic region.

Relative value fee schedule   Fees based on procedural units and multiplied by a conversion factor to determine the fee paid.

Staff model HMO   A delivery system that owns facilities and providers (physicians) are employees of the HMO.

Third-party administrator (TPA) An organization contracted to provide administrative services such as claims payment, utilization review, and customer service.

Utilization management A group of processes used to review appropriateness and quality of care. These processes encompass prevention and wellness, demand management, utilization review, peer review, which includes practice guideline implementation and monitoring, and case management.

There are other terms that may be used or are related to the managed care industry and the reader is directed to two references that have listed a comprehensive list of terms related to managed care. These are:

Managed Care: A Resource Guide for a New Language, 1995. (Oklahoma State Department of Health, Oklahoma City, OK)

Managed Care Glossary, Texas Medical Association, Medical Student Section, Austin, TX, 1996.

THE MANAGED CARE CONCEPT

The managed care concept involves understanding health care delivery systems based upon the components of access, expense, and efficiency. The ideal organizational structure of such a delivery system should be formed so as to minimize bureaucracy, thus making the delivery system itself as transparent to the consumer as possible. The HMO Act of 1973 and the subsequent additions to this act established minimum standards for the industry to provide these components.

Access. The measurable outcomes of access to care generally are measured by customary health statistics. These include, but are not limited to infant mortality rates, immunization rates, and average life expectancy. The inherent design of HMO regulations broadens access to care by defining premium rating structure, mandating services, requiring geographic access standards, limiting out-of-pocket expenses, and limiting eligibility clauses designed to protect the insurer from adverse risk. The most serious failing of U.S. health care is the failure to guarantee access to care (Woolhandler, 1990).

Premium rating limitations allow access to the health delivery system by keeping premiums within an affordable level for the consumer. Prior to 1988, HMOs were limited to a **community rating** system and its variants. Community rating uses the same rate structure for all subscribers, regardless of their past claims experience or potential loss. This rating system applies to both group and individual coverage. The community rating approach which began with Blues plans, fulfills the HMO mandate that coverage should be available to the widest range of persons at an affordable cost (Beam, 1995) The 1988 amendment to the HMO act permitted HMOs to establish advance rates for a single employer of more than 100 employees, based on that employer's claims experience (Beam, 1995). The advance rate cannot be more than 10% higher than the other community rates used in the HMO. Rating methods used by traditional insurers include **manual rating** and **experience rating**. Manual rating established premium rates for broad classes of group insurance business.

Claims experience is included as part of the aggregate claims experience for the entire business class. Experience rating considers an individual group's claims experience when determining the premium rate for that group. Premium rates can be a barrier to access. Managed care plans are required to reduce that barrier.

Mandated service requirements assure that comprehensive health services include those services necessary to promote health, prevent disease and permit acute care diagnosis and intervention. These health service requirements are usually listed in the HMO schedule of benefits, and are uniform throughout the industry. These service benefits include physicians' services, outpatient services (diagnostic and treatment), inpatient hospital services, short term rehabilitation services, emergency health services, mental health services, diagnostic laboratory and diagnostic and therapeutic radiology services, home health services, and preventive health services. Preventive health services include family planning, infertility, well-child care from birth, eye and ear examinations, pediatric and adult immunizations.

It is within these mandated service requirements that the HMO Act successfully moved traditional public health preventive services from the public to the private sector. Traditional medical insurance at that time did not cover preventive care service while most medical insurance carriers sought to indemnify a person against catastrophic medical expenses.

Geographic access standards are subject to HMO regulation. The HMO must have services which are available and accessible to each enrollee within reasonable promptness. These services include geographic location, hours of operation, and emergency services which are available and accessible 24 hours a day, seven days a week. These provisions assure access to the enrollee when services are needed, and does not place the enrollee in the position of having to "shop" for health care.

Out-of-pocket limits are subject to state and federal regulation. These regulations attempt to limit the effects of underinsurance, a situation in which a person has insurance but, because of high deductibles, copayments and exclusions, finds that using the insurance for a major illness may well impoverish him (Woolhandler, 1990). Regulations also may specify that an HMO cannot impose copayment changes that exceed 50% of the total cost of providing a services or services to an enrollee. An HMO also may not impose copayment charges which exceed 200% of the total annual premium. This ensures that copayments are not a barrier to the utilization of health services or enrollment in the HMO (OSDH, 1996).

Eligibility clause limitations imposed upon HMOs. Traditional carriers have limited risk through the use of exclusions and limitations of benefits. This attempt to prevent adverse selection of a plan also included preexisting clauses which limited or excluded payment for any illness or injury or limited payment after a qualifying period elapsed after the issuance of the insurance policy. HMOs may not limit enrollment nor coverage based on health status, health care needs, nor age of an enrollee (OSDH, 1996). The existence of this regulation lowers barriers to obtaining health services.

Expense. Cost containment has been a major emphasis of HMOs. Available health care dollars are limited. Both employers and governmental entities who purchase health care have turned to managed care as a means for reducing the national health care debt. Unfortunately, some employers place emphasis only upon projected cost savings and ignore the associated benefits of managed care delivery such as health promotion programs. Employer groups of less than 500 employees tend to look at cost and provider selection in choosing a managed care system. Employers with more than 500 employees tend to look at quality indicators in addition to cost savings, and have the sophistication to see the correlation between price and quality (McBride, 1996).

Managed care cost containment is based on the concept of risk. The basis of risk is the awareness that all components of the system, (payers, physicians, patients, facilities, and ancillaries) must share congruent incentives in order to achieve maximum cost effectiveness (NAMCP, 1995). Shared risk among all participants imparts a sense of ownership to employer, provider and the health plan. The sense of ownership coupled with shared risk agreement should lead to cost reductions by giving all participants an incentive to become more cost effective.

While traditional insurers pay for physician services on a fee-for-service basis, either at billed charges or with a percentage discount, most HMOs pay for some services on a capitated basis as part of risk sharing arrangements. Capitation is money paid to a provider on a per capita basis prior to delivery of services for each member the provider expects to serve. This money is a fixed amount. The amount may be demographically adjusted (primarily age/sex) for primary care services, or may be fixed based upon the type of service the provider agrees to provide. Fixed capitation would be applicable for services such as mental health, allergy, pharmacy, or clinical laboratory, where the amount is based upon the aggregate population, and intensity of service may not vary according to demographic variables.

Mode of compensation is being increasingly scrutinized as a quality issue. Capitation, while not inherently so, sometimes is targeted as a reason for doctors to withhold care (Spragins, 1995). Fee-for-service reimbursement encourages a "more is better" mentality of delivering services; more services maximize more reimbursement. Capitation encourages maximizing volume while limiting services. While there are no valid comparisons between reimbursement mechanisms and quality of care, anecdotal evidence is enough to prompt responsible HMOs to look carefully at physician reimbursement issues. HMOs must find a medium where both services and reimbursement are appropriate. It is the responsibility of the HMO to find the acceptable service range where neither underutilization nor overutilization practices are rewarded.

The risk sharing concept prompts the problem of divided loyalties. Traditionally, physicians have stated that their loyalty is to the patient (Hillman, 1991). However, that sentiment may be argued against based on the escalation of health care costs, that some physician loyalty shifted to maximization of income without regard to optimization of care after the advent of health insurance reimbursement. Managed care demands for shared risk divides physician loyalty between the patient and the health plan. The inference is made that divided loyalty may compromise care. It then becomes the responsibility of the plan to balance incentives and reimbursement with practice guidelines to allow the physician to concentrate on providing appropriate health care.

It also is the responsibility of the HMO to determine its mission, its philosophy of delivering care, and to define its responsibility to the member. It is after that definition is made, that the HMO can decide how much money should be dedicated to medical claims payments. One measurement of this decision is reflected by the **medical loss ratio**. The medical loss ration (MLR) is the amount of medical expenses paid divided by the premium income. Simply stated, the MLR shows how much money is spent on medical care instead of administration and overhead (Spragins, 1995). Although MLR alone is not a sole indicator of quality, there seems to be a correlation between perception of quality and MLR. The higher the MLR, the better the quality rating (Spragins, 1995). The best rated mature HMOs have a medical loss ratio between 87 and 96. A ratio above 96 indicates that the plan may not be financially sound, for the medical costs exceed premium income. A ratio below 87 indicates that a plan may be spending too much on administration or is skimming profits before medical expense budget is set.

Efficiency is an integral part of the managed care concept. A managed care plan must have money to pay for health care, but it is imperative that this money be spent wisely. Efficiency of health care delivery is paramount in producing a viable plan. Efficiency can be fostered by development of several approaches (NAMCP, 1995). It should be noted here that the relationships between cost and quality of care has been described in detail in Chapter 11 of this book.

Team building among both physician and non-physician providers is vital to the shared risk idea. Physicians historically have been poor team players (Delbecq, 1990). Integrating physicians with nonphysician providers (case managers and therapists) in order to plan appropriate treatment for patients is difficult but vital to the efficiency of a plan. This team building must be achieved through physician acceptance. Plans which to not achieve physician acceptance fail (Shulkin, 1995).

Integration of delivery systems is a plan's responsibility, where the treatment becomes transparent and seamless to the patient. Emphasis should be placed on the holistic treatment of the patient by provision of those services available within the plan; preventive, mental health, medical. Replacement of a fragmented specialty driven treatment regimen with an integrated team headed by the primary care physician is more efficient and more cost effective.

The creation of **congruent financial and performance incentives** for all providers has been discussed in the previous section on finance. Many plans place performance incentives solely at the primary care level. This strategy produces disproportionate burden on the primary care physician to manage care cost-effectively without placing any responsibility on the specialist. An efficient plan applies rules and incentives at all provider levels.

The **definition of best practices and requiring use of accepted standards of clinical practice** not only is a means of assuring uniformity, but also provides a structure from which to measure the treatment process and patient response (outcomes). These clinical practice guidelines are instructions on how a health care provider should or should not act in specific clinical situations (Hillman, 1991). Issuance of specific practice guidelines or "expectations" of clinical practice forces physicians who, under traditional fee for service practice, choose not to keep abreast of new treatment regimens, to do so.

Concepts of disease prevention and promotion of healthy lifestyles were embodied in the HMO Act. Attempts to change behavior produce results slowly. Outcomes

from these programs do not show immediate positive financial impact, and have
been underdeveloped in many managed care programs. Some high quality plans
have dedicated prevention and wellness programs. Others have thrust prevention and
wellness into the marketing effort as a competitive gimmick. The problem with
prevention and wellness programs is that it is the HMO member who is the risk-
sharer. Members must be educated about cost-effectiveness (NAMCP, 1995). Many
members have an entitlement attitude toward any insurer, and must be educated
about their ability to impact their own health. This requires aggressive effort by all
providers as well as the plan staff. HMOs have developed strategies to increase
member responsibility. These strategies are known collectively as **demand management** as described in Chapter 13 of this book.

COMPONENTS OF MANAGED CARE PROGRAMS
AND ORGANIZATIONAL STRUCTURE

Five distinguishing characteristics of a managed care plan were identified in the
introduction to this chapter: (1) restricted network and control of payment for
services, (2) benefits designed to maximize intervention, (3) aggressive care management, (4) formal, organized quality improvement, and (5) data gathering and
dissemination of information.

The functional components of an HMO which, when fully operational, blend to
create the unique health care delivery system that is an HMO. These components
are discussed in terms of functionality and do not imply organizational reporting
structure.

The **board of directors** or governing board is a committee whose purpose is to
be accountable to the owners. It is the responsibility of the governing board to
identify the wishes of the owners and carry out directives as effectively as possible
(Griffith, 1994). It is the responsibility of the governing board to be responsible for
everything that goes on in an organization, as well as what might go on (Griffith,
1994). Essential functions of the governing body are:

1. to appoint a chief executive officer.
2. to establish the mission, vision and plans.
3. to approve the annual budget.
4. to monitor performance against plans and the budget.
5. to be responsible for the quality of care the plan delivers.

Board membership will differ depending upon the structure of the HMO; whether
the HMO is for profit, not-for-profit, provider owned, independently owned, or
owned by an insurance company. There are regulations governing the membership
and responsibility of the board, as well as requirements by accrediting bodies such
as those promulgated by NCQA or JCAHO.

Measures of governing body performance are profitability, pricing against com-
petitor plans, access to care, patient satisfaction, employer satisfaction, provider
satisfaction and employee satisfaction.

The **chief executive officer** is required to implement decisions of the board and to assist the board in making decisions (Griffith, 1994). This individual is the key manager for the plan. It is this individual who fulfills the vision and mission of the plan. This individual is responsible for the operational aspects of the plan, although the operational implementation may be delegated to a subordinate. The chief executive officer is responsible for general administrative operations and public affairs. These operations include but are not limited to general plan operations, human resources management, legal services, public relations, health services and quality improvement.

The **human resources department** is responsible for establishing and administering benefits, compensation, hiring, recruitment of plan employees. Functions are similar to any human resources department.

The role of the **legal services department** is directly affected by the nature and risk of the product sold. Health care is subjective in nature and it is particularly important that contract language, benefits language and interpretation be consistent and in accordance with the many regulations governing this industry. Health care involves many interpretations and expectations by both providers and consumers. This leads to frequent disputes. The legal department must offer opinions involving thousands of dollars in potential liability. The legal department also may be responsible for fraud investigation and risk management. **Corporate affairs** may be a function of the legal department or may be separate in larger plans. The role of corporate affairs is to keep abreast of the legislative activity which involves the plan and to intervene appropriately in lobbying efforts which set health care policy.

The **quality department** is responsible for overseeing all quality management activities. This includes guiding departments in the setting of standards, aid in design of quality measurement, report of findings and impact of improvement initiatives. It is this department which is responsible for building cohesiveness between all departments, the providers and customer. This department usually is responsible for gaining and maintaining accreditation, and for fulfilling regulatory reporting requirements. This department has the responsibility to report status of quality indicators to the board of directors.

The **chief financial officer** or finance director is responsible for the oversight of financial and accounting operations. This person is responsible for the initial development and analysis of the plan and appraisal of the overall operating results. This person is responsible for establishing and overseeing the management and enforcement of underwriting practices and policies in a manner that will meet the objectives of both the financial and marketing goals of the plan. Finance functions may include billing and collections, management information services, enrollment, accounting, and underwriting. Billing and collections involves billing of premiums and collection of premium income. It is imperative that billing be notified of changes in employment status within all employer groups, and that collections notify the enrollment department when an employer or member is past due on payment of premiums. Most companies allow a grace period for premium payment. However, enrollment must be prepared to disenroll groups within terms of the group master contract when premiums are not paid. If a plan offers more than one type of coverage such a life insurance, disability insurance, or dental insurance, in addition to the managed care coverage, billing may be combined into one monthly statement.

The **underwriting department** examines the risk the plan is to assume before agreeing to cover a group. Particular attention is paid to determining if a prospective group meets underwriting guidelines. Underwriting guidelines include verification that the group is a legitimate business entity that does not exist sole to obtain health care coverage, medical claims history of the group, and existing diseases within the group population which may cause increased risk to the plan, demographics of the group, and financial stability of the group. Underwriting not only rates new groups, but also examines claims trends on existing groups in order to decide if the plan can continue to assume risk for a group. Rates may be adjusted from year to year with a rate ceiling established for some groups based on medical loss. These rate ceilings may be guaranteed for a three–five year period. Underwriting of small business is subject to specific state legislation and varies from state to state. Some HMO products may be sold on a **guaranteed issue** basis; that is, a rate is guaranteed without underwriting evaluating the medical risk of the group. Some group products may be sold as **guaranteed to issue**, where a rate may be adjusted within a narrow range based upon the medical risk of the group. Underwriting guidelines for HMOs are unique to HMO rules and regulations and are considerably different for traditional indemnity underwriting.

Management information services works at the heart of the managed care plan. Data management and interpretation is the bricks and mortar of a managed care plan. Management information services has the dubious function of "being all things to all people" in a managed care plan. It is this service which must be operational all the time for all departments. Not only is data required for the internal operations of the plan, but also it is vital to determining the operational efficiency of the plan. Mundane operations such as printing member identification cards are an inherent part of MIS services. Maintenance of enrollment files, patient authorization files and claims files requires strict adherence to quality data management methods. Information management is so critical, that one accrediting body has a complete subsection dedicated to it. Information management must assure complete confidentiality of patient information, for this data is as sensitive as that contained in the medical record.

The **marketing director** is the key person responsible for marketing the plan. The **marketing department** is essential for the survival of any plan. Most financial planning is based upon growth projections which result from marketing research of the HMO service area. Marketing includes oversight of marketing representatives, broker relations, advertising, enrollment forecasting, and client services. Marketing processes are specialized and complex. Processes change frequently due to demands from employers, organized labor and regulatory agencies (Beam, 1995).

Marketing representatives are commonly salaried employees of the HMO who receive commission. HMOs also may market through brokers who are agents of the buyer rather than the HMO. Brokers are compensated solely on a commission basis. Brokers may specialize in other types of insurance such as life insurance and not be familiar with managed care. The HMO should make every effort to educate brokers about managed care and maintain quality broker relationships. It is conceivable that brokers should also be allowed to enter into risk sharing agreements with the managed care entity. Marketing representatives may also work with benefits consultants who are hired by employers to recommend health coverage.

The buyers of health care include employers, trusts and associations (Beam, 1995). Some insurers will not underwrite trusts or associations. Approximately half of all employee benefit plans are written for groups of less than 25 employees. These groups, usually defined as small group accounts, account for 50 percent of plans but only 10–15% of total dollar volume (Beam, 1995). States which have passed small group insurance reform acts usually define a small group as a group of less than 50 employees. Small group business is labor intensive for the plan and has inherent increased risks based on size alone.

Twenty-five to 30 percent of employer groups have 25–100 employees. These groups account for 10 percent of group benefit plans, but represent 25 percent in total dollars. Groups of 500 or more employees represent half of the benefit dollars spent (Sadler, 1995).

Marketing must not only sell accounts, but must service those accounts. Service after the sale keeps the confidence of these insured and continues to keep the group at renewal (Soule, 1994). Marketing representatives may service the accounts they sell, or the account may be turned over to a service specialist, a marketing representative specially trained to retain groups. Good service not only increases the employer's satisfaction, but minimizes the possibility of losing a group at renewal time.

The **operations director** or chief operating officer usually oversees the claims department, customer service, office management and other operational functions. Operations if responsible for setting performance standards, internal quality control and management reporting. **Claims administration** requires unparalleled service and accuracy. It is here that the true worth of a policy is measured, and it is here that the insurer has its most important communication and interface with the consumer (Soule, 1994). Claims administration, customer service, and health services are the most highly visible services to the consumer. Two of these three service areas are assigned to operations. It is in these areas that quality indicators measure the response of the plan and predict consumer reaction.

Customer service involves servicing and communication with the managed care member. The importance of this function cannot be underestimated, as it is frequently the consumer's only contact with the plan and may determine the image of the plan (Nash, 1994). Customer service not only services the members, but the providers as well. A managed care plan must service both providers and members, for without one group, the other has no reason to exist.

The **medical director** and associates are responsible for quality of care, provider recruiting, provider reimbursement, peer management, utilization management, credentialing and medical policy. care management is critical to the managed care effort. The success or failure of a plan largely depends upon care management function to control medical costs, yet not withhold necessary care. The continuum of care management starts with demand management. Demand management is the portion of the plan which puts the patient into the risk sharing concept. Utilization management involves inpatient critical pathway management, clinical practice guidelines management, case management and individual disease management. These functions are measured in terms of outcome data and practice profiling of physicians. The medical director must monitor and report on expected vs. actual quality of care performance and target improvement areas. This is best achieved through the judicious use of other plan physicians who are cultivated to look at issues and lead or participate in peer activities.

The medical director and the associated departments for health service delivery also are responsible for benefit interpretation and administration. This is in contrast to indemnity insurance plans where benefits administration and case management are historically claims department functions.

Prevention and wellness services are an integral part of health service delivery. These services start with the evaluation of a member through the use of a health risk appraisal. The member's health risk is assessed and the results communicated to the primary care physician and to the member. All members are encouraged to adopt healthier lifestyles, and are reminded to receive regular screening and preventive services. These services may include immunizations, mammogram screening, PAP smears, prostate exams, and prenatal care. It is from this function that the basic public health services mandated by the HMO Act are delivered.

ROLE OF PHYSICIANS

Managed care plans which score high ratings in the marketplace are successful because of close relationships with physicians (Spragins, 1996). HMOs which carry out all the functions of delivering care, but do not ask physicians for input into HMO operations, fail to recognize the physician as a customer as well as front line delivery person of the very product the HMO sells: health care. At the entry level to the system is the primary care physician. This physician has been named the "gatekeeper" of the system. The term "gatekeeper" implies that the physician only controls initial access to the health delivery system. In the traditional insurance system, it is the patient who enters and navigates the system on his own. If not initiated to the system, the patient may travel the wrong route, thus increasing charges and delaying diagnosis. Therefore, the role of the primary care physician is more than that of the gatekeeper, it is that of "guide" through the maze of health delivery. This person should be as any other guide; knowledgeable of the terrain, have demonstration of competency, have proven success in health care delivery, and employed to keep the safety and success of the member in mind, while providing efficient and quality care.

The managed care plan determines the competence of the physician through a process known as **credentialing**. This process, while cursorily carried out, may not determine competence unless standards are developed and rigorously applied to all applicants. The managed care plan should as a minimum conduct primary credentialing verification and not rely on information provided by providers or hospitals. The credentialing standards should apply to all practitioners, not only physicians. These standards, when applied, should tell the consumer that this provider meets absolute standards of training and practice performance.

The credentialing process should be done more than once, usually every two years. This repeat process known as **recredentialing**, uncovers any adverse information related to physician practice during the preceding two-year period. The process also allows the plan to incorporate any practice patterns documented during the previous two year period. The process is done by practitioners for practitioners. This is part of the **peer management** process.

In addition to assuring that a provider meets standards of practice, the role of the HMO physician broadens into several areas of responsibility. The physician who seeks admission to practice in a managed care plan is obligated to *understand and manage risk*. This knowledge is vital to creating the culture shift (Haglund, 1996) required to practice successfully in managed care. Some physicians may well understand the mathematics of risk without understanding the equally important concept of the psychology of risk (NAMCP, 1995). The mathematics of risk involves knowing how many patients create a successful environment, how many patients are too many, patient population demographics (age is the most predominant variable), and the type of practice (primary care or specialty). The physician must know how much it costs to see one patient, not how much is charged.

The psychology of risk is more nebulous. The physician must decide how to maximize the use of the most cost-effective care delivery options available. This requires research into "best practices" around the country and instituting behavioral modification of both the physician and the patient to assure compliance with proven delivery methods (NAMCP, 1995; Haglund, 1996).

Physicians and managed care plans must address and plan around the issue of **defensive medicine**. Defensive medicine has been used as an excuse for adding more tests than necessary to offset the implied threat of lawsuit. It is true that the threat of litigation has altered practice behavior and increased costs, however attorneys argue that physicians need not order extra services as long as the judgment used in diagnosis and treatment is "right" and justifiable (NAMCP, 1995). This argument supports the use of practice guidelines that are based upon proven practice with documented outcome based upon statistically valid findings. The development of these practice guidelines is precluded by **peer interaction**.

Peer interaction requires a physician to look at established referral patterns and practice outcomes based upon data rather than friendship, convenience and social amenities. Risk sharing will cause the wise physician to associations with practitioners who have cost-effective methods of achieving good outcomes. As practice patterns change, so do referrals to facilities, which now must meet the same standards of optimum outcomes at cost-effective prices. Primary care physicians also begin to rate specialists based on quality of practice; prompt consultation, feedback to the primary care physician, communal planning of treatment and judgment of efficacy.

Practice management techniques may change as physicians are forced to become more efficient. This may involve more use of physician extenders; physician assistants, nurse practitioners, and nurse midwives. The use of office staff to assure uniformity in processing of patient data and efficiency in managing patient care is extremely important. Also at the disposal of the physician is the use of the managed care plan itself. The managed care plan that has practice data to allow physicians to compare their own practice to those practices of their peers, is the plan that fosters physician loyalty within the plan, thereby creating the symbiotic relationship so necessary to the well-being of each. The goal of practice management is to create a solid, stable patient-physician-plan relationship (NAMCP, 1995).

Whether physicians are employees of an HMO, contracted to an HMO through an employer, member of a group which accepts risk from an HMO, or an independent practitioner who contracts directly with an HMO or through a physician organization, it is the physician who is the manager of care. It is imperative for the physician to be an active participant in the managed care continuum. This includes not only patient care, but also interaction with peers to improve the quality of the delivery system itself.

In order to be successful in managed care, the physician must understand and manage risk. This includes reimbursement methods, patient mix, distribution of patients among different plans, and practice management. The primary care physician is the central manager of patient care. It is up to the primary care physician to develop, control, and implement a plan of treatment. The role of the care manager demands that the primary care physician must be skilled in team building, and be secure in his or her own practice patterns to assure appropriate care.

STATISTICS AND DEMOGRAPHICS

Before there were health care delivery systems, there were statistics on health. The source was not the health industry: The keeping of statistics began with the insurance industry. Mortality statistics were collected as early as the 1700s. Morbidity data collection is a newer science, and the data is not as reliable. The insurers began collecting data in order to calculate risk. Calculating odds based on sound statistical evidence allows one to more closely calculate the probability of a person having a disease and determining how much it will cost to treat that disease, therefore allowing a company to make more reliable underwriting and actuarial judgments. Morbidity data is less reliable than mortality data. This is because morbidity data are less in volume and are more volatile in nature. The more morbidity data are collected and pooled, actuarial decision making becomes less of an art and more of a science (Weston and Friis, 1996). Insurance statistics are collected according to demographic variables: age, sex, lifestyle status such as smoking, occupation class, and type of insurance coverage. Some insurers have medical examination results such as blood pressure, height, weight, and medical history. In addition to these data elements, there are large claims data warehouses which give information as to dates of service, diagnoses, procedures, physician and specialty. All these elements give the insurer some idea of patterns of health, health service use, and estimation of risk. The value of data is that if an organization is able to capture the information produced by its activities and return it to the business operations, the result will be higher operational performance (Weston and Friis, 1996).

There are inherent pitfalls in interpreting quality of health services based on claims data alone. Most managed care computer systems evolved from the insurance industry claims payment systems, and are limited to the data received on standard physician and facility claims. The most common form for physician claims submission is the HCFA 1500 form. The most commonly used facility form is the UB92.

Thus, in the information age, managed care still is tied to its ancestral roots in the insurance industry. These rudiments of data collection fulfill the requirements for rating and actuarial estimation. The data required to analyze practice patterns, utilization patterns, outcome monitoring, practice guideline monitoring and the improvement of health status in a population are still in infancy stages. Claims data is well suited to population oriented analysis, and do not have the depth to determine outcomes. Claims data are easily retrieved, inexpensive to retrieve and are relatively unobtrusive in the collection process.

Most managed care plans do not have enough of their own data from which to assess all aspects of plan operation. There are data sources available from which to base cost and medical decisions. Public data are available on hospital information from several governmental and private sources. Medicare data are available from the Health Care Financing Administration. Medicaid data may be available from state agencies who act as intermediaries for Medicaid programs. Private financial and health data are available from private corporations. If a plan is purchasing data to calculate costs, local payers can provide the utilization and claims history for a defined population within a geographic area for a defined period. There are potential limitations to using payer data bases. Data integrity, or the quality of the data base, may lead to skewed results when analyzing data. Common errors are duplicate data, incorrect coding, incomplete data entry and inconsistent classification (Larsen, 1995). Procurement costs for this data can be high. Programming or processing errors can occur when transferring data from one system to another. These errors lead to unexplained variances in utilization and cost. It is best to use multiple data sources to minimize these variances (Larsen, 1995).

Internal database development is preferable so a plan can establish and maintain good quality control standards. However, the plan is faced with years of data collection before norms can be established.

Managed care plans most often use outside data to compare their costs with other plans. Cost analysis for medical services involves many variables which must be considered before a true cost can be calculated. These variables include population demographics of the insureds with identification of the benefits package for each insured. Utilization may vary widely according to the type benefits the group has. Diagnosed illness is an important variable, from which, when combined with population demographics, the incidence rates for diagnosed illnesses can be calculated. Prescribed treatment regimen can be analyzed for identification of those regimen which are cost effective and have consistently positive outcomes. Within this process is an identification of the resources consumed for treatment. These variables combined can produce a picture of provider activity, i.e., physician profiling, to see which practitioners are effective and efficient. In turn, the plan can combine data into a "report card" of plan activity and compare against other plans.

The near future offers arrays of exciting possibilities in data interchange in managed care. The practice of insurance companies holding data as trade secrets is giving way to free exchange of data through the use of electronic data interchange. The Internet offers many possibilities in helping to harness managed care. Services currently offered on the Internet involve the ability to monitor regulatory issues and health care delivery trends, retrieve practice guidelines, find the latest strategies for promoting wellness, watch the shake-out of mergers and acquisitions among managed care companies, and see what the competitors have on the net. The Internet, or local intranet, also offers operational management opportunities for managed care. Referrals, ordering prescription, and transferring medical information are a small part of the prospects.

More exciting than information exchange are projects that allow comparisons of utilization and practice guidelines from one population to another. John Wennberg's *The Dartmouth Atlas of Health Care*, which catalogs hospital and doctor concentration in 306 health care markets across the nation and compares differences in costs and health care within each of these markets, is a fine example of use of data from multiple sources. Dr. Wennberg has concluded from 30 years of research that there is no health system in the United States, and that his numbers show that supply generates demand (Hudson, 1996). Although Dr. Wennberg's work has its critics, it is up to professionals in the health care industry to either substantiate or disprove this magnanimous work.

Demographic data is an important gauge for managed care plans as the industry evolves. Early arguments against managed care used by traditional insurers was that HMO "cherry-picked" healthier people because of preventive care benefits, and left the sick people to the traditional insurer. Today, the HMOs feel the effects of **adverse selection**, where sicker people gravitate toward HMOs because of lower copayments, no deductibles ,and no preexisting clauses found in the traditional plans. It is important for a plan to track changes in its population demographics over time, so as to better plan for the needs of its population and to better predict costs based upon demographics.

There are many reasons why a person elects coverage under a managed care plan. Most large employers offer a choice of benefit plans, usually a dual option (HMO and a PPO), or a triple option (HMO, PPO, and indemnity) plan. People who choose the HMO option usually do so based upon the following:

1. The reputation of the managed care plan, especially established plans, will attract large numbers of people. Reputation of the plan is largely based upon service and claims payment.
2. Established relationships with physicians will lead members into a plan. People do not wish to sever an established physician relationship. Physicians may lead patients into a plan, especially if the physician participates in several plans, and the person is offered a choice of HMO plans. Again, physicians usually base judgment upon plan reputation, established by service and claims payment.
3. The attitude of the employer steers people toward a managed care plan. The employer who is enthusiastic about managed care will have greater numbers of employees enroll in managed care plans.
4. Costs play a significant role in choosing a managed care option. Where premium rates are lower and there are few out of pocket costs, group penetration by a managed care plan will be greater (Beam, 1995).

As attitudes from employers and employees alike change, the demographics of HMO populations also will change. The workforce is aging. Ten years ago, the mean age of an HMO enrollee was 28 years. Some employer groups now have a mean age of 44 years or greater. Data collection and statistical analysis needs to be meticulous, so managed care plans can predict changes and plan to deliver care to a different population than was seen in the early 1970s.

TRENDS AND CURRENT MARKET ACTIVITIES

There is prediction that there will be continued rapid growth of managed care. As Medicare and Medicaid populations have stayed relative steady since 1988, there has been continued growth in the managed care market and a loss of market share in the traditional insurance market. Although HMOs and PPOs have not reversed the escalation of health care costs, they have slowed that escalation. There is a concentration of market power in large HMOs, although small, regionally owned and operated plans produced had the best investment earnings. There continues to be a consolidation of the large HMO market as acquisitions are made.

Government entities are taking advantage of managed care successes and growth of Medicare HMOs has doubled since 1988. Medicaid plans are moving to managed care with 38 states now having a federal waiver to shift Medicaid populations to managed care. There are currently 7.8 million Medicaid beneficiaries in managed care programs. Benefit changes will be needed as more chronically ill people are absorbed by the managed care plans. HMO benefits are designed for emphasis on preventive care and acute crisis intervention. HMOs will have to consider methods to provide for the long-term chronically ill as Medicare enrollees increase and as Medicaid programs shift the disabled and institutionalized patients into managed care.

There have been dramatic reductions in utilization in certain markets. These differences are dramatic when one looks at geographic distribution. This can be seen not only in average length of stay for certain diagnoses and procedures, but also in the number of chronic disease management programs developed for home and outpatient use.

Managed care has prompted the acquisition of physician practices by proprietary physician management companies, managed care organizations, hospitals, and insurance companies. Predictions are that in some areas of the country, the independent practitioner no longer will exist. However, the rush to purchase physician practices has put some purchasers on the endangered species list. Some hospitals and staff model HMOs are privatizing or divesting their physician practices as lessons in loss. There have been integrations of specialty groups and primary care groups, especially those groups who have accepted full-risk contracts with managed care entities. Because of problematic issues regarding delegating care with accrediting bodies, HMOs are reneging on delegated services associated with risk contracts.

Because many physician groups who assume risk are paying claims, conducting utilization management activities, and generally looking like unlicensed managed care entities, there are regulatory concerns which will be addressed in the legislative arena. Physician groups may be required to have an insurance license, may be required to put up reserves to protect members from insolvency, may be required to carry liability and reinsurance coverage far in excess of normal practice. There may be activity to require that the consumer be informed of the reimbursement arrangements made between the managed care group to which he pays premiums and the physician from whom he seeks care. This is also informed consent.

There are new partnerships forming, not only among providers and managed care entities, but also in the public sector providers and managed care entities. The HMO mandate to provide preventive services was in essence a transferring of traditional public health services to the private sector. There now are efforts to bring a partnership between public health entities and the managed care providers (McBride, 1996).

The paradigm of health care coverage has shifted. This process will continue to evolve. Coverage has shifted from provider payment mechanisms which were fee for service and retrospective (indemnification), to prepaid and performance based (capitation and incentives). Traditional health coverage was cost based and focused on the individual. This has shifted to a population focused price based economy. care under the traditional coverage was individually focused, episodic and interventive; this is shifting toward continuous, preventive care. The shift is beginning with providers from services as revenue generation to resource conservation (Kongstvedt, 1996). Health care providers and health care insurers should become what the name implies; purveyors of health care, not payers for sick care.

REFERENCES

Beam, Burton T., Jr., *Group Health Insurance,* The American College, 1995, 125.

Delbecq, Andre and Sandra Gill, "Justice as a Prelude to Teamwork in Medical Centers." *Health Services Management,* 1990, 274.

Griffith, John R., *The Well Managed Community Hospital,* 144.

Haglund, Mark, "Making Managed care Second Nature." *Hospitals and Health Networks,* April 20, 1996.

Hillman, Alan L., "Managing the Physician: Rules vs. Incentives." *Health Affairs,* Winter, 1991, 142.

Hudson, Terese, "Mirror, Mirror," *Hospitals and Health Networks,* April 5, 1996, 24–28.

Kongstvedt, Peter R. "Ideas for the paradigm shift," described by Peter R. Kongstvedt in a keynote address at the AMISYS Users Conference, May 1996.

Larsen, Roger, II, *Collecting and Using Data to Develop Cost and Utilization Assumptions for Risk contracts,* Thompson Publishing Group, January 1995, 45.

McBride, Susan H., "Meet Your Future." *Managed Healthcare,* June, 1996, 34.

McBride, Susan H., "Partnering for Prevention." *PharmaCare Economics,* May 1996, (?????) s36.

NAMCP, " Demystifying Managed Care." *Managed care Strategies for Today,* National Association of Managed Care Physicians, Inc., 8.

Nash, David B., *The Physician's Guide to Managed Care,* Aspen, 1994, 19.

Oklahoma State Department of Health, *Health Maintenance Organization Licensure Rules.* 18.

Sadler, Jeff, *Disability Income,* National Underwriter, 1995, 95.

Shulkin, David and Alan H. Rosenstein, "Toward Cost-Effective Health Care." *The Physician's Guide to Managed Care,* 118.

Soule, Charles E., *Disability Income Insurance,* Business One Irwin, 1994, 135.

Spragins, Ellyn, "Does Your HMO Stack Up?" *Newsweek*, June 24, 1996, 63.

Spragins, Ellen, "Examining HMOS." *Bloomberg Personal*, October 1995, 10.

Weston, Cathy and Jacob Friis, "Getting the Most Out of Medical Claims Data." *Profitability Bulletin*, Ernst & Young, Winter, 1996.

Woolhandler, Steffie, "A Failing System of Health Care." *An International Comparison of Health-Care Systems*, Harvard Community Health Plan Annual Report, 1990, 23.

2 Historical Evolution of Managed Care Quality

A. F. Al-Assaf

CONTENTS

This book is about quality in managed care, but whether it is in managed care or not, quality as a concept is implemented in the same manner and is practiced in the same fashion in any setting. Health care quality, in general, focuses on the concept that health care has three major cornerstones; quality, access, and cost. Although one is dependent on the other and each can impact another, quality has a stronger impact on the two other cornerstones. Quality is achieved when accessible services are provided in an efficient, cost-effective, and acceptable manner. A quality service is one that is customer oriented. It is a service that is available, accessible, acceptable, affordable, and controllable. Quality is achieved when the needs and expectations of the customer are met. In health care, patients are the most important customer. (Al-Assaf, 1993)

All quality concepts, when properly applied should ensure that services rendered in an organization are quality services and that outcomes are quality outcomes. Total quality, in particular total quality management (TQM), originally was introduced by certain quality experts in Japan before it was "imported" to the United States. This "new" management concept was introduced shortly after World War II to help the Japanese manufacturing industry to improve its products and ultimately its services. It is with the major improvements of their industries that our industries took notice and started a search for the factors behind this remarkable product of quality improvement. TQM was not introduced "en mass" in the U.S. industry until the early 1980s.

Let us examine the history of this management concept and its evolution into a leadership paradigm. We also will take a look at the shift of emphasis in health care from structure standards to process and lately outcome standards.

1-57444-073-X/97/$0.00+$.50

THE EARLY DAYS OF QUALITY ASSURANCE

Quality assessment and control in health care date back to the mid 19th century, where Florence Nightingale was a leading nurse during the Crimean War (Bull 1992). She was the first to notice the positive correlation between the introduction of adequate nursing care to wounded soldiers and the decrease in the mortality rate among this group of soldiers. This concept triggered her interest in attributing quality of care to positive outcomes. She then began documenting this fact after the war in several studies that looked at other components of quality. She started looking at the extent of services and resources utilization and quality outcomes, and was instrumental in writing up several quality criteria in nursing care. A period of testing of these concepts was passed and few other clinicians attempted to further study the correlation between care and outcome. During the early part of the 20th century in the United States, several physicians conducted studies on health care quality assessment. In 1914, Ernest Codman, a surgeon at Massachusetts General Hospital, was able to study general surgeries and their follow ups and was responsible for influencing the adoption of follow up progress exams after one year of surgery. This prompted the American College of Surgeons in 1918 to create the Hospital Standardization Program that provided criteria and standards for accreditation which were later adopted by the Joint Commission on Accreditation of Hospitals.

Just prior to this time, an interest started to develop structure criteria. Abraham Flexnor in 1910 presented his famous report after his study of the education of physicians in the U.S. and was quick to point out the deficiencies in the medical education system. He further pointed out that the education of physicians is directly related to the quality of care the patient receives and that medical education needed substantial reforms. As was expected, this report forced a considerable number of medical schools to close their doors for their inability to meet the report's reform criteria. It should be noted that with this report the emphasis shifted from process elements to structure elements, i.e., the human and the physical resources. Education, certifications and licensure became very important in "qualifying" a health care professional and an educational organization. Several professional associations were established to provide these services, with state licensure and examining boards spreading slowly but gradually throughout the country. For health care organizations, the same interest in structure quality started taking place influencing the American College of Surgeons in 1952 to establish the Joint Commission on Accreditation of Hospitals or JCAH. JCAH later changed its name to the Joint Commission on Accreditation of Healthcare Organizations or JCAHO. JCAH, as it was then called, published its first list of accreditation standards for hospitals. Hospitals that met those standards were accredited and certified as a "quality" institution. It is interesting to note here that this first list of accreditation standards fitted on one single page. The list today is compiled in a number of manuals of few hundreds pages each. JCAH standards were structure standards that emphasized the quality of the credentialing process and the risk management standards. Basically the objective of the accreditation process was to ensure care was delivered in a safe physical environment and by qualified providers. Of course the then JCAH thought that meeting structure criteria is equivalent to providing a quality medical care.

The interest in quality measures continued in the 1950s. In clinical practice at least three physicians studied the quality of medical care delivered by practitioners in the U.S. Unlike JCAH, those studies primarily were process oriented that looked at the process of care delivered. According to Brook and Avery (1975), one study by Dr. O. L. Peterson looked at the care provided by general practitioners. Dr. Peterson looked at the processes and procedures conducted during patient examinations and follow-ups. Another physician, Dr. M. A. Morehead, looked at the ambulatory care practice of physicians compared to their peers. The third study was conducted by Dr. B. C. Payne, who compared the care delivered by a select group of physicians in acute care hospitals with a set of predesigned criteria of care. All three studies concluded that there are deficiencies in patient care and that the quality of care need to be continuously monitored and improved.

HISTORY OF TQM IN MANUFACTURING

In 1948–1949, Japan was trying to recover from its losses in World War II and to find ways to revive its economy. An observation was noted by several Japanese engineers that quality improvement almost always will lead to improvement in productivity. (Deming 1986) This observation was extracted through earlier work of Walter A. Shewhart (1931) and from literature supplied by Bell Laboratories (through the staff of Gen. Douglas MacArthur). This simple observation became the impetus for the Japanese management to learn the methods of proving it. In 1950, W. Edward Deming, an American statistician, was invited to Japan to introduce and teach the methods of improving quality and TQM. He was instrumental in showing the Japanese engineers that improving productivity is dependent on decreasing the variability of processes in a plant. He emphasized Shewhart's earlier Statistical Quality Control principle that errors are predicted and further prevented from happening before producing a product. Therefore, a defective product almost never is produced and the consumer is unlikely to see one. The Japanese learned quickly that to survive, four major issues need to be addressed: (1) the consumer must be studied and looked after, (2) total systems, not components, need to be studied in detail, (3) teamwork must be the way to do business, (4) and decisions must be based on data. They also understood that focusing on meeting customer needs and expectations was the only way to improve their economy.

Japan at this time was bankrupt. It had no natural resources, such as oil. The only resource was its people. They also knew that for these people to be fed, manufactured products needed to be marketed successfully and sold to an outside market. Of course such markets were receiving higher quality goods that the Japanese were not producing. Therefore, a need for improving the quality of products was a must for Japan to survive. Hence, management started to make quality the most important target. Management further communicated this defect-prevention paradigm to its workers — a paradigm that predicts costs will decline with improving quality because of less rework, waste, and errors, and will lead to better use of human and physical resources, improving productivity. As productivity improves more markets are captured, which is paramount for staying in business, maintaining and creating more jobs, and so on. This paradigm further was communicated to every worker that producing affordable, dependable, defect-free, and acceptable products was important to keeping his or her job and for Japan to buy its basic needs. Therefore, it became obvious to the worker that improving quality was not only a requirement of his job, but also an individual and personal responsibility. TQM started spreading in Japan's corporations and institutions for the next 20 years. During the same time the American industry was almost unopposed in its products and services. This period although was dominated by American goods and products was detrimental to the American industry due to the lack of incentives for marked improvements and "breakthroughs."

It was not until 1973, as the oil embargo wass felt, that American industries started to realize their dependence on other countries for survival. Suddenly, the automobile industry started noticing that foreign cars are getting more and more of the market in the U.S. The same was noticeable about other products, especially those from Japan. From cameras to electronics and watches, Japanese products started to gain further markets on the expense of the local American industries. Japan became an exporter of many other products to not only the U.S. but also to Europe, Asia, and the rest of the world. American corporations started looking for answers to these successes and began studying Japanese companies to find answers. Soon it became obvious to U.S. industries that quality is dependent on the worker and that tapping this potential is important for improving productivity. A number of programs sprung from American companies that were based primarily on worker participation and involvement in problem solving. From quality circles, to employee involvement and quality of worklife, all were based on participative management. These programs and others continued through the 1970s with varying successes and outcomes.

For those companies that understood the *cultural change*, quality improvement was achieved, while others were not as successful. When commitment of management was lacking, all these programs that encouraged employee participation started to wane as employees felt their work was not being encouraged and appreciated. Management of these companies — and those were the majority — did not realize that stagnation in the economy and problems facing the American industry mainly are system problems, not those of employees. These companies apparently were unaware of these facts until June 1980, when NBC aired the TV landmark program "If Japan Can, Why Can't We." Dr. Deming was interviewed about his experiences and successes with the Japanese manufacturing industry. He stated that the combination of basic management skills with statistical process control to reduce variability were the major principles for improving quality and productivity. It was only then that major U.S. corporations took this philosophy to the test and introduced it to their settings. This philosophy started to spread in popularity between other companies and for the next several years this "quality movement" became a reality to several industries in the U.S.

GOVERNMENT INFLUENCE ON QUALITY IN HEALTH CARE

Returning to health care, several events occurred before organizations started adopting TQM or quality improvement principles. TQM did not become a known entity in health care until the late 1980s. It primarily was a business management practice somewhat foreign to health care. Of course in health care, quality was "assured" through efforts of several quasiregulatory agencies that demanded the application of certain care standards. This was evident in the sequence of events that are discussed below.

In 1965, President Lyndon B. Johnson signed into law the two major amendments of the Social Security Act — Title 18 (Medicare) and Title 19 (Medicaid). The main objectives of these amendments were to increase access to health care services by certain beneficiaries and in particular the elderly and the poor. However, the act also provided mechanisms that promised to ensure the provision of quality health care services to those benefiting. Here again quality of care is promised through emphasis on structure (providers and institutions) and to a lesser extent on process (the way care is delivered). Nevertheless, Medicare and Medicaid did provide certain incentives for providers to deliver "quality" service. During and after this time JCAH was encouraged by the government to "enforce" its accreditation requirements and tighten its standards for certifying the quality of hospitals. This role which is considered by some as a semiregulatory role had a major influence on the establishment of quality assurance departments in health care organizations.

In 1966, Dr. Avedis Donabedian, a university professor and physician, introduced his famous three measures of quality: structure, process, and outcome. He urged health care organizations to look at **all** three measures when monitoring and assessing care quality. He further suggested structure include both human and physical resources in delivery of health care to the patient. Processes, as he described them, include all the procedures and activities required to deliver medical care by providers and support systems. Outcome, on the other hand, includes results and outputs of the care process, for example, morbidity and mortality rates, patient satisfaction, etc. This model prompted different players in health care to use it but misinterpretation led to use of these measures separately and independently from each other.

During the 1970s, the government concerns over health care cost escalation continued. Therefore, in its attempt to control cost and preserve quality, the U.S. legislature passed two bills during this period that have direct impacts on the quality of care delivered. One bill in 1972 established the Professional Standards Review Organizations (PSROs). These organizations were to review the standards of care provided to inpatient Medicare patient and to ensure the delivery of adequate and appropriate treatment to these patients. PSROs, however, received several negative reactions from interest groups. JCAH looked at them as competing organizations for the same market. With the PSROs being physician oriented, other groups beleived their nonrepresentation was counterproductive to effective evaluation of care processes. Physicians, on the other hand, believed their work and humanitarian efforts to preserve life was being questioned. Representatives of physicians on these organizations found themselves ostracized by their peers and often were looked on as "traitors" to their profession. All these factors hindered the real function PSROs originally were created to fulfill. Despite the failure of PSROs in achieving their objectives, they were the first to influence the emphasis on process quality. This notion opened the door for a new paradigm shift in quality monitoring and assessment.

Two years following the PSROs' creation, another bill was passed and enacted to establish Health Systems Agencies (HSAs). The functions of these agencies were to act as analysts of health care needs and requirements and to maintain the quality of care provided. HSAs were quick to flag their inefficiencies to improve quality as interest groups found ways to limit the authority of these agencies. These agencies gradually began to disappear as the need for their services ceased and the funding of their existence stopped. It is interesting to note that during this same time period another bill to decrease health care costs was passed in 1974 to open the door for the creation of Health Maintenance Organizations. The concept of decreasing rising health care costs by controlling access to "costly" health services and beginning the process of "managing" care seemed novel at the time. Even though this concept had potential, it was slow to be adopted by the insurance industry and did not show major breakthroughs until the late 1980s.

This trend continued as the government looked for ways to contain sharply rising and seemingly uncontrollable health care costs and maintain quality at the same time. Government was first to realize that after a decade of PSRO activities, health care costs still were rising and the quality of care was not improving. Therefore, funding ceased for PSROs. HSAs received the same treatment. This further prompted legislators to pass the Tax Equity and Fiscal Responsibility Act (TEFRA) of 1982. TEFRA introduced a new ceiling to reimbursement for Medicare inpatient services. This act also paved the way through mandated studies to introduce the DRGs (Diagnosis Related Groupings) as the basis for reimbursement of Medicare providers (inpatient services). Reimbursements were to be made under a prospective payment system (PPS). The Health Care Financing Administration (HCFA) was empowered to enforce and administer this system. PPS then was enacted as an amendment of the Social Security Act and was signed into law by President Ronald Reagan in October 1983. The act again provided for a mechanism to ensure both access and quality of care associated with an efficient cost reduction effort. Therefore, besides their mandate to control costs, the Social Security amendments required the establishment of Peer Review Organizations (PROs) by October 1984.

PROs were established to replace PSROs in their attempt to assess and improve quality of care delivered. Similar to PSROs, PRO services extend only to Medicare inpatient services, meaning their impact on care quality is limited, but considerable. Again PROs look at the process of care. Unlike PSROs, PROs membership is not limited to physicians, but should have liberal access to them. PROs can be a for-profit or a not-for-profit organization. Hospitals are required to contract with a PRO to review their services. PROs have the authority to enforce quality improvement measures on the provider by either an extensive evaluation process or through monitory fines. PROs also have a mandate to review other professional services rendered in a hospital and may refer to these professions for advice on specific care standards.

Starting in the 1970s and especially during the 1980s and beyond, QA departments and units became very active in collecting and analyzing data on patient care and health risk management. The pursuit of ensuring and maintaining quality of care became painful as the objectives placed emphasis on the structural aspects of a program, in particular human resources, e.g., credentialling and certifications. QA professionals felt new "power" of searching for "bad" providers. These "bad" providers felt harassed by the system and once their "mistakes" became public, medical liability lawsuits started to spread. This trend negatively affected the providers, including their institutions, and their patients. Patient–provider relationships started to erode and providers lost the anticipated trust owed to them by their patients. Also administration–physician relationships started to show some stress, as one started blaming the other for the cause of the problems. This situation was exacerbated further after the physicians started practicing medicine defensively. Physicians started ordering more (usually unnecessary) tests before making any diagnosis on a patient's condition in an attempt to protect themselves from the potential of a malpractice suit. The legal system did not help alleviate this situation, but, on the contrary, made it worse. Lawyers started prompting patients to question their providers of any unexpected outcome of care. The same lawyers "volunteered" their services to these patients on a contingency basis and would accept payments only until a financial settlement or judgment was reached, earning themselves 33–50% of the award. This trend continued to escalate the misuse and misallocation of precious resources and, of course, the expenditures on health care kept rising, but not the quality. (Al-Assaf, 1994)

Again the government stepped in and, as a reactionary measure to the malpractice crisis, passed the National Healthcare Quality Improvement Act of 1986. This act had two major provisions encouraged patients to become informed consumers on those providers with a record of malpractice. It called for the creation of a national clearing house of providers malpractice records in the U.S. Further, it made it mandatory for health care institutions to report malpractice incidents to this clearing house. The act encourages this effort by providing immunity against violations of privacy lawsuits that may be initiated by those providers. This information, therefore, could become available to licensure boards and other entities inquiring about practicing providers in different states. Due to inadequate funding, the act was not implemented until 1989. It is obvious that this act was passed in an attempt to "improve" the quality of medical care delivered, but again the emphasis is put primarily on structure without involving process and outcome measures.

By the late 1980s, the focus of government suddenly shifted away from the PROs' process-oriented review and the JCAH structure-oriented review to a renewed emphasis on outcomes. The December 1987 *HCFA* published the Medicare Hospital Mortality Information list. (HCFA 1987) It made headlines when excerpts of this list were published in *The New York Times*. Major reactions came from the hospital industry, which refuted the validity and usefulness of the list. They pointed out that this list did not take into consideration the case-mix index, i.e., they asked for a differentiation between acute care and cancer treatment hospitals. Despite the flaws associated with this list, and the annual lists thereafter, it triggered many organizations to start looking at patient outcomes. JCAHO changed its name to include other health care organizations besides hospitals, as it already was including other institutions in the accreditation process. About the same time, in an effort to continue its tight grip on the market, JCAHO announced its Agenda for Change (O'Leary 1987) which calls for a gradual refocus its of standards on outcomes. These events stimulated several other groups to start looking at clinical outcomes and physician practice patterns as qualifiers for care quality (Daley 1991).

Outcome assessments later were explored further by researchers and more funding became available, especially in the area of clinical outcomes research. Also in its quest for better outcomes with limited resources, the health care industry started looking outside its field for answers. This thinking prompted TQM to enter into this industry in the late 1980s. Starting with hospitals and followed by other health care organizations, the principles of TQM began its infiltration into this industry. Leadership paradigms that originally were designed for manufacturing were modified in an attempt to make them applicable to health care. Quality experts were quick to realize that the amount of work necessary to bring this giant industry to the realms of quality management was tremendous. Thus several of these experts started setting up companies and subsidiaries to educate the masses in health care on this relatively new philosophy. Health care professionals, on the other hand, found a tremendous appetite for learning more of this concept and started flocking to institutes and workshops designed for them by these quality experts. This trend continued throughout the first half of the 1990s and still was active in 1997. Now most hospitals (AHA 1996) either have started the journey for TQM or are making headway towards it. Similarly, managed care organizations adopted quality and its concepts in their services. Actually, these organizations now are mandated by their accrediting and certifying agencies to introduce and practice quality improvement in their daily operation and services. This was evident by the creation of one of the most aggressive and quality improvement-oriented accrediting bodies, the National Committee on Quality Assurance (NCQA), in 1990. NCQA was created first as an affiliate of the Group Health Association of America, but then became an independent not-for-profit organization devoted for the surveying and accreditation of HMOs. (NCQA 1997) Other health care organizations, however, especially long-term care and mental health organizations, were not as fast in adopting this leadership cultural transformation. To date several of these organizations have a adopted only a rudimentary model of QA.

It also should be noted that the concept of assessing quality based on outcomes received A further boost with the introduction and funding by congress of the U.S. Agency for Health Care Policy and Research (AHCPR) in 1989. This move by Congress was in direct response to the call by the Institute of Medicine Report of 1989 (IOM, 1989) which called for the need to emphasize patient outcomes in the delivery and improvement of health care. This agency was created to enhance the quality of care by the search and development of clinical practice guidelines (CPGs) based on patient outcomes. AHCPR became active in sponsoring several activities in the area CPGs and, to date, at least 18 general CPGs have been developed (AHCPR, 1996). This trend, however, also is changing and the emphasis on outcome for quality assessment, although still strong, is being overshadowed by a more traditional trend where processes besides clinical outcomes are being highlighted.

NCQA now is considered the most influential organization in the accreditation of HMOs, having surveyed in excess of half the approximately 600 HMOs in the U.S. As the NCQA 1997 standards for health plans accreditation was published, another version of the Health Employer Data and Information Set (HEDIS) was issued. HEDIS 3.0 has a number of changes from the older version HEDIS 2.5 and seems to be more aggressive on quality improvement and benchmarking. Requirements for HEDIS 3.0 again are based on the U.S. Task Force on Preventive Medicine guidelines and is geared towards the improvement of preventive care services to HMO members. (HEDIS, 1997) NCQA, on the other hand, has taken the position of adopting HEDIS 3.0 as one important component of the accreditation process and no HMO will be accredited without showing evidence of following the HEDIS requirements. This mandate has started a new trend since the early 1990s, where health consumers and purchasers are demanding comparative performance data of health care organizations. This has spawned a new field of data reporting in the form of "report cards." Several of these report cards are out on health care organizations ranging form hospitals and HMOs to individual providers. It is believed the trend will continue throughout the 1990s as consumers are becoming more prudent in "shopping" for health services.

It is evident that quality, especially quality improvement and management, is fairly new to health care. When they first were introduced, these concepts received a mixture of reactions. Since health care quality calls for cultural change of the organization, traditional bureaucrats (which are abundant in Health care) fought against its quick adoption. They since have accepted the change reluctantly as this leadership paradigm moved through the levels of management with swift steps backed by support from consumer groups, regulators, and accrediting agencies. In the next two chapters this issue of health care quality and its late adoption is further explored and the factors behind the change is discussed in detail.

REFERENCES

Al-Assaf, A. F. and Schmele, J. A. *The Textebook of Total Quality in Healthcare*, St. Lucie Press, Delray, FL, 1993.

Al-Assaf, A. F. "Quality Improvement in Healthcare: An Overview." *Journal of the Royal Medical Services*, 1(2):, 1994.

Brook, R. and Avery, A. *Quality Assurance Mechanism in the U.S.: From There to Where?* Rand: Santa Monica, CA, 1975.

Bull, M. J. "QA: Professional Accountability via CQI." *In Improving Quality: A Guide to Effective Programs*, C. G. Meisenheimer (Ed.), Aspen: Gaithersburg, MD, 1992.

Codman, E. "The Product of a Hospital." *Surgical Gynecology and Obstetrics*, 1914.18:491-494.

Daley, J. "Mortality and Other Outcome Data." In *Quantitative Methods in Quality Management: A Guide to Practitioners*, Longo and Bohr (Ed.'s), AHA: Chicago 1991, 27-43.

Deming, W. E. *Out of the Crisis*, MIT: Cambridge, MA, 1986.

Donabedian, A. "Evaluating the Quality of Medical Care." *Milbank Memorial Fund Quarterly*, 1966, 44:194-196.

Health care Financing Administration, *Medicare Hospital Mortality Information: 1986*, GPO No. 017-060-00206-9, Vol I– VII, U.S. Department of Health and Human Services, Washington, DC, December 1987.

HEDIS 3.0 Requirements. NCQA: Washington, DC, 1997.

O'Leary, D. S. *The Joint Commission Agenda for Change*, JCAHO: Chicago, IL, 1987, 1–10.

NCQA. *Accreditation Standards for Health Plans*, NCQA: Washington, DC, 1997.

3 The Concept of Health Care Quality

A. F. Al-Assaf

CONTENTS

INTRODUCTION AND BACKGROUND

Quality is rapidly becoming a global issue and is of concern to both the suppliers of services and the consumers of those services. In health care, quality is reaching a new dimension in that it is being demanded and expected and providers are judged by it. Health care quality is becoming a required attribute to providing care whether in the United States, Europe, Asia ,or any other part of the world.

One issue related to quality involves communications and sharing of information. The world certainly is becoming smaller through advances in communications technology and transportation linkage. Therefore, advances and accomplishments in health care quality in one place must be communicated with other places. Sharing ideas and learning from one another is an attribute of quality as well. Furthermore, quality in health care and services no longer are being judged solely on a local or even a regional level, but on a national, if not international, level

As mentioned in Chapter 2, the concept of quality in health care usually is associated with two other concerns — access and cost. This triad has been the center of much heated discussion and many important decisions in the United States. These three issues are equally important in health care decisions made on the international scene. These same issues are equally applicable to countries around the world, but we still find that these same issues center around one important aspect of care — quality. (Al-Assaf, 1993)

Before we discuss the concept of quality, one must understand in broad terms the relation of quality health care to access, a pivotal issue related to the mission of the World Health Organization, and to the cost of providing such care. What access mean here is that appropriate and necessary care actually is received by the consumers regardless of race, age, sex, and geographical distribution. This involves physical access, availability of appropriate health services and personnel, financial access, and intellectual access. This last dimension — intellectual access — is as important as availability and affordability. It deals with the issues of acceptability, awareness, and perception of the type and quality of care being delivered. If the consumer perceives the care as inadequate or contradictory to his or her expectations and culture, this care will not be accepted and there will be no cooperation between the provider and the consumer. Care quality is related directly to the level of acceptability of that care by the consumer and is equally dependent, if not more so, on the other variables of availability and affordability. Therefore, anytime health care quality is discussed, the issue of access must be met in order to achieve an optimum level of quality. (Al-Assay, 1994)

In this chapter, I will discuss issues related to health care quality in general. Emphasis will be made on such areas as definitions, dimensions, reasons for quality, history, principles, and applications of health care quality. An overview of the introduction of quality in health care also is presented as an introduction to a later chapter. Let me preface the discussion by choosing to use the word *health care quality* as the umbrella term for all other terms used in quality, some of which will be defined later on. In addition, I will attempt to differentiate between quality assurance, quality improvement, quality management, and the totality of any one of these under the rubrics of total quality management or total quality improvement.

THE MYTHS OF QUALITY

According to Peter Drucker, a management expert, people have different stereotypes and beliefs about quality. He calls them "myths of quality," and they are:

- Quality means goodness, luxury, shininess, or weight.
- Quality is intangible and, therefore, is not measurable.
- There is an "economics of quality"; e.g., "We can't afford it."
- Quality problems are originated by the workers.
- Quality originates in the quality department.

The first myth describes the notion that quality has to be the most expensive or most prominent approach or product. Quality can be as simple as continuously doing one's job better. A quality car, for example, does not have to be a Mercedes Benz or a Rolls–Royce. It very well may be a small or medium sized car that is reliable, economical, and has low maintenance. A car that can take you from point A to point B with the least hassle. Similarly, a quality care does not have to be only that provided in the most expensive setting by the most eminent practitioners. Health care quality can be as simple as providing appropriate and necessary care to the consumer in the most efficient manner utilizing available resources.

The second myth describes the belief by many people that quality is "magical" and undefined. They often believe it is an ideal that cannot be calculated or attained. However, quality is tangible and measurable. Health care is a system. Therefore, according to the simple system theory as it was applied to health care by Dr. Avedis Donabedian (1966), each health care system can be divided into three components: structure — human and physical resources, processes — the procedures and activities of care and services, and outcomes — the results of care and services. Each of these components has a number of quantifiable elements that can be defined and measured accurately. For example, under structure, one might look at the quality of physicians in terms of training, experience, and education as one attribute of the total quality of the health care system in which they work. In the process component, one may calculate the variance of current procedures to a standard set of steps for the same procedure. For outcomes, one example might be to calculate the level of patient satisfaction as a proxy measure of the total quality of that system.

The third myth is about the issue of the relationship between cost and quality. Quality is based on the principle of cost saving. If it is applied correctly, it should save money — not cost more. Initially, certain "new" resources are needed to start the quality process, but cost savings rapidly become a reality. Quality calls for the elimination of waste, of rework, and of duplication. One of the major principles of quality is efficiency. According to Suver et al. (1992), there are three costs for quality: prevention, appraisal, and failure — both internal and external. Implementing quality in a health care system requires resources to provide training in quality methodologies, secure monitoring capabilities, measure performance and improvement accomplishments, and to collect necessary data for documentation of the status and level of care. Quality, however, reduces the costs incurred by the system by gradually cutting costs associated with failure. Internal failure costs, such as rework, duplication, and waste, can be reduced and eventually eliminated if resources are used wisely and processes are streamlined. It also is an objective of quality to eliminate errors and mistakes that may have a detrimental effect on the customer, primarily the patient. External failure costs, usually are the highest, sometimes being tied to malpractice and liability issues. Hence, quality and cost may have an inverse relationship in this model. If quality is high, savings are byproducts and, therefore, cost is lower. Quality definitely is inexpensive.

The fourth myth suggests that workers are responsible for system problems and, therefore, errors must be attributed to them. Some people go even further, saying these workers should be "hunted" and swiftly removed for the system to function properly. This notion sometimes is called "the bad apple theory." (Berwick, 1989). Several quality experts proved this theory was wrong. Deming (1984), Crosby (1979, 1985), and Juran (1988), all found that more than 85% of all the problems are really system errors, while only 15% actually are worker errors. They emphasized that if one instituted a quality system of proper training in the right work environment, these workers would not make mistakes. Mistakes happen when the system lacks adequate policies, standard procedures, and tools. Errors also happen when there is a lack of systematic methods to document processes, study them, and act proactively before problems can occur.

The last myth suggests that quality is the responsibility of the quality department. This department should only act as a facilitator, an advocate, or a coordinator of the quality efforts in the system. It is the responsibility of every worker to provide quality, to practice quality, and to ensure improvements toward quality. Quality is everybody's responsibility and should originate from the system's units and the system's workers. In a quality environment, there is no need for a quality department as everyone is responsible for his or her own performance quality. If all workers in an organization are aware of their responsibilities and abide by their standards of performance, there is not need for a separate department to tell them what to do to achieve quality.

WHY QUALITY?

Several reasons can be cited for why we need quality and why we ask for quality. Some of these reasons follow, but the reader is reminded that these are just few of the many one can recite:

1. Increased demands for effective and appropriate care.
2. Need for standardization and variance control.
3. Necessity for cost saving measures.
4. Benchmarking.
5. Accreditation, certifications, and regulation.
6. Report cards on provider performance.
7. Requirement to define and meet patient needs and expectations.
8. Pressure of competition, and to enhance marketing.
9. Need for improvements in care and services.
10. Desire for recognition and the strive for excellence.
11. Competition
12. Ethical considerations.

One of the most fundamental reasons for quality is to meet the needs and expectations of the customer — both external and internal. Patients, as one important external customer, have certain needs and expectations that providers are required to study, investigate, understand, and implement methods for meeting them on a continual basis. Basically it is a process of effective communication between the supplier or provider of care or health services and the consumer or receiver of that care or services. It is a continuous process of dialogue and understanding between them. Additionally, one must not forget others in the system — internal customers, employees, and other external customers, such as families of patients, visitors, and payers. Each has special needs and expectations, and it is the obligated duty of health professionals to know them. Therefore, meeting the needs and expectations of the customer is a requirement for quality, and it is the reason we must have health care quality whether private or public.

As item 12 suggests, quality is the fabric of the very existence of the health care professions. Ethics dictates that one must provide the best and most appropriate care accessible to the patient. It is the basis of the humanistic aspect of the health care field. It is the duty of health care professionals to provide quality care and service to fulfill this ethical code.

Other reasons listed above ,such as effectiveness, appropriateness, and efficiency, are basic elements of a quality system and quality care (Nicholas et al. 1991). You cannot provide any care without addressing the available resources. While we all would like to provide and receive the best care there is, it is prudent to do that within the limits of current resources. If this is not considered, quality is not achieved. Quality requires efficient use of health care resources and effective delivery of care and services. This is discussed further in *The Dimensions of Quality* section later in this chapter.

Based on the previous discussion, quality can be achieved most effectively once we know our baseline data and what are we striving for. It is the issue of setting specific, but incrementally improving, standards of care. Identifying and selecting appropriate standards for the structure, the processes, and the outcomes of care and health services provides a guideline and allows minimum variation from these standards. By doing so, one would is able to control variance, reducing failure and appraisal costs.

Important to the reasons we strive for quality is the issue of competition. In the current era of cost constraints and limited resources, even health care institutions must demonstrate their ability to provide their services most effectively and efficiently. It is a matter of survival in today's volatile market. Nonprice competition is becoming increasingly important as consumers are demanding better care and access to appropriate care. Quality fits into this competition, where health care organizations work hard to achieve the desired level of quality care in order to attract new resources and expand to their horizons. Quality stimulates confidence, which leads to improved performance, ultimately building consumer trust, increasing marketability and membership.

One cannot speak about quality without speaking about excellence. Every prudent health care professional must aim for excellence. It is what Crosby (1979) calls *zero-defect*. In other words, health professionals should improve their work processes and procedures, and perform them with no defects. Errors need to be minimized and eliminated. This status of excellence, whether it is at the individual or organizational level, will gain recognition, encouraging other individuals, organizations, and systems to follow suit. Such *benchmarking*, the process of identifying centers (or practices) of excellence specific to certain processes or procedures to study and emulate in one's own system, stimulates reorganization, innovation, and improvements, all towards a higher level of quality.

WHAT IS QUALITY?

There are different perspectives to health care quality. To the provider, it might mean offering the best possible care available to the patient. To the administrator, it might mean providing effective care in a cost-conscious environment that may include rationing, especially when resources are limited. To the patient, quality is getting care "when and where I need it by whomever I choose to cure my symptoms in the fastest possible way." What is quality? And how can we define it?

> Quality is never an accident; it is always the result of high intention, sincere effort, intelligent direction and skillful execution; it is the wise choice of many alternatives.

Quality is something you work for to achieve. It does not happen by itself. It must be planned, it must have strategies, actions, and scientific methods. It requires sophisticated learning and adequate training, and must be conducted by leaders with skills leading to consensus building and teamwork. It will be achieved only if a process of effective selection is followed when choosing the implementation strategy, i.e., decisions are made as informed decisions.

Another definition of quality is that it is achieved when the organization's processes and activities are designed and implemented to continuously meet the needs and expectations of the customers and the organization. (Al-Assaf, 1996) We need to stress the *needs* rather than the *wants*. Patients tend to want more than what they really need. The prudent health care professional is able to know patients' expectations and establish a good rapport to get their trust in understanding their needs and meeting them. One effective way to achieve this is to survey patients periodically. Surveys provide valuable information on patients' needs and expectations. Surveys also can be designed for the other external customers and internal customers. It is up to the providers to analyze the information obtained and identify ways to meet the expectations and needs of those surveyed.

In health care, another definition of quality may apply. Quality is doing the right thing right the first time and doing it better the next. Think of a scenario where a patient is seen by a physician at a clinic. The physician's objective is to learn as much as possible about the patient's signs and symptoms and medical history in order to make the right diagnosis, thus rendering the right treatment. The physician strives to accomplish as much as possible on the first visit, so that updated knowledge on a medical condition means the next patient with the same medical condition receives even better and more current care. This is exactly what this definition calls for — you do only the right things; you do them right at the first time; and you do them better the next time. This follows the Prophet Mohammed, who said: "God likes that when one of you does a job, he does it perfectly."

Quality assurance, as distinguished from quality improvement (QI) or quality management (QM), is the process and subprocesses of planning for quality, development of objectives and goals, setting standards, communicating standards to users, developing indicators, setting thresholds, and collecting data to monitor compliance with set standards. As a consequence of QA, the degree of variance of the current performance from the set standard can be measured, the extent of which defines what steps need to be taken to minimize this variance. QA supports the theory that by standardizing care there will be less chance for variance and a better opportunity for controlling patient care outcomes. (Al-Assaf, 1994)

By having a specific plan, one is able to allocate resources more efficiently, monitor progress more effectively, and possibly able to predict outcomes earlier, avoiding the practice of crisis management where resources are expended to put "down fires rapidly" without due attention to efficiency. Additionally, by having a specific plan, you are able to map strategy more effectively and able to judge progress and evaluate achievements based on planned objectives. QA provides a venue for proper documentation and standardization of key processes, thus controlling variance and better predicting outcomes. It also provides for the development of an ongoing monitoring system where one is able to measure progress towards compliance and

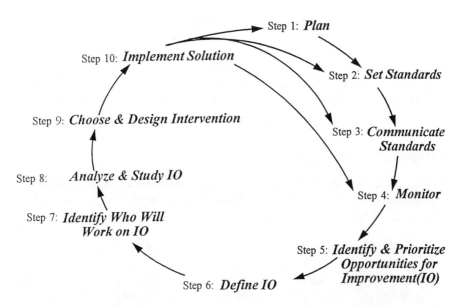

FIGURE 1   USAID Quality Management Cycle. (Nicholas et al., 1991; Blumenfeld, 1993)

able to select areas needing improvements first. In an operational situation, QA will include activities related to such ares as utilization management, risk management, case management, credentialing, and peer review.

Quality Improvement (QI) is the process and subprocesses of reducing variations of performance or variance from standards in order to achieve a better outcome to the organization's customers. The key issues are the ability of this process to identify and act on variance. It is a process of enhancing processes to control outcomes. Activities must revolve around the customer as the driving force for any improvements.

Obviously, QI has a number of necessary specific activities, skills, and tools to accomplish its tasks. Adequate and appropriate training is paramount for its success and proper implementation. Because of this, several models and techniques for performing QI have been developed. Examples of such models are the FOCUS-PDCA model developed by Hospital Corporation of America, the world's largest health care management organization; the 10-step model of JCAHO; and the Quality Management Cycle designed by the QA Project of the U.S. Agency for International Development (USAID). (Figure 1)

Quality Management (QM), on the other hand, is a structural umbrella over all processes and activities related to QA and QI. QM is responsible for the coordination and facilitation of these activities in an organization. Specifically, QM is involved in the selection of health care quality personnel, the allocation of other resources, the monitoring and evaluation of plans, and the launching of improvement teams.

Other terms used in the field include **Continuous Quality Improvement** (CQI), **Total Quality Management** (TQM), **Total Quality Improvement** (TQI), and **Total Quality Leadership** (TQL). The newest term is **Performance Improvement** (PI).

The term an organization chooses is irrelevant as to what the organization is set to achieve and how to achieve it. The key point is that quality can be achieved only if there is adequate preparation, understanding, and proper application of its principles in a health care organization, region, or country. Organization-wide involvement and adequate participation of employees in improvement efforts are critical. The environment must be ready in order to introduce health care quality, as discussed in Chapter 5: *Implementing Quality in Managed Health Care*.

DIMENSIONS OF QUALITY

Health care quality has several attributes and dimensions. Data collected from several national and international surveys of consumers and quality providers describe these dimensions in this sequence:

- Effectiveness
- Efficiency
- Technical Competence
- Safety
- Accessibility
- Interpersonal Relations
- Continuity
- Amenities

Both effectiveness and efficiency are at the top of the list, stressing the fact that quality only can be achieved if processes are performed appropriately and in a cost-conscious environment. (Binns, 1991; Jensen, 1991) Only appropriate and necessary care should be provided. Waste, duplication and rework should be eliminated. Only the most economical and effective ways to provide care should be stressed. In a system of higher demands for quality care, coupled with the reality of limited resources, prudent decisions regarding best possible combinations of effective and efficient care are required and expected.

Providing effective health care in an efficient manner requires high technical skills of professionals who follow the practice of doing the right thing the first time and doing it better the next. Providers and other health care professionals must be well educated and trained to face the everyday challenges of meeting the needs and expectations of their customers, in particular their patients. Health care is a complex field and without a good technical background the chance of a professional survival is weak. Quality must be associated with high technical capability.

It is obvious that no one would provide or receive care in an environment that is unsafe or perceived as unsafe. From a risk management standpoint, the health professional must secure a safe environment for the patient. Unsafe conditions may lead to liability, physical and emotional injury, a loss of goodwill, and damage the facility's reputation in the community. An unsafe environment is counterproductive, time will be spent answering complaints and fending off lawsuits. Safety is an expected and a required dimension.

Accessible care is care that is available, acceptable, affordable, and this includes physical, financial, and intellectual accessibility. The latter is even a more important in an environment where there is a multiplicity of cultures, beliefs, and educational background, as it is the case with the international health care community. Quality care need to be communicated to the "users" in their own setting and under their own conditions to be truly accessible. Therefore, good communication skills are essential.

Personnel interaction is important to providing quality care, which is provided by highly educated, sophisticated, and skilled individuals. These individuals cannot provide holistic care to the patient without relying on teamwork. Interpersonal relationships, therefore, play a tremendous role in shaping the processes of care and ensuring a positive outcome to the patient. Consider a highly specialized hospital with all the "bells and whistles" of technology and a highly competent technical staff, but no real care teams. Each provider works on his own without regards to others, and no coordination of activities or collaboration between providers. It would be almost impossible to deliver any care, let alone quality care. Such an environment is not conducive of quality processes and the hospital is doomed to failure. Effective teamwork is a must for health care quality, as are good interpersonal relationships.

Health care quality is a process, not a program. A program has a beginning and an end, while a process is continuous with no end. Therefore, care should be provided in a continuum — it should be initiated, rendered, evaluated, improved, and continuously monitored even after the patient is cured of his current illness. Care is extended to include wellness, health promotion, and disease prevention. Additionally, care started by one provider should be continued and followed by the other provider in cases of transfer to ensure continuity of care. Fragmented and disconnected care is not a quality system.

Finally, it is always more pleasant to have the care provided in an aesthetically acceptable environment. A facility that pays attention to the minute details of its customers' comfort and well being is certainly a quality facility. Whether it is cleanliness, decor, or service, health care quality only can be enhanced with such a valuable dimension.

PRINCIPLES OF HEALTH CARE QUALITY

Thre are four tenants of health care quality:

1. Focus on customers.
2. Team-work and employee participation.
3. Focus on systems.
4. Data driven.

Health care quality is system oriented. Since systems are comprised of structure, processes, and outcomes, quality focuses on studying the elements of each of these components and finding ways to improve their status collectively. A basic principle is that the health care system is mutually dependent on its parts and elements, no one part being more important than another in order to achieve a better outcome for the patient. Therefore, all system elements need to be considered when improvements are sought.

The last tenant is that health care quality is driven by data. As described earlier, the processes of QA, QI, and QM are based on documented and calculated incremental progress. Without data, quality cannot be measured and improvements cannot be documented. Health care quality requires training on the effective use of meaningful data, through proper collection techniques, appropriate analysis, prudent use of tools and management protocols. Based on data, improvement opportunities are identified and further tackled.

What are the other principles of health care quality?

The following is a selective list of principles applicable to all sectors of health care and others, but is by no means complete. Most are self-explanatory.

- Not only effective management, but also leadership
- Commitment of management
- Customer focus
- Process oriented and outcome driven
- Participative management; consensus building
- Individual responsibility, "...quality originates with the worker."
- Employee empowerment; given the right tools and trained appropriately.
- Proactive improvements; continuously looking for improvement opportunities.
- A continuous process, not a program
- Data driven decision-making
- Teamwork
- Interdisciplinarity, not multidisciplinary
- Education and retraining; professional development
- A system of employee rewards and recognition
- Preventive management before problems are occur
- Variance control to predict outcomes
- Benchmarking or positive competition; emulating the best processes

According to Deming (1984), the organization is made up of thousands of processes. Therefore, health care quality calls for identification and flowcharting of key processes and the early identification of opportunities for improvements in these processes in order to initiate early intervention. Deming also was sensitive to the issue of leadership commitment. He suggests that without this commitment quality will not succeed. In health care this is partly true. Leadership commitment still is important, but not a must for health care quality to succeed. Leaders can facilitate the process, making it work faster and produce faster results. However, in health care leaders change more frequently and total dependence on their commitment may not be prudent. Starting health care quality even at the staff level may produce positive results that will attract the attention of top leaders, thus earning their active support. This approach is a "bottom-up" approach, as opposed to the "top-down" approach described by Deming. In other experiences, both approaches might be implemented in the same system and this may be the most applicable

Another principle needs to be emphasized — **preventive management**. In health care especially, there is a need to look proactively for improvement opportunities. You should not wait for problems to occur and then try to fix them. This approach leads to failure and is very costly. Instead, health care quality requires individuals must know their job processes very well and identify those areas needing improvement early to prevent potential problems. In this way, the system is spared of the consequences of errors and this will increase the its efficiency and effectiveness.

In the next chapter, quality in managed care is explored from the perspective of the provider. Issues related to clinical practice guidelines and requirements of an effective managed care plan also are presented.

REFERENCES

Al-Assaf, A. F. and Schmele, J. A. *The Textbook of Total Quality in Healthcare*, St. Lucie Press, Delray, FL, 1993.

Al-Assaf, A. F. "Quality Improvement in Healthcare: An Overview." *Journal of the Royal Medical Services*, 1(2), 1994.

Al-Assaf, A. F. "International Health care and the Management of Quality." In *Quality Management n Nursing and Healthcare*, Delmar Pub., 1996.

Berwick, D. M. "Sounding Board: Continuous Improvement as an Ideal in Health Care." *New England Journal of Medicine*, 320(1): 53-56, 1989.

Binns, G. S. "The relationship among quality, cost, and market share in hospitals." *Topics in Healthcare Finance*, 18(2):21-32, 1991.

Blumenfeld, S. N. "Quality Assurance in Transition." *PNG Medical Journal*, 36:81-89, 1993.

Crosby, P. *Quality is Free: The Art of Making Quality Certain*, McGraw-Hill, New York, 1979.

Crosby, P. *Quality without Tears*, McGraw–Hill, New York, 1985.

Deming, W. E. *Out of the Crisis*, MIT Press, Cambridge, MA, 1984.

Donabedian, A. "Assessment and Measurement of Quality Assurance in Health Care." *Milbank Memorial Quarterly*, 1966.

Joint Commission on Accreditation of Healthcare Organizations. *Agenda for a Change*, JCAHO, Chicago, IL, 1987.

Jensen J. "Marketing hospital quality." *Topics in Healthcare Finance*, 18(2):58-66, 1991.

Juran, J. *Quality Control and Planning*, ASQC, Milwaukee, WI, 1988.

Nicholas, D. D.; Heiby J. R.; Theresa H. A. "The Quality Assurance Project: Introducing Quality Improvement to Primary Healthcare in Less Developed Countries." *Quality Assurance in health Care*, 3(3):147-165, 1991.

Reerink, E. " Quality Assurance in Health care of Developing Countries." *Quality Assurance in Health Care*, 1(4):195-196, 1989.

Sawyer–Richards, M. "Innovations and Excellence." *Journal of Nursing Quality Assurance*, 5(1):85-88, 1990.

4 Perceptions of Quality in Managed Care: Defining and Improving Providers Performance and Quality

Philip Mosca

CONTENTS

So cheat your landlord if you must, but do not try to shortchange the Muse. It cannot be done. You can't fake quality any more than you can fake a good meal.

William S. Burroughs

However, no two people see the external world in exactly the same way. To every separate person a thing is what he thinks it is — in other words, not a thing but a think.

Penelope Fitzgerald

INTRODUCTION

Precisely defining quality medical care is as elusive as trying to grasp smoke. Everyone believes they know quality medical care when they see or experience it, but few succinctly can define the parameters that differentiate good from poor medical care. It has been noted that value is said to be quality divided by price. Price certainly can be quantified, but the equation breaks down when one tries to define the quality moiety precisely. Some have defined quality as good outcomes. However, outcomes and outcomes measurement is almost as difficult and elusive to define as quality itself. Quality has been defined by others as patient satisfaction. I, as well as many other physicians, can relate tales of patients very satisfied with their medical care, where we as physicians were, shall we say, less than impressed by the processes or outcomes experienced. Oftentimes quality is construed to mean access to or availability of medical care, with little attention to specific patient interactions or outcomes. Thus, the central issue becomes: Who defines quality? Is defined by the patient? Is it defined by the provider? Does the employer or purchaser of the product determine its quality, or is the plan itself the sole arbiter of the quality of the product it offers to its subscribers? Regardless of who defines the quality of the health care offered (provided), it is the responsibility of the plan and plan providers to measure the quality and improve performance if it is deemed lacking.

OPERATIONAL DEFINITION

An operational definition of quality is much the same as the childhood fable of the blind men and the elephant. The opinion of quality is totally dependent upon which aspect is viewed or touched. In general, four basic views enter into any serious discussion of the issue: medical, social, patient, and fiscal.

MEDICAL

The medical or provider view of quality is the classic medical outcome definition. Is the cancer patient cured of the disease? Has the cardiac patient reached optimal performance level? Is the diabetic's blood sugar under good control and is he/she getting the proper screening examinations and optimal medical management to prevent/control complications of the disease? In essence, the clinical issues of mortality, morbidity, complications, screening examinations, and physical performance evaluations are the elements reported in classical medical outcomes.

SOCIAL

The social or societal view of quality is more of a functional assessment on a continuum. Have the psychosocial aspects of the patient's disease been addressed? How well does the patient understand the disease? How may it affect them in their job or family life? Is it apt to affect their reasoning or thinking? May it alter their body image? Will it affect their sexual functioning or ability to enjoy sexual activities? Will it limit their ability to care for children or otherwise interfere with their family life or social obligations? Will they pose any risk of contagion to their spouse, children, or community? How much pain are they liable to experience now or can they expect in the future? If they will suffer from pain what will be the availability of pain medications? If they are having trouble accepting their disease or if their family is overly worried or concerned, is counseling needed or available? Will their general level of energy, and physical functioning be effected and for how long? If their disease is likely to be fatal how long are they likely to live? If they are likely going to die soon, how will they make arrangements for/with family, children, spouse, etc.? How well the provider(s) and health plan itself address these issues will determine the functional quality aspects of the plan or health product.

PATIENT

The patient's view of quality is usually a combination of those found in the medical area, as previously noted, and the measures of patient system/physician interaction. The latter usually are referred to as *patient satisfaction*. Patient satisfaction is a critical element in the definition of quality. How the patient felt about his/her interaction with the physician or other heath care provider is as important, if not more important, than the actual medical outcome. The old retail adage, "if you please a customer, they will tell a friend." is true in health care. More important, the same adage notes, "if you upset a customer, they will tell 10 people." Not only is this true in health care, it is axiomatic. These patient/subscriber tales of woe and discontent can bog down even the most smoothly running operation. The critical elements of patient satisfaction in my opinion are broken into four areas, *access*, *time*, *attitude*, and *outcome*. All of these will be discussed in detail later in this chapter.

COSTS

No discussion of quality can be complete without mention of costs. It is well accepted that the cost or rate of change of costs in the health care arena is what rekindled the flames of the managed care fire. Some would argue that costs alone are being used to determine value, and quality *per se* does not enter into the equation. I believe the two are inseparable.

The cost of health care must be considered in both traditional and nontraditional areas. Traditional costs relate to dollars as costs *per* member *per* month, or costs *per* encounter, or costs *per* disease process. We are all familiar with these costs because they all relate to money spent. Nontraditional costs include: lost time from work, need for hospitalization, length of illness, and intensity of services needed to return the patient to his/her premorbid condition.

OPERATIONAL SYNTHESIS

If we are not mindful of each of these areas in the arena we call quality, then any action taken to effect change in any area is apt to have untoward effects in another area. Much like the child's balloon toy, if you squeeze one area without attention to the whole, the response is simply to *bulge out* in another area. Whenever we are trying to influence quality, we must view our interactions from each of these perspectives before we institute them. Failure to address these areas in our thought processes may result in an outcome which is more harmful to the overall quality than the perceived problem we were trying to address.

PRACTICAL CONSIDERATIONS FOR THE PLAN

With the ethereal and philosophic behind us, what are the practical considerations necessary to attempt to measure quality of care and the performance of physicians and other health care providers? I will discuss the issue as if all health care providers are physicians; however, I fully recognize this is not the case. My reasoning for this tunnel-visioned approach is that although physicians are not the only health care providers, as a group they perhaps are the most difficult to deal with. It has been estimated that 80% of the health care expenditures originate with the physician's pen. As such, from a strictly financial perspective, this is the single most important group to address. There are several elements which must be examined in any practical discussion of this process.

Medical Director

The medical director is the vision of the medical management of the health care plan. The attitude and philosophy of the medical director will pervade many, if not all, of the plan–provider interactions. The medical director must have a clear vision of the direction in which health care is moving. As health care has not been static the past few years and is not expected to undergo any major diminution in its rate of evolution in the near future, the medical director must be amenable and able to change in attitude, process, and operations. However, it is truly the medical director who never must waver in the mission to keep the plan's vision as a beacon to guide all of the plans medical management. When medical providers call a plan's medical director — usually because they are angry or about to become angry about some policy issue, communication, coverage issue, etc. — the first two questions they ask about the medical director before they speak to him/her are "What is the medical director's specialty?" and "Does the medical director still practice medicine?", e.g., see patients. These questions are utmost in the provider's mind for several reasons. The average provider always feels more comfortable discussing patient issues with someone of their own specialty, a luxury a health plan can ill afford if it expects to have a medical director of each specialty. In addition, they feel that a practicing physician is *one of us* and not *one of them*. The *one of them* is a physician who no longer is involved in the direct care of patients, but now has passed over to the other side of solely administrative medicine. Worse yet, the medical director's credibility plummets if he or she never has practiced clinical medicine.

A consideration of the plan should be to have a primary or chief medical director of one specialty and several part-time medical directors of different specialties who can address specific concerns of various provider interest groups. At least one of these physicians still should practice medicine. In some plans that use the group model, each group often selects a medical director from among its own ranks. In the IPA models this is also possible. However, if the preponderance of physicians is not in large groups, then it is the plan that will need to provide the bulk of the medical management. From the plan's perspective, at least one primary care medical director is needed — a family physician is more appropriate than an internal medicine physician or pediatrician, as the latter still are thought of as semispecialists. An obstetrician–gynecologist also is a near necessity. Obstetrics and other women's issues not only are in the societal spotlight, but also they almost always are among a plan's most common procedures. The ob–gyn physician can take on the role of the specialist physician, or if the plan's finances allow, a specialist physician also would be asset. Mental health issues, and diagnostic issues also are important to the plan and at least having physicians of these specialties on contract for administrative consultation is an operational issue that should be addressed. The medical director's must convey to all of the other plan employees the medical management philosophy. If the medical director does not convey this well, the interface with plan providers, employers, subscribers and officials of state and national regulators will be inconsistent and, therefore, in question.

The attitude of the medical director will set the tenor of all of the plan's interactions with its providers. If the attitude is haughty or dictatorial, resistance will be forthcoming. If the attitude is condescending, providers will be quite passive aggressive. If finances always are of utmost concern, underutilization issues may result. The attitude of the medical director should be of partnering with the plan providers to assist patients in getting the health care they need. Dissemination of information and performance are central issues in motivating physician performance. Never fail to compliment and congratulate plan providers for jobs well done in meeting quality goals, in going the extra mile for their patients, and for working with the plan to assist patients in their needs.

MEDICAL SERVICES DIRECTOR

If the medical director represents the executive arm of medical management, the medical services director is the administrative or operations arm of medical management. The interface between the medical director and the medical services director should be as seamless and transparent as possible. They should be able to communicate freely and well. They should share similar values relative to plan management and medical management goals. The medical services director is the implementation arm for case management, peer management, utilization review, and authorizations, if any and all of these management techniques are in use by the health plan.

CLINICAL GUIDELINES

Clinical Guidelines are the two--edged sword of medical management. In group model or staff model HMO plans, they can be quite useful and may result in significantly better changes in practice patterns. The formation of guidelines often is difficult, time consuming, and may not modify physician behavior to a degree to make it seem worth the effort, especially in the IPA or PHO model HMO. The first issue in guideline implementation is whether to adopt a guideline already promulgated or develop one locally. From a practical standpoint, it is best to start with a national guideline and modify it for local conditions and community medical practice. Although this sounds ideal and is said to provide the best of both worlds, personal experience with this method has proved it is time consuming, difficult, and tends to codify the current existent behaviors of the majority or at least the most vocal of the plan's physicians. This is not to say one should not attempt to implement guidelines, but rather to enlighten those getting ready to implement this stratagem. Implementation may not be quite as simple or direct as some authors or conventional wisdom might allow you to believe.

A recent trend in guideline development has been the development of *ideal patient flowcharts*. These are guidelines, but on a benchmarked ideal patient protocol. In the few studies I have reviewed, they seem to reduce costs without altering favorable outcomes. I believe they will require a great deal more study; however, the concept appeals to me because it places in front of the eyes of the clinician the best case scenario as opposed to the average case scenario. Any use of guidelines or ideal patient flowcharts needs to be accompanied by sites of objective data collection to determine compliance as well as predetermined medical outcomes. Most guidelines, as currently developed, deal with surgical procedure, or in-patient care. Cooperative guidelines between specialist physicians and primary care providers for appropriate testing and referral would be far more helpful to physicians in general and would obviate the argument that the patient is being referred too late.

DATA, DATA, DATA

Physicians are data driven. I can't think of any truer statement concerning physicians or medicine in general. It has been demonstrated time and time again that when presented with valid compelling data physicians almost always will change their behavior. The problem is in obtaining the data, being certain that it is valid, and presenting it in a manner that is easy to understand. It also must provide for peer group comparison and best-in-class comparison. If the data is financial in nature, additional medical outcomes data also should be provided. Easy? **Not!** Designing studies, collection of data, analysis of data, and presentation of data is a complex and time consuming set of tasks associated with numerous perils and pitfalls.

In addition, data must be severity adjusted or the comment that "my practice is unique" or "my patients are sicker than average" invariably will be forthcoming. There are several software packages that can interface with claims systems and perform this function, as well as provide excellent utilization and variance reports. True severity adjustment, however, requires the existence of the computerized medical record designed to collect the data necessary for disease state ranking or other forms of clinical status adjustments based on *clinical* rather than *administrative* or *claims* data.

PROVIDER COMMUNICATION

If data is important, communication is vital. You must keep the lines of communication open between the providers and the plan or PHO, or medical group. The communication should exist in many forms and forums. For the PHO's presentations to their boards, as well as their membership, meetings of various aspects of the plan usually are well received. Meetings with individual medical groups to answer questions or to attempt to ferret out problems and correct the same go a long way towards having satisfied providers. Presentation of data in a nonthreatening format is useful to provide the tenor or mission of the plan regarding medical management. Of course if a particular area needs addressing, it may be necessary to provide data which is more pointed towards findings of less than uniform practice patterns as well as significant variations in outcomes and/or costs. The development of teams to assess particular disease processes and to help with the development of ideal patient flowcharts and guideline tools as well as data collection forms and the format for data presentation will help obtain buy-in from the local physician community. Communication cannot be overdone. The plan must share with its providers as much data in as many formats as possible. We must remember that we all learn in different fashions. Some of us are auditory learners; others visual learners; and others kinesthetic learners. By providing data in more than one format or media, we stand the best chance of educating the provider. It is through education that we stand the best chance at modifying behavior if this is needed, or enlisting cooperation in any number of initiatives designed to improve the quality of the health care provided to the membership.

PRACTICAL CONSIDERATIONS FOR PROVIDERS

From the provider's standpoint, the practical considerations relative to quality are *responses* to external pressures. The practices which have instituted their own patient satisfaction surveys and acted upon them will be viewed quite favorably by all. The provider should have all necessary licenses and inspections as required by law, e.g., CLIA, OSHA, and fire. Further, if the practice has instituted any special programs to increase patient satisfaction or enhance patient care and/or understanding, these items should be brought to the attention of the plan at contracting time. An introduction to the practice booklet explaining how to reach the physician for questions, prescription refills, emergencies, etc. goes a long way to enhance a practice's reputation, please patients, and ultimately improve patient care quality by creating a more educated patient population whose expectations are grounded in the "reality" of practice patterns rather than preconceived ideas. In addition, explanation of how to access a specialist or why one needs to obtain a referral before returning to see a specialist goes a long way towards educating the patient population about the nuances of managed care. These items are valuable whether the practice is primary care, specialty service, or a mixed practice model. For other plan providers this becomes even more important if the patient's expectations are to be met in the somewhat more restrictive environment of the managed care world.

No discussion of quality from the provider's perspective can be considered complete without mention of the **medical record**. This perhaps is the single most important document relative to the "quality" of care rendered to the patient. Whenever a question arises as to what happened, the expectations, what conversations ensued, the treatment plan, how the outcome was perceived, etc., the first request is to review the medical record. Inpatient or outpatient, the patient medical record is the single most important document relative to the type of care rendered and the medical decision process involved in those treatment decisions. I believe physicians finally are coming to the realization that if it was not documented, it did not happen. The content of the medical record or patient chart varies according to whether the physician is a specialist or a primary care physician. Regardless, check with HMOs in the area or obtain copies of the Health Employer Data Information Set (HEDIS) chart review guidelines to define the standards to which your medical records will be compared. The issue is not whether you agree or disagree with the standards, as this really has no practical value. The employer and the plan usually have adopted the standards and they will compare the provider's records to those standards regardless of the provider's opinion of their validity. In general, the most stringent requirements will be those imposed by the HMOs as opposed to the PPOs in the area. As the HEDIS quickly is becoming a national standard regarding access, quality, satisfaction, etc., it would behoove providers to familiarize themselves with these standards. The provider must be aware of the perceptions of the health plan, the patient, and the employer in this milieu we call quality of care and outcomes measurement.

PRACTICAL CONSIDERATIONS FOR PATIENTS

The patient has very little objective data from which to draw conclusions. It has been noted that plan specific, as well as physician specific, data will be published on the Internet in the near future. Public presentation of hospital data has been available in a few places in the United States for several years. With the advent of the Internet, it is not surprising that this data formatted for employers as well as consumers soon will be available. The patient has only a few objective and subjective measures of their encounters with the health care system. How easy was it to access the system? Did it take several calls to get an appointment? Was the time from the call to the appointment date reasonable to the patient? How were they treated by the staff making the appointment, and did their attitude seem caring and genuinely concerned? Once they arrived at the physician's office, were they greeted cordially? Was the registration process difficult? How long did they wait between arrival and seeing the doctor or other health care provider? Did the provider seem interested? Was the provider's attitude condescending or curt? Did the provider seem to have compassion? Did they have enough time with the provider? Did they have their questions answered? How satisfied were they with the thoroughness of their exam? Were they happy with the initial outcome of their visit? Did their health status improve as a result of having sought out medical care?

Although patients may not be in an expert position to provide answers to these questions, they will be asked, and the patients will provide their perceptions as the answer. If you are a provider and have not reviewed the HEDIS questions and standard or the SF-36 question set, I would recommend you do so to more fully understand the manner in which the issues of access, time, attitude and outcome are addressed.

PRACTICAL CONSIDERATIONS FOR EMPLOYERS

For the employer, picking the *right* health plan coverage for your employees is of paramount importance. Seen as a major retention and bonus agent, health care coverage not only is important from an employee satisfaction standpoint, but also usually is a major expenditure for most small and many large employers. The following issues usually are raised to the health plan by the employer, while more recently with physician groups increasingly approaching employers for direct contracting, they are asked of the physicians' groups as well. From the employers standpoint the single most pressing question involves who are the physicians, hospital, and other providers? Where are they located relative to the homes or worksites of their employees. Are the providers considered high quality? A measure of quality from the employer standpoint is hospitals which are accredited by JCAHO and other accrediting bodies and physicians who are board certified or have some other standard of credentials that they have attained. Once a panel is chosen, the employer is interested in wellness programs provided to help keep their workforce healthy. These programs might include smoking cessation programs, prenatal classes, exercise or health club discounts or facilities. How accessible are the providers to the employees? Is it easy to get an appointment and in a relatively short time frame? Are the employees generally happy about the health care they receive? Does the benefits manager have complaints with the health plan or with the provider panel? What are the additional costs beyond premiums that must be paid? How do the health care costs of the employee group this year compare to prior years? If health care costs are rising, has the *rate* of increase remained constant? As can be seen, the employer generally sets the tone of the health plan's Explanation of Benefits Coverage (EOC). It is the EOC, along with the employee demographics and prior years' heath resources utilization, which drives the actuarial projections which translate into premium rates or levels. Today price is the single most important determinant in the employer's selection of health care coverage. However, as risk is shared or moved into the provider's camp, it will become quality, within certain price constraints, which will determine the health care plan selection of the future.

SUMMARY

The steps necessary to define and improve a provider's performance and quality in the provision of health care services are:

1. Measure current performance of the provider from the standpoint of the health plan, the consumer, and the employer in a defined area of interest. Be certain the measurements are severity adjusted, and that you are in fact measuring what you intended to measure.
2. Present the data obtained and the analysis thereof to the provider panel to be certain they agree with the finding that the area in question needs improvement. If there is no agreement that the area in question needs to be improved. the process will stop at this point. Be certain there is agreement on both the "area" and the measurement parameters.

3. Develop a "process" with the provider to address the parameters of each of the constituent groups, e.g., employer, patient, and health plan. Be certain the process involves agreement on any new measurement parameters.
4. Institute the process and provide ongoing incremental data to the provider at short enough intervals that they do not lose interest in the project, and can make real time adjustments to their practice style to ensure the outcome.
5. After the predefined interval, provide the "final" data on the study to all the provider groups, and, if appropriate, to all the constituent groups.
6. Assess the performance of the plan in the process. That is, did we do what we intended to do? Did it have any untoward negative effect in any of the constituent groups? Would the entire project bear the scrutiny of an outside observer from a cost/benefit ratio, or a return on investment analysis from either a fiscal, image, marketing, or community standpoint?

Remember, If the provider does not perceive the need for change, it will not occur. If the provider does not participate actively in the development of the parameters of the improvement process, the endeavor will fail before it can be implemented. If the health plan has not done its homework to develop the systems to provide for the proper instrument to provide accurate and complete data capture, severity adjustment, and valid analysis of the data, the provider will see this as incompetence, and will react with distrust and anger.

The path to improving the provider's perception of quality and acting as the nidus for positive change is not easy. Do **not** jump into the arena until you have examined the necessary processes to determine if you posses the required tools to implement the process. Keep in mind that the market is currently in a great state of flux and is expected to remain in flux for the near future. Whenever a system is in a state of flux, it is difficult to understand the operative forces driving the internal changes. However, if one examines the system closely by examining each of its subsystems carefully, a reasonable model can be constructed. Although I may have projected a negative image of the efforts required to effect provider change and improvement, there is nothing further from the truth. I not only believe it can be achieved, but also I have seen it done time and time again. These efforts only can succeed, however, when they are well planned and carefully implemented. If you are reticent about instituting a quality improvement activity within the managed care environment; if your vision of the problem seems obscured, I encourage you to reflect upon the following passage found in the new translation of the recently discovered Ma-Wang-Tui texts of the Te-Tao Ching ascribed to Lao-Tzu. From the section of the *Tao* (the way):

If you take muddy water and still it, it gradually becomes clear.
If you bring something to rest in order to move it, it gradually comes alive.

REFERENCES

Banks, N. J. and Palmer, H. P. "Clinical Reminders in Ambulatory Care." *HMO Practice*, 4: 131–136, 1990

Brailer, D. J. "Clinical Decision Support: Managing Quality in Integrated Delivery Systems." *Quality Management in Health Care*, 4: 24–33, 1996.

Cangialose, C. B., Edward, K. S., and Ballard, D. J. "An Economic Evaluation of the Healthcare Quality Improvement Program." *J. Outcomes Management*, 3: 4-9, 1996.

Cotterell, C, C., Dobbroske, L., and Fischermann, E. A. "Comprehensive drug-use evaluation program in a health maintenance organization." *Am. J. Hosp. Pharm.* 1712–1717, 1991.

Dunn, E. F. and Brown, C. J. "Patient Satisfaction Studies: What Do the Results Really Mean?" *J. Outcomes Management.* 3: 10–14, 1996.

Foundation for Acountability(FAcct). *Guidebook for Performance Measurement.* Portland, OR. October 1995

Gottlieb, L. B., Margolis, C. Z., and Schoenbaum, S. C.. "Clinical Practice Guidlines at an HMO: Development and Implementation in a Quality Improvement Model." *QRB.* 80-86, Feb. 1990.

Gottlieb, L. B., Sokol, H. N., Murrey, K. O., and Schoenbaum, S. C.. "Algorithm-Based Clinical Quality Improvement." *HMO Practice*, 6:5-12, 1992.

Gross, P. A. "The Missing Links in Guideline Implementation." *Quality Management in Healthcare.* 4:34-36, 1996.

Hanachak, N. A. and Schlackman, N. "The Measurement of Physician Performance." *Quality Management in Healthcare.* 4: 1–12, 1995.

Hillman, A. L. "Managing the Physician: Rules Vs. Incentives (Commentary)." *Health Affairs.* 138–146, Winter 1991.

Horn, S. D. and Hopkins, D. S. P., Eds. *Medical Outcomes and Practice Guidlines Library.* Vols. 1–3, Faulkner and Gray, New York, 1994

Integrated Healthcare Report. The Minneapolis Business Coalition RFP. 4-7, June 1993.

Kamerow, D. B. and Schlackman, N. *Practice Guidlines and Managed Care: Fact or Fiction.* AAHP 1996 Annual Meeting, Session Number 28.

Kenkel, P. J. "Consolidations in Minnesota help bring about the demise of the state's health coalition." *Modern Healthcare.* 32, June 1992.

Kemnitz, D. H. "An Employer Model for Reform." *Journal of Healthcare Benefits.* 12–17, May/June 1994.

Lassa, J., Asadi, M.J. "Comparing Physician Outcomes and Influencing Change." *HIMSS Proceedings.* 2: 165–175, 1995.

Leigh, B. "Case Management in a Health Maintenance Organization. Improving Quality of Care." *AAOHN Journal.* 41: 170–173, 1993.

Matthews, P., Carter, N., and Smith, K. "Using Data to Measure Outcomes." *HIMSS Proceedings.* 3: 295–307, 1995.

McHorney, C. A.,Ware, J. E., Rogers, W., Raczek, A. B., and Lu, J. F. R. "The Validity and Relative Precision of MOS short- and Long-Form Health Status Scales and Dartmouth COOP Charts." *Medical Care.* 30: MS253–MS265, 1992.

Nash, D. B. "Quality of Measurement or Quality of Medicine?" (Editorial). *JAMA* 273: 1537–1538, 1995.

Nash, I. S. and Pasternak, R. C. "Managed Care and Quality." *JAMA.* 273:1483–1484, 1995.

Nelson, E. C., Mohr, J. J., Batalden, P. B., and Plume, S. K. "Improving Health Care, Part 1: The Clinical Value Compass." *Journal on Quality Improvement.* 22: 243–258, 1996.

Norling, R. A., McLaughlin, D. B., Schultz, A., and Borbas, C. "The Minnesota Clinical Comparison and Assesment Program: A Resource for Clinical Quality Improvement Programs." *The Quality Letter.* 14–17, June 1993.

Rosen, R. R. "The Place of Healthcare Standards in Quality Assurance." *HMO Practice.* 3: 173–177, 1989.

Rubin, H. R., Gandek, B., Rogers, W. H., Kosinski, M. A., and McHorney, C. A. "Patients' Ratings of Outpatient Visits in Different Practice Settings." *JAMA.* 270: 835–840, 1993.

Schlackman, N. "The Quality Care Cycle." *QRB.* 360–364, November 1991.

Singer, C. A. "Utilization Review and Case Management Systems Update." *The Singer Report.* Report Number 30, 1995.

UPDATE: The Newsletter of the Health Outcomes Institute. 2: 2; 1–3, 1995.

Using Clinical Practice Guidlines To Evaluate Quality of Care. U.S. Dept. HHS; AHCPR AHCPR Pub. No. 95-0046, 1995.

Webb, M. Z., Kuykendall, D. H., Zeiger, R. S., Berquist, S. L., Lischio, D., Wilson, T., and Freedman, C. "The Impact of Status Asthmaticus Practice Guidlines on Patient Outcome and Physician Behavior." *QRB.* 471–476, December 1992.

Weiner, J. P., Parente, S. T., Garnick, D. W., Fowles, J., Lawthers, A. G., and Palmer, H. "Variation in Office Bases Quality." *JAMA.* 273: 1503–1508, 1995.

Winslow, C. "The Role of Guidlines in Achieving Rational Health care Management." *The Internest.* 14–16, May 1990.

Witter, D. M. "Transforming Paradigms for Provider Information Systems." *Quality Management in Healthcare.* 4: 7–13, 1996.

5 Implementing Quality in Managed Health Care

A. F. Al-Assaf

CONTENTS

INTRODUCTION AND BACKGROUND

Health organizations worldwide are beginning to introduce quality in their care systems. This mainly is due to the fact that providing care — any care — no longer is an acceptable option. Patients and purchasers alike are asking for and sometimes demanding that this care is provided with quality. (Al-Assaf, 1993, 1994) Providing mediocre care no longer is acceptable. Providing care without regard to optimum resource utilization no longer is acceptable. And certainly, care that is provided in a haphazard way also is not acceptable.

Other reasons are cited for this increasing demand. Implementing health care quality has resulted in cost savings and a satisfying environment. Quality accomplishments have made patients happier and turned providers into highly effective professionals. (Linsk, 1990) In quality systems, care is provided more appropriately and there is less waste and unnecessary rework. Purchasers are reaping the benefits of a leaner, more efficient system as they too are learning to become more prudent in achieving the organization's objectives. (Sawatzky and McDonald, 1994) In essence, health care quality, when implemented correctly, can lead to patient satisfaction, higher employee morale, and lower costs of care and services delivery.

Obviously, introducing health care quality is not an easy task. It also is not an easy solution to age-long problems, but it certainly is a step in the right direction.

Implementing health care quality requires dedication, perseverance, and patience. It requires real commitment. It thrives on leadership. It cultivates champions. So, what is health care quality? How can it be implemented? And what are the stages a system might go through to achieve health care quality?

To answer the first question, we will borrow the definition and discussions presented on health care quality from the earlier chapter on the subject. Health care quality is the structural umbrella of all the processes associated with quality assurance, quality control, monitoring, and quality improvement in one system and culture of quality applied to health care. It is a cultural transformation towards excellence. Health care quality is related to **total quality management**, TQM, or **to continuous quality improvement**, CQI, in that it is also an organization-wide or a system-wide management intervention strategy. Its objectives revolve around improving organizational processes based on meeting customers' expectations and needs on a continuous basis.

In this chapter, I will present a broad discussion on the introduction of health care quality in a system. I will provide a discussion of the strategic planning process towards health care quality as well as a broad discussion of the stages of implementation of such a process and conclude with the lessons and challenges of institutionalizing health care quality in an organization, or a system.

STRATEGIC PLANNING FOR HEALTH CARE QUALITY

The process of planning for health care quality is divided into two components: strategic and operational. In **strategic planning** the level of involvement is higher in the organizational hierarchy, where initial decisions and broad policies are made for the proper implementation of health care quality. It involves management commitment and securing additional support (financial and technical), as well as structural support organization for quality implementation. It is a complex and necessary process that should take place before any implementation activities are begun.

Operational planning, on the other hand, is more specific and elaborate in design, process, and activities. It involves the detailed planning for any and every activity that will be taking place during partial or full implementation of health care quality. In this planning stage, the right individuals actively are setting resource allocations, training requirements, employee participation, type and number of projects to be performed, etc., all at the intervention level(s). This level of planning involves much more time and details than the strategic planning level and it, too, is an essential step before proper implementation of any process, especially health care quality. What follows is a discussions of the steps and activities that should take place under each of these planning processes.

MANAGEMENT COMMITMENT

There are not enough words to describe how important management commitment is to the success of quality, at least in other industries. Time and time again, experts have demonstrated the value of management commitment to the quality process. In health care, however, the personnel are somewhat different and their values also are different. Health care professionals are interdependent, but less so on management — although this model is changing rapidly with managed care. Also, health professionals in the most part have been attracted to health care not because of profit-making, but for serving humanity. Therefore, the values in health care revolve around helping another human being without need for management reminders. Hence, in health care, management commitment is encouraged, but not vital. Boerstler et al. 1996 However, it is preferred if one wants to achieve results rapidly. Management can open doors, facilitate interventions freely, and coordinate resources easily. In most cases, management has the final say on things, making the final decision. Therefore, health care quality implementation can be enhanced with management supporting and pushing it.

What is commitment? Deming (1984) says if top management's commitment is not there, he would not even bother implementing quality in such an organization. His words echo his theory: "If you can't come, send no one." Commitment to a cause means being involved, supportive, active, and participative. Commitment also means leading efforts, facilitating activities, and providing resources to make that cause a reality and a success. Commitment to a process or a program means taking pride and joy in supporting it and learning more about it. It is not just rhetoric and oral support, although even that is better than no support at all.

In my opinion, commitment cannot be achieved without adequate understanding of what you want to commit to. Therefore, paramount to this step is increasing knowledge and awareness on the subject needing commitment. For health care quality, it is even more difficult to get unequivocal commitment from management without demonstrating results. Manager usually are quick to say: "Show me that it works!" Health care quality then must be based on data and always should be driven by outcomes. With adequate planning and process design, commitment will be cultivated and positive results can be achieved.

ROLE OF CONSULTANTS AND ADVISORS

As seen from the above, at least early in process, the need for objective perspectives and specific expertise may warrant the call for consultants and advisors. (Newman 1991) With the help of experienced organizations and professional associations, a collaborative effort of identifying and selecting the right consultant needs to be initiated before actual implementation occurs. Identifying the right consultant is necessary — one that has demonstrated expertise in the specific area needed with past experiences in similar environments and cultures. Another important characteristic for a useful consultant is one with the knowledge and sincere desire for technology transfer, one that is interested in establishing and fostering local expertise.

Early in the process of implementation, the managed care organization should select a suitable short-term consultant to assist the designated key person(s) in the strategic planning effort for health care quality. At this stage the consultant may be useful by assisting in the identification of internal qualified individuals to work on this effort, provide an organization-wide awareness seminar on quality to key personnel, draft with key personnel the mission and vision statements of the organization, and help design and map this new initiative. A consultant can be extremely helpful in identifying milestones towards complete implementation of health care quality in that organization, which in turn makes it easier to monitor progress and ensure sustainability.

Once strategic planning is accomplished, either the same consultant or another should be selected to guide the operational implementation of the process. This individual should have practical expertise in training, facilitation, and process improvement team-building. This type of consultancy requires long-term involvement — at least a year or until internal expertise become available. Quality assurance expertise, on the other hand, will be needed on an *ad hoc* basis, patricularly during the stage of standards development and indicator selection. This kind of expertise usually is more specialized to the specific areas needing standards and internal resources should be included along with the external consultant to ensure continuity of the process.

ASSIGNING RESPONSIBILITY

At this stage of strategic planning, the person in charge of the organization, usually the president, CEO, or COO, needs to identify an internal **coordinator of health care quality**. This position need not be full-time, but requires an individual possessing leadership skills and given sufficient authority. Direct link is necessary between this individual and the top administrator for maintaining credibility and authority. This position is so important that in some organizations a key person in top management assumes this role. This approach has advantages and disadvantages. A prominent person would give instant recognition and support to the quality movement. It would establish commitment from day one, which sends a message to the rest of the organization that quality is important and everyone must follow. One disadvantage is that this person usually is not in a permanent position, thus causing discontinuity of the process if there is a change. Regardless of whom this person is, this individual needs to be trained extensively in health care quality techniques and prepare for the organization of the quality council. Of course the responsibilities of the quality coordinator are numerous, among which are:

- advocate and speaker for health care quality,
- facilitator of the quality council,
- designated counterpart of the consultant,
- coordinator of strategic and operational planning for health care quality activities and the allocation of resources,
- initiator of process improvement teams,

- coordinator of the selection of key personnel in quality,
- coordinator of the health care quality training plan.
- facilitator of future expansions strategies.

The **quality council** (QC) is formed to act as the steering body that will directs the health care quality process throughout the organization. It works as a coordinating committee of individuals representing the different aspects of health care in the organization to formulate corporate policies towards quality. Organizing the QC is not a must, but from experience I found it to be a necessity. Certainly the council's membership is as important, and careful selection of these individuals should rest with the top administrator, with advice and assistance from the quality coordinator and the consultant. Members should be prominent individuals in the organization representing different departments and disciplines. Membership may be broadened to include other prominent individuals from the provider network, thus giving it a global flavor while gaining invaluable expertise and perspectives from outside individuals. Once members are identified, a charter needs to be developed with specific roles and responsibilities delineated. The roles of the council are somewhat similar to the roles of the quality coordinator, giving it collective perspective and establishing itself as the organization's resource in health care quality that the rest of the organization may tap into when necessary. QC members need to be prepared adequately and should be exposed to the concept of health care quality and its principles early in the process.

Once formed, the council's first agenda item should be to ratify its charter. Each member should believe in the charter, and should get actively involved in its revision and redrafting to reflect actual involvement in the council. Other agenda items to be addressed are the **mission** and **vision** statements, which should reflect the desire for health care improvements and the goal of quality. Both statements need to be drafted by council members, with input from all key personnel in the organization. These statements are important in establishing the organization's constancy of purpose and will serve as a constant reminder of the organization's path and a map for its future. Mission and vision statements reflect what the organization's current activities are, the purpose for its existence, who its customers are, and what it wants to achieve. Mission and vision statements should be concise, clear, realistic, and reflect the true desire of the organization. That is why input from other key individuals is necessary. Once drafted, approved and finalized, these statements should be communicated to the rest of the organization actively and consistently. Some organizations opt to post these statements in prominent places throughout the organization, even printing them at the back of personal business cards

ALLOCATION OF RESOURCES

Early in the process, both physical and human resources are needed to initiate change. Resources are needed initially for the necessary training and the acquiring of consultants. Resources also are needed for dissemination and increasing health professionals' awareness in the concept of health care quality. Additional resources may be required later to disseminate the concept at the grass-roots level and to the professional staff. Funds also should be set aside for potential structural changes and redesigns in processes or units to fit required improvements. In some organizations, funds were used to buy reading material and to establish a central library on health care quality. Others used them to hire full- or part-time individuals as internal quality coordinators, while others used the additional funds to publish a newsletter on quality and to hold internal and periodic seminars on the subject. Still others opted to offer monitory and capitol support to successful units or individuals who have demonstrated substantial improvements.

Another aspect of resource allocation is establishment of a new unit within the organization dedicated to health care quality. This unit can be organized with a number of health professionals from within the organization and linked directly to top management. This unit also should be given the mandate for setting organization's quality standards and indicators, disseminating information related to health care quality, monitoring the quality of care delivered, and to act on opportunities for improvements in the system. The unit should have financial and political support from the top administrator, with broad authority for inspecting any record within organization. The objective is to start a nucleus of a quality unit that will take the responsibility of coordinating health care quality for the organization, thus ensuring sustainability. This unit also could take responsibility for preparing and coordinating all activities related to certification, licensure, and accreditation. Other duties may include coordination of all committees related to quality, such as peer management, credentialing, and utilization management, as well as the actual processes of provider credentialing, delegated services oversight, and preventive services provision and monitoring.

INCREASING AWARENESS OF HEALTH CARE QUALITY

Health care quality as a concept has different facets, principles, techniques and tools. There is also a vast amount of literature that has been written about it in the professional arena. Therefore, an early activity of the QC is for its members to participate in a seminar on health care quality. This seminar should be followed by intellectual discussions with the consultant as to the application of this concept in that organization, taking into consideration available resources, the culture, and the current health status and structure. A similar activity should be organized to present health care quality to other key personnel to get further support, and to increase dissemination of the concept. One method introduced in one organization was the preparation of newsletter articles, with examples for potential internal application in clear and operational language. Another organization sponsored an organization-wide "scientific day on quality" in which the concept and application of health care quality was introduced. This received instant attention from all levels of the organization as it perceived top management's commitment to quality. The consultant's services could be used to present a number of short discussion sessions with other key personnel and middle managers. These sessions, which should be attended by at least the quality coordinator and some QC members, can serve as focus group sessions to get feedback on quality implementation and applications in health care, as well as an avenue to increase awareness on the concept. Information and feedback collected from these sessions can be used in the next planning phase of implementation at the operational level and in launching pilot projects.

MAPPING HEALTH CARE QUALITY INTERVENTION

It is found that once strategic planning and a basic organizational structure have been completed, early testing or preimplementation activities need to be sponsored in the form of small pilot projects or process improvement teams. This step is not mandatory, but can be very useful in the early identification of gaps in communication, planning, and intervention. Lessons learned after the completion of such projects can be extremely valuable in correcting these shortfalls.

In collaboration with the QC and with information collected during the planning phase, the quality coordinator may identify areas in the system having an opportunity for improvement. These areas should be selected carefully to include simple projects that require the least amount of resources and have the highest probability of success and potential of affecting a large number of beneficiaries. Examples of such projects may include improvements in the reception area, improving the aesthetics of the customer service area, or selecting a few areas that receive high complaints from the public. Other examples may include the initiation of a simple national campaign on promoting health awareness to the members or conducting an immunization campaign or a health fair during a special event. Other projects may involve the formal identification and selection of an improvement opportunity, either clinical or administrative, and the organization of an interdisciplinary team from the affected area to initiate improvements. The key here is to start somewhere and start with simple projects that have a higher possibility of success.

At the completion of pilot projects, the QC should analyze the lessons learned and based on the criteria, listed below, prioritize those services for further implementation of health care quality:

- high volume,
- problem-prone,
- high risks,
- high impact and
- high costs services, procedures, units, etc.

The QC in the next two steps needs to decide on whether to start partial implementation within a certain service area or within a number of services organization-wide. In either way, using these criteria, the council will be able to choose the area or service specific for implementation. The use of objectivity in selecting a system or an area for intervention is crucial for successful implementation and future expansion. At this stage, the council is ready to plan for the operational level of health care quality implementation.

OPERATIONAL PLANNING FOR HEALTH CARE QUALITY

Although the scope of this chapter is to present broad strategies for the introduction of health care quality into a managed care organization or a system within a specific organization, it is imperative to present briefly the operational planning stages. As mentioned earlier, this level of planning is highly specific and detailed and usually is carried out by same individuals responsible for carrying out the implementation process at the selected service or system.

At this stage the key individuals from the selected intervention service or system are the ones with the primary responsibility for assisting the QC in planning the implementation strategies at the operational level. This type of planning usually is carried out by the QC and in collaboration with middle managers. These individuals in direct participation with the quality council are asked to develop the operational plan. The final outcome of planning meetings should be the development of operational strategies for quality implementation. The following strategies are suggested:

Strategy 1   Initiate communications and secure commitment of other professionals

Council members and/or the quality coordinator should start early communications with the "leaders." (Kaluzney et al. 1995) Leaders should be contacted for support of the initiative and to solicit their willingness of having their area be part of an organization-wide strategy on health care quality. At this stage a discussion is necessary as to the benefits of the initiative and the advantage of being an early implementation site. A note of caution here is to include everybody who is considered a leader in that organization. Being too selective might have negative effects.

Strategy 2   Introduce the concept of health care quality

Hold a number of small group discussions or small seminars on the concept of health care quality. Emphasize the principles, and the advantages. Discuss the resource requirements and the importance of the commitment of the internal customers on the success of the process. Try to answer the question regarding the benefits of implementing such a process in that organization.

Strategy 3   Develop broad internal objectives of health care quality

Again with key leaders in the community develop a number of broad, yet realistic, objectives along with a timetable for accomplishments. Objectives need to reflect the local needs and expectations of the community at large, not individuals. Therefore, issues regarding health status improvements need to be associated with data, if available, or rely on credible sources.

Strategy 4   Discuss plans for and secure needed resources

This is a preliminary planning stage for the estimated resources needed. Once the next strategies (discussed below) have been completed, a more rigorous resource allocation must take place. However, at this stage only a broad description of the type of resources needed and its uses should be discussed. Specific resource allocation is directly dependent on the extent of quality interventions needed, which will be established at a later stage.

Strategy 5 Establish the health care quality organizational structure

There are several schools of thought regarding the implementation of this strategy. The question is whether to establish an elaborate, but solid, organizational structure or to keep the structure loosely linked. The suggested advice is that a structure is needed to ensure sustainability, but the extent and the mapping is dependent on several factors that need to be considered in determining the best approach in that organization. Another bit of advice is to develop structures slowly and gradually, never a complex structure at the outset, as this will distract the focus on the main issue of improvement and concentrate on committee memberships, responsibilities, and meetings. One other issue is that one type of structure in one organization may not be as effective in another. A review of the experiences in similar organizations may be of help in accomplishing this strategy.

Strategy 6 Collaboratively plan training requirements

Again, based on only actual needs, training may be planned. The goal is to plan for optimum training. Too much training also may have negative outcomes. Another issue to be considered is: In what mechanism training should be delivered? i.e., should it be delivered in the form of preparation workshops for potential participants in health care quality or should it be delivered on needs basis and only at the time of the actual improvement process? Deming suggests that training should be as an on-the-job training, but others have done it differently and successfully. In whatever mechanism it is delivered, in general, training in QA and QI skills is required for proper implementation of health care quality. Also, under this strategy issues related to training venues, training material, objectives, type of participants, method, content, trainers, timetables, and expected outcomes should be developed. Here again, relying on previous experiences from other organizations and with the help of an experienced consultant, a good training strategy can be accomplished.

Strategy 7 Plan preimplementation assessment

A full assessment of the quality of health care services in that organization should be done. Planning for that assessment activities is required. In planning for such activities, issues related to method, assessment population, by whom, how long, and resources needed should be addressed. The objectives of this assessment are twofold. First, is to identify problem areas to aid in the selection of improvement interventions areas. Second, is to provide planners base-line data of the status of health services (and potentially their members) of that organization before improvements. Any future improvements then will be easily measured using comparative data.

Strategy 8   Develop progress reporting mechanism and methods for evaluation

This is the strategy that is so crucial yet missed or de-emphasized the most. Progress toward meeting the objectives of the quality initiative need to be documented and communicated to the quality council and the coordinator. In this way, obstacles can be identified and corrected early. Thus, adjustments to plans can be made effectively. Agreement should be reached at this stage on the method, the type, and the frequency of self reporting, as well as on the method for evaluating and monitoring the progress of improvement efforts. Reporting and evaluation should be encouraged for the purpose of learning and not judgment. Health care professionals should be given assurances that this intention will be followed.

Strategy 9   Establish an effective mechanism for incentives

Agreeing on the type of incentives is one issue and making them work is another. From experience, it is found that this area is the most sensitive and the most deficient in health care quality implementation for answers. Questions such as "What's in it for me?" and "Why should I do it?" continue to be asked. Answers to these questions include providing monitory incentives, nonfinancial rewards, different kinds of recognition, and making quality a job requirement. As one individual says in summarizing an employee appraisal system having no provision for rewarding improvements, "As long as you stay away from making changes, the likelihood of making mistakes is low and, therefore, the likelihood of being scrutinized is low." This is the type of attitude that needs to be changed and a system of incentives very well may be linked to the employee performance and appraisal systems that already are in existence in health care organizations.

IMPLEMENTATION STAGES

In this section, again only broad strategies will be presented as specific approaches cannot be developed for all scenarios and for different settings. The intent of this section is to introduce the five different stages of implementation with a brief description of each stage. There is an abundance of literature on planning, training, improvement, and evaluation of the implementation processes and the reader is encouraged to seek additional information.

STAGE I   ASSESSMENT

In the last section, we discussed the issue of planning for a comprehensive assessment of the status of health services in the organization. In this stage of implementation, actual assessment activities should take place. Again, depending on the method, the resources available, and the time table allotted in the plan, thorough assessment should be completed before any intervention can be planned, authorized, or carried out.

To explain one method of assessment, here is a description of one organization's experience. In that organization, assessment took different approaches. A team of consultants was assembled and met with key leaders representing the different service areas of that organization. After presenting their intended methods of assessment, they were teamed with a number of internal health professionals to assist in data collection. A predesigned survey instrument was used to conduct personal interviews with key health professionals of the organization. Focus group sessions were organized with a few staff members and others with members. Additionally, actual review of existing health care documents and medical records was carried out to review the quantity and quality of health services rendered. Statistical reports on services utilization in that organization also were collected. A number of random sample satisfaction surveys were conducted for members as well as for physicians and staff. This extensive data collection effort took a period of two weeks, while data analysis and reporting took an additional four weeks. Based on the findings, the quality project steering committee selected the areas of intervention that required the most improvements using a specific prioritization scale. Problems were divided into three categories; those requiring low cost to fix, others with moderate cost, and those costing the most. One aspect missing in that organization's experience was measurable base-line data. The objective of their assessment was to identify problem areas and not to measure indicators. However, it is highly recommended that the development and the measurement of indicators be part of the assessment outcomes.

STAGE II   REORGANIZATION AND TRAINING

Decentralization of intervention and improvement activities should be the objective, although a combination of both approaches is more practical. One consideration need is whether early standards — clinical and administrative — development or adoption is useful coupled with the development of key indicators for future monitoring. If so, then a specialized or several specialized committees should be formed to tackle these tasks. One effective method to develop key indicators is to ask a representative from each service unit in the organization to develop or identify three to five key indicators specific to that service unit. Prioritization of these indicators then will be made to select the most effective ones in measuring compliance to quality standards.

Quality committees can be formed gradually to address specific issues related to health care quality, such as peer management, credentialing, utilization management, member services, health promotion and prevention, and operations. The key issue here is form these committees very gradually and only as needed. Each committee should have a separate and specific charter, a defined membership, and an identified reporting mechanism. All committees will be reporting their findings and activities to the institution's quality coordinator, if present, which in turn present the reports to the QC or to the top administrator of the organization for monitoring and further action.

In regard to training, several seminars have been developed and delivered. Again, the objective here is not to overtrain, but to optimally train on the needed skills and to the right individuals. In some organizations several workshops have been delivered on health care quality. There are workshops in awareness, basic and advanced skills of quality improvement, standards and indicators setting workshop, team-building workshops, customer service, and cost analysis workshops. Other organizations delivered only few workshops and only to active process improvement teams, while still others delivered a set of workshops in gradual complexity in an effort to rapidly develop a cadre of inhouse professionals that will take the burden of training others later on. The most important piece of advice is to deliver training according to a well-written training plan with well thought out objectives in order for it to be accomplished on a systematic manner.

STAGE III   IMPROVEMENTS

Under this heading, a total process of quality assurance and improvement should be carried out. Any model of the process can be used. Figure 1 in Chapter 3 shows the model used by the QA project of the USAID in countries around the world with very positive results. The major issue to be considered is how to measure and monitor improvement and that is where standards setting could be of importance. (Benneyan and Kaminsky, 1995) Ideally, a set of key quality improvement indicators and data analysis are developed at the central level while data collection and reporting would be carried out at the service levels.

It is outside the scope of this chapter to discuss the specific steps of quality assurance, monitoring, and quality improvement presented in Figure 1. Several chapters in this book discuss these issues in much more detail. The reader also is encouraged to seek additional information from the literature available on these subjects.

STAGE IV   REASSESSMENT, EVALUATION, MONITORING, AND CQI

A practice that should be encouraged is to measure pre- and post improvements of every project. In this way reassessment will be much easier to accomplish. Reassessment and evaluation may use the same method applied earlier at the assessment and planning phase through different methods of data collection and analysis.

Monitoring, on the other hand, is based on specific and measured indicators related to standards. It is a process of measuring variance to standards and initiating processes for action to reduce this variance. Monitoring is a necessary step for proper selection of and consideration of quality improvement projects and studies. It also can provide the organization an indication of the status of care and services provided at any point in time. In advanced health care systems, elaborate and comprehensive monitoring has been developed that utilize members' medical records for the abstraction of specific data elements which in turn are fed into a central data base for analysis and monitoring. Each service unit then receives a periodic report showing aggregate data of health care indicators compared to their specific set of data for the same indicators. Variance from the mean is studied and acted upon using the QA/QI process mentioned above.

A few words need to be said about the issue of continuous improvement here. Improvements are not one-time activities. When a team has worked on a process and improvement was accomplished, this does not mean that it should abandon this process for ever and move on to the next one. Improvement is a process and a process is continuous. Monitoring should continue and improvements should be initiated every time it is needed. The other principle involves incremental improvements in the standards once compliance is achieved. If high or even perfect compliance to a specific standard has been documented, then upgrading this standard is the next prudent step. Otherwise the organization will stay at status quo without further improvements.

STAGE V DISSEMINATION AND EXPANSION

A successful process ought to be taught to others and accomplishments shared with others. Even failures give us ideas for improvements. For these reasons, dissemination of activities in health care quality is encouraged locally, nationally, and internationally.

The process of dissemination may have different approaches. This may include the organization of a monthly lecture on health care quality progress in the organization, or quarterly or annual seminars on quality activities, development of a newsletter, or including a section in an already established newsletter. One country, for example, began organizing study tours of professionals from other parts of the country to the health care quality implementation site. Similarly, study tours could be organized to visit other successful organizations for benchmarking. Dissemination is essential to attract further support and to maintain momentum of staff. It also provides an avenue for recognition of staff and can prove to be a useful incentive method.

Expansion, on the other hand, includes the spread of implementation to another location or nationwide. Expansion should be done very slowly and gradually only when complete assessment and planning has been performed. Hasty mistakes may jeopardize the success of the whole process. Caution should be practiced when choosing the next site and at what time, as readiness of the staff for expansion is essential for its success. Similarly, methods of expanding the process to another location can follow the same path outlined in the partial implementation process discussed above.

I stress that this model is by no means the only model for implementation. There are a number of different approaches to achieve the same outcome and the reader is advised to seek more knowledge on the subject from other sources to get an idea of the different perspectives. A model that may be applicable in one setting or country may not be applicable in another.

Implementation stages which are typical of new processes include:

- **Perception** — "We already are doing this."
- **Awareness** — "We can improve."
- **Education** — "Let's learn how to do it."
- **Partial implementation** — "Let's start pilot projects."
- **Full implementation** — "Let's involve everybody."

- **Culture** — "The way we do things."
- **Achieved quality** — "Let's share accomplishments."

The process of health care quality implementation is a long and hard road, but is certainly worth walking it.

REFERENCES

Al-Assaf, A. F. and Schmele, J. A. *The Textebook of Total Quality in Healthcare*, St. Lucie Press, Delray, FL, 1993.

Al-Assaf, A. F. "Quality Improvement in Healthcare: An Overview." *Journal of the Royal Medical Services*, 1 (2): 1994.

Al-Assaf, A. F. "International Health care and the Management of Quality." In *Quality Management n Nursing and Healthcare*, Delmar Publications, 1996.

Benneyan, J. C. and Kaminsky, F. C. "Another View on How to Measure Healthcare Quality." *Quality Progress*, 120–124, February 1995.

Blumenfeld, S. N. "Quality Assurance in Transition." *PNG Medical Journal*, 36: 81–89, 1993.

Boerstler, H., Foster, R. W., O'Connor, E., O'Brien, J. L., Shortell, S. M., Carmen, J. M., and Hughes, E. F. X. "Implementation of Total Quality Management: Conventional Wisdom vs. Reality." 41(2):143-159, 1996.

Brown, L. D. "Instittutionalization Issues for Quality Assurance Programs." *International Journal of Quality in Health Care*, 8 (1), 1996.

Dwyer, J. and Jezowski, T. "Quality Management for Family Planning Services Practical Experience from Africa." *AVSC Working Paper*, 7:1-8 1995.

Kaluzney, A. D., McLaughlin, C. P., and Kibbe D. "Quality Improvement: Beyond the Institution." *Hospital & Health Services Administration*, 40 (1): 172–188, 1995.

Linsk, J. A. "The Quality of Health Care: The Practical Clinical View." *Quality Assurance in Health Care*, 2 (3/4): 219–225, 1990.

Newman, J. J. "Lessons in quality from other industry experiences." *Topics in Healthcare Finance*, 18 (2): 1–6, 1991.

Nicholas, D. D., Heiby, J. R., and Theresa, H. A. "The Quality Assurance Project: Introducing Quality Improvement to Primary Healthcare in Less Developed Countries." *Quality Assurance in health Care*, 3(3):147-165, 1991.

Sawatzky, J. and MacDonald, M. M. "Challenges to Achieving Quality Care: Efficiency, Effectiveness, and Beneficence." *Int. Nurs. Rev.*, 41 (1): 27–31, 1994.

Walker, G. J. A. "Medical Care in Developing Countries: Assessment and Assurance of Quality." *Evaluation & Health Professions*, 6 (4): 439–452, 1983.

6 Quality Assurance Activities

Dennis Zaenger and A. F. Al-Assaf

CONTENTS

In this chapter, the activities of **quality assurance** (QA) are presented in detail as it applies to health care organizations in general and managed care organizations in particular. QA is described here as all the processes and subprocesses of planning for quality, setting of standards, indicators, and thresholds of expected quality, and the active communication of the expected quality in measurable terms to the appropriate audience and the direct users.

Although planning is an integral part of the QA process, it is not included in this chapter as it was presented in Chapter 5. In this chapter, we will concentrate on presenting the basic elements of a QA plan for a health care organization. Following the process of planning for quality, a new set of steps should take place in the implementation of this initiative in the organization. One of the early steps in this initiative is the setting of standards. Setting of standards does not necessarily mean the development of standards from zero level, but includes such activities as the search for the system to standardize and the selection of the right standards for adoption, modification, or redevelopment. These newly set, developed, or adopted standards then would need to be tested for reliability and validity and further communicated (actively) to the intended audience and the appropriate users. Once standards are communicated to health professionals, a set of steps should take place in measuring compliance to these standards using an adequate number of key indicators related to those standards. The measurement of the *variance* between current practices and the set standards is what monitoring all about. Monitoring as a system, will be discussed further in the next chapter.

In this chapter only one method of setting standards is presented. Here the scenario given assumes that the organization actually is developing its own standards. Therefore, a step-by-step approach of how to develop standards and indicators is presented. Most managed care organizations, however, rely on other specialized organizations, such as the National Committee on Quality Assurance or the Joint Commission, to use their standards of expected quality. These same organizations may use the method described in this chapter to develop additional standards or to develop their policies and procedure, clinical practice guidelines, or algorithms, which are all different forms of standards.

PLANNING THE QA PROGRAM

The QA plan is a document developed by the organization that defines the conceptual understanding of quality in that organization, and provides a description of the organizational structure, the resources, and the materials allocated to that organization's quality program. This plan also may outline the methods for applying quality standards to delivery of care and service of that organization. Therefore, sources and type of data will be discussed, as well as information offered on the methods of data collection and type of reporting mechanism. These plans usually are designed according to the Joint Commission's 10-step model of quality assessment. This model includes the following steps: (1) assign responsibility, (2) delineate scope of care and service, (3) identify important aspects of care and service, (4) identify indicators, (5) establish a means to trigger evaluation, (6) collect and organize data, (7) initiate evaluation, (8) take actions to improve care and service, (9) assess the effectiveness of actions and assure improvement is maintained, and (10) communicate results to affected individuals and groups. Accordingly, an organization may be able to define each step more appropriately as it pertains to its operation and quality program and prepare its QA plan as such. Following is an example of a managed care organization's QA plan synopsis:

> **Title page:** 1997 Quality Management Plan of Great Health Plan, Inc.
> **Table of contents**.
> **Background and History of the Program.**   A description of the chronology of establishing the program and the actions taken to secure resources for it. If the program has been in place for a long period, you may include

an abstract of the program changes that have taken place since its inception.

The Organization's Mission and Vision.   Describe how does the organization's mission fits in the overall goal of the QA/QM program.

Objectives of the program. A list of measurable goals for quality.

Who is involved?   Describe the positions of the different personnel associated with the QA/QM program. List the main duties and responsibilities of each position and what are their major activities in the program. A short list of the expected qualification of a person in each of these positions provides a better understanding of the caliber and competencies desired. Also provide an organizational structure of the program, outlining each position and its hierarchy within the organization. Include the position (for reporting purposes) of all the committees associated with the operation of the program.

List and Brief Description of all Quality-related Committees.   Include a general description of each of the committees, membership composition, main tasks and duties, reporting mechanism, and frequency of meetings.

Scope of the Program.   List all the major activities of the program, e.g., risk management, utilization management, case management, and credentialing.

Important Aspects.   Here you may include a list of all those key indicators that the program identifies and collects data on regularly. List only those areas that the program is regularly measuring and monitoring. e.g., member complaints, provider access, claims management, HEDIS requirements, medical records completeness, and problem identification and improvement. For each of these areas a level of acceptable standard should be provided, i.e., what is the threshold of minimum accepted standards beyond which evaluation is automatically triggered?

Linkages with other Services.   List and briefly describe all those departments, services, or units that either have a direct or indirect link or association with the QA/QM program. Provide a description of these activities and tasks related to quality in each of these entities.

List of Reports and Communication mechanism for the Program.

Synopsis of the Annual Evaluation of the Program.

Once the QA plan is developed, it should be circulated to all the key individuals of the program and then sent for review and approval by the organization's top administrator and its board of directors. Any subsequent modifications should follow the same route for approval. This requirement — developing a QA plan and having it appropriately approved — is based on the standards prescribed by most accrediting agencies, thus making it almost mandatory for all health plans to follow.

In the chapter on quality implementation, we discussed the steps of implementing quality in a health care organization in a broad scenario. As mentioned earlier, QA must include a stage of adequate planning both strategic and operational to assure the availability of resources, and facilitate quality assessments and improvements.

Therefore, a comprehensive and well-developed plan is essential not only for accreditation, but also for ensuring the success of the quality program in that organization.

In the following section, a method for setting standards in health care is presented. Again this is only one method of setting standards. There are several others that follow the same format, but the objective is the same — the development of a standard that is valid, reliable, clear, applicable and timely. Setting a standard does not necessarily develop one *de novo*, but it may include the adoption or the modification of an existing standard. Actually, a standard that has been developed for one organization may not be applicable for another and a standard that is developed for the average organization may not be adequate for higher quality organization. Additionally, the more effort put into the development or adoption of a standard, the more acceptance it will receive. This is especially true when one is dealing with the development of clinical standards, and in particular clinical practice guidelines.

SETTING QUALITY STANDARDS

Standards are an important part of health care and have taken a new prominence in the trend to address quality-of-care issues. Once an organization makes a commitment to addressing its quality-of-care, it must define "quality" in operational terms. Standards do that. The organization ensures consistent, high-quality services through the correct application of standards.

This section outlines a methodology that has been used in at least two countries to date and in a number of health care organization worldwide. Early indicators are that it is useful for helping an organization begin its quality improvement "journey."

WHAT ARE STANDARDS?

Standards, broadly defined, are statements of expectations for the inputs, processes, behaviors, and outcomes of health systems. Simply put, standards tell us what we expect to happen in our quest for high-quality health services. Standards are important because they are the vehicle by which the organization translates quality into operational terms and holds everyone in the system — patient, care provider, support personnel, management — accountable for their part. Standards also allow the organization to measure its level of quality. Standards, indicators, and thresholds are the elements that make a quality assurance system work in a measurable, objective, and qualitative manner.

Among health care professionals, there are many definitions and uses of the word "standard." The term standard sometimes is used to describe protocols, standard operating procedures, specifications, and practice guidelines. **Guidelines** are statements by experts that describe recommended or suggested procedures. (Eddy and Couch, 1991) Guidelines serve as a flexible technical reference that describe what the health care provider should or should not do for a given clinical condition, e.g., guidelines for vascular injury in frostbite cases. (Imparato and Rites, 1989) A **protocol** is a more precise and detailed plan for a process, such as the management of a clinical condition. A protocol implies a more stringent requirement than a guideline, such as WHO protocols for diarrhea case management. A **standard operating proce-dure** (SOP) is a statement of the expected way in which an organization's staff carries out certain activities, such as standard operating procedures for billing patients. Standard operating procedures usually are more stringent than guidelines. A **speci-fication** is a detailed description of the characteristics or measurements for a product, service, or outcome.

In essence, these are all standards. They are varying ways that an organization explicitly defines what it expects for: (1) inputs (resources), such as the materials, drugs, supplies, and personnel, (2) the delivery processes and procedures, and (3) the desired outcome of these processes. (Donabedian, 1980)

WHY USE STANDARDS?

In every process, there is a certain amount of variation. In every task we perform, we vary the way it is done each time. A surgeon performs open-heart surgery differently each time by changing the angle of incision, the manner of suturing, and other small details of the operation. While the surgeon strives for perfect perfor-mance, it is impossible to perform surgery exactly the same each time. Variation is natural and is to be expected in every process of health care. However, through continuous quality improvement techniques, health workers can increase their knowledge of and control over variation in the health care system. (Berwick, 1991) The objective is to keep variation within limits of control. (Deming, 1986)

Many sources of variation in medical care should not be standardized completely. Treatment plans and other aspects of care need to be tailored to each patient's specific care requirements. However, quality of care can be improved by eliminating or minimizing unnecessary variation in the way that care is provided. "It is simply unrealistic to think that individuals can synthesize in their heads scores of pieces of evidence, accurately estimate the outcomes of different options, and accurately judge the desirability of these outcomes for patients." (Eddy, 1990) Standards help to reduce variation by defining what the organization expects for the day-to-day inputs, processes, and outcomes of health care and services.

For example, input standards for open-heart surgery help to ensure that surgeons have the necessary and appropriate equipment and staff needed to perform the procedure. Process standards, such as guidelines and protocols, help ensure that the surgeon is using up-to-date techniques and technology. Outcome standards define what the organization expects as results for the procedure.

Much of the attention in recent decades to establishing standards has been driven by payment reimbursement and litigation requirements. Hospitals must demonstrate adherence to NCQA and JCAHO accreditation requirements and to HCFA standards for reimbursement through Medicare and Medicaid programs. Licensing require-ments and litigation concerns also influence a health care organization to establish minimum standards for quality of care. (Mills and Lindgren, 1991) Due to these and other influencing forces, standards for almost any aspect of health care now exists in some shape or form in most health care organizations.

Health care organizations have a growing interest in establishing standards, partly to set minimal expectations for health services rendered and partly to help reduce adverse health outcomes and variation within existing health services.

A METHODOLOGY FOR SETTING STANDARDS

The methodology for setting standards described here can be used step-by-step, although it is not necessary to do so. This method usually is used for the development of new standards, but the method also may be used to develop organizational policies, while few of these steps may be used to modify other developed standards. As the organization moves from one task to another, it may need to return to certain tasks as more information is gathered. The approach is designed to guide the organization and the people assigned to the task of setting standards through the various questions it must consider to define what is quality for the organization and what standards are needed to meet that quality.

Step I   Identify a Function or System

When starting to develop standards, the organization will need to identify systems or subsystems requiring standards and select one or two that are high priority. These systems are the clinical and nonclinical functions the organization engages in regularly. Some primary care examples are acute respiratory infection (ARI) case management, maternal and child care services, and immunization services. Some hospital-based clinical examples are cæsarean sections and emergency care services. Some nonclinical examples are patient admissions and the use and maintenance of medical records.

The organization can identify high-priority functions through a two-step screening approach. The first identifies high-volume, high-risk, and problem-prone functions or systems. (JCAHO, 1990) High-volume functions are those that are performed frequently or affect large numbers of people. High-risk conditions or functions are those that expose the client to a greater risk of adverse outcomes because of the nature of the disease or the case management process. Problem-prone functions are those that have produced problems for the organization and/or clients in the past.

The list produced by the first screening most likely will be long enough that the organization will need to narrow it further. Initially, most organizations cannot afford the time and expense to develop standards for every function or system that is high volume, high risk, or problem prone. To narrow the list further, the organization will need to select additional criteria by which to judge all the possible functions or systems. These are some commonly used criteria for selecting among the possibilities:

Importance — Having more significance, consequence, and/or value relative to the other functions or systems.

Feasibility — Any changes recommended for the function or system can be carried out by the organization and personnel.

Impact — The recommended changes for the function or system will produce the most positive result relative to other choices.

Cost — Changes that can reduce cost and produce savings.

Step II Identify a Team or a Panel of Experts

Up to this point the critical decisions concerning what functions or systems need standards are made usually by managers and department chiefs. Once they have decided where to begin, the organization typically assigns interdisciplinary teams who know the most about a given function or system for which standards will be developed.

These teams should include the right people in order to address issues necessary to complete this task. (Brassard, 1989) The "right" people are those who are best qualified by virtue of their experience, training, and role in the organization. They are the people who are most involved or most knowledgeable about the function or system. In particular, consider who is involved with each step of the function or system, consider including a technical expert, and consider including someone of authority within the organization.

Step III Identify the Inputs, Processes, and Outcomes.

The team or panel of experts must identify the elements for each of the components of the function or system. These are the inputs required to make the processes happen, the processes that are necessary for the expected outcomes to occur, and what is expected as outcome(s) for the function or system.

Some teams find it useful to look at the system backwards to better list the elements for inputs, processes, and outcomes. In this manner, a team first lists the desired outcomes for an activity, then lists the processes necessary for those outcomes to occur, and the inputs that the processes require.

Once the team identifies all the elements, it should decide which of these elements are critical, or key, for the function or systems to be carried out and outcomes to occur in manner that the organization expects. Not all inputs, processes, and outcomes are critical for a function or system to be of the quality that an organization expects.

A number of tools are useful for identifying inputs, processes, and outcomes, then gaining consensus on which are critical to the quality of the process. An Affinity Diagram (Al-Assaf, 1993) is a useful technique for gaining consensus on the various inputs, processes, and outcomes of a health care function or system. Some teams couple this technique with flowcharting (Scholtes, 1988) to lay out the steps visually for the function or system and to gain consensus on critical inputs, processes, and outcomes.

Step IV   Define the Quality Characteristics

Quality characteristics are the distinguishing attributes of inputs, processes, or outcomes that the organization or team decides are essential for how it defines quality health care. They are the traits or features by which we judge the quality of health care elements. For example, a team of physicians and laboratory technicians may use "timeliness" as a characteristic of quality (among others) when setting or evaluating standards for hospital diagnostic tests. Once the team understands and agrees on a quality characteristic, it then can define a standard for it. In this example, the team's next step is to define what it means by "timeliness" in measurable terms.

A team should use whatever decision-making process that feels comfortable to decide which are the key elements and the quality characteristics. Some decisions and choices may have consensus among the group members with little need for discussion. Other decisions may require more discussion, time, and the use of some decision-making tools and techniques. (Scholtes, 1988; Al-Assaf, 1993) Some groups may not make decisions by consensus, but rather the leader may make the decision or the group may vote. No one decision-making process is universally better than another. The group must decide which is the best way for it to make decisions.

Step V   Develop/Adapt Standards

Once the team has decided the quality characteristics for the elements of a function or system, it must decide which quality characteristics require standards, then set the standards. A team may decide it does not need a standard for all quality characteristics, and instead focus on what it feels is most important. In completing this step, teams usually do the following at some time.

   A. **Choose a Format for Standards.** Standards can use several different formats to describe what is expected for inputs, process, and outcomes of a system. Most often input and outcome standards take the form of statements, but many health professionals and organizations have developed a variety of formats for process standards. Below are just a few of the more common formats you will find for standards.

   1. **Statements.** Standards often are written statements of what is expected to happen for a function. The statements can be written as specifically or as generally as the team or organization decides is necessary, e.g., NCQA's Standards for Accreditation of MCO's (NCQA, 1997).

   2. **Algorithms.** Process standards can be in the form of an algorithm, which are presented as a list of steps, or as a few sentences in paragraph form, or as a map that outlines a stepwise approach to solving a clinical problem. A common algorithm is a flowchart, sometimes called a decision tree, that will guide the user through a variety of steps and decisions to lead them to the most appropriate outcome, e.g., Comatose Patient Management Algorithm.

3. **Case Management Plans.** These are patient care plans that "outline the anticipated usual or standardized length of stay and set out the expected clinical outcomes, intermediate goals, and interventions involved in the care of a given case type of patients." (Grossman 1991) These plans include care provided in all clinical settings, such as admissions, routine patient floors, and intensive care units in the case of, e.g., CABG patient care.

4. **Critical paths.** Process standards can be in the form of a critical path, which is "an optimal sequencing and timing of interventions by physicians, nurses, and other staff for a particular diagnosis or procedure ..." over a period of time. (Coffey et al. 1992) Critical paths are designed to minimize delays in health services and resource use and to maximize the quality of care. The terms critical pathways, critical paths of care, and care maps all refer to the critical paths described here, e.g., critical path for a myocardial infarction patient care episode.

5. **Clinical care protocols.** Process standards also can be in the form of clinical care protocols. They are "practice guidelines which are explicit, criteria-based plans for specific health care problems." (Benson and Van Osdol, 1990) Protocols are used to define the process of care for a primary care problem, including history, physical exam, assessment, diagnostic procedures, treatment, and patient education, e.g., hypertension care protocols.

Developing process standards can be complicated and require extensive technical knowledge of a health care function or system. They can be presented in a variety of forms in addition to the ones described above. The NCQA, JCAHO, AHCPR, American Medical Association, physicians, and other health care organizations have developed many input, process, and outcome standards for a variety of health care functions. Many health care organizations are developing process standards for common health care functions and systems which are specific to their organizational and environmental requirements. A team or organization can use these sources, but if it decides that it needs to develop new and original process standards, then the team may require additional training and resources.

B. **Gather Background Information.** Developing or adapting standards requires the team to gather background information, then process that information to derive appropriate standards. Teams can gather information through methods such as those listed below.

1. **Literature review.** A worldwide body of knowledge for most health care functions and systems exists and can be accessed numerous ways. Much of this knowledge is found in current health care literature in most medical school libraries. The Internet may have a number of sites that are dedicated to certain health care organization and may have a listing and full text of a large number of clinical practice guidelines ap-

plicable to that organization. Whenever possible, teams should consult the medical literature to determine what is commonly accepted for a given health care function or system before inventing, or possibly reinventing, standards.

2. **Confer with experts.** Sometimes the team does not have all the expertise it needs to develop or adapt standards. If so, then the team can include an expert as an *ad hoc* member to help guide them in the technical nature of a chosen function or system. Or the team can confer with an expert and bring the information back to the team.

3. **Benchmark.** Benchmarking is a technique for learning from others' experiences for a function or system where the team is trying to set standards. (Watson, 1993) The term benchmarking means using someone else's successful standard as a minimal measure of what you would like to achieve. Benchmarking can be used to stimulate creativity by gaining knowledge of what has been tried by other similar organizations and modifying it to make it work better for your organization.

4. **Review past experiences.** This method is similar to benchmarking, but the team examines their own organization's experiences to discover what has worked and not worked in the past. This is important because if there is some organizational constraint that has prevented the adherence to standards in the past, then that constraint may prevent any new effort to set standards from being successful.

C. **Draft the Standard.** Experts in setting standards suggest that a team begins with a "seed" standard. These usually are input, process, or outcome standards from other organizations or some other proposed standard which a team can consider to help it start thinking. After beginning with the "seed," there are several techniques a team can use to draft their standard. You can use the Delphi Method (Dalkey et al., 1972) to exchange and build on each other's ideas, flowcharts to illustrate sequence of steps in a process, or interrelationship diagrams (Brassard, 1989; Al-Assaf, 1993) to show the relationship among the parts of a standard. When disseminating new or a dapted standards, be sure to describe the rationale for its recommended use and the consequences for following the standard. (Eddy, 1990)

Step VI   Develop the Indicator for the standard

Once the standard is developed, an indicator can be drafted by using measurable terms to convert the standard into an indicator. For example, if the standard is "physicians associated with an X managed care plan should be board-certified," then the indicator will be "the percentage of those physicians associated with the X managed care plan that are board-certified." Indicators are important to the monitoring of compliance to the standard and measuring variance from the desired level of achievement of that standard. However, only key indicators should be selected.

Too many indicators and too many nonkey indicators can overburden the system with excessive and probably ineffective data collection and analysis.

Step VII   Assess Appropriateness of Standards and Indicators

Standards should be assessed to ensure that they are appropriate for the organization. The team or the organization should determine if the standards are valid, reliable, clear, and applicable before they are disseminated. Indicators should have the same characteristics plus be measurable. All too often health organizations develop or adopt standards with little or no assessment. Consequently many standards are not appropriate or unrealistic and are simply not followed by intended users. In general, the assessment should be carried out on a small scale, using qualitative rather than quantitative data when necessary. The following procedure may be followed to assess standards.

Determine all those in the organization who will use or be affected by the standards and select a representative group to review the standards. Since the number of users of standards in a given facility is small, statistical samples and rigorous qualitative analysis are not advised unless a national or systemwide effort is underway.

Determine the method to use for obtaining information about the standards from the sample group. Possible methods are staff meetings, anonymous questionnaires, and face-to-face interviews.

Analyze the feedback and make any necessary changes before disseminating the new standards. Analysis should include a compilation of strengths, weaknesses, and recommendations. The standards team should review and develop a plan to revise and implement the standard.

Additionally, the assessment should determine if the standards have the characteristics described below. (IOM, 1990) If they do not, the team should revise the standards and reassess them to ensure that they meet these criteria.

Assess standards for validity. Assessment should determine if there is a strong demonstrated relationship between the standard and the desired result it represents. The team should confirm that, if the inputs are provided as they have defined them, and, that if the processes are carried out as they have defined them, the desired outcomes should occur. Expert advice may be required to affirm validity of the standard.

Assess standards for reliability. Assessment should determine if the same results occur each time the standards are used, i.e., the standard's measure reproducibility. A reliable standard will result in a small amount of variation in the way the standard is applied every time it is applied.

Assess standards for clarity. Assessment should determine if the standards are written in clear, unambiguous terms so that the workers who use the standards do not misinterpret them. It is important that the sample of workers that test the standards represent those workers who ultimately will use the standards.

Assess for applicability. Assessment should determine if the standards are realistic and applicable given the available resources and training of the health care workers responsible for complying with them.

A word of caution: When assessing standards with a sample population, make sure the sample is adequate and representative of the target population that will use and comply with the standard. Assessing sample size and representation of a target population is beyond the scope of this article, so refer to a statistical sampling text for further discussion. (Williams, 1978)

CHALLENGES TO SETTING STANDARDS

In spite of a large resource of existing standards to adapt to specific needs and the growing interest in establishing standards by various health care organizations, certain challenges to this process still exist:

A. **Reliance on explicit criteria.** Physicians, nurses, and other health care professionals may resist on the basis that standards impinge on their subjective judgment they have developed through their practice. Some professionals contend that medicine is partly art, partly science, and that standards may require them to diagnose and treat without allowing them to use their professional judgment. Others may fear that standards will be used in a punitive manner, to identify and punish professionals who do not perform within strictly defined limits. Still others may feel that the presence of standards make the practice of medicine "cook-book medicine," and that may impede their creative ability in the diagnosis and treatment of patient. Of course the other issue is the legal impact such standards might have or are perceived to have on the practice of medicine. These are legitimate concerns and require the organization to address them in some constructive manner before developing or implementing standards.

B. **Identifying appropriate resources, human, physical, and financial.** Developing or adapting standards takes time and personnel. Sometimes the organization must go outside its staff to use experts in the field. Throughout all this the organization will incur certain costs that should be evaluated beforehand to determine if the effort is worth the cost.

The process of setting standards is an integral part of a cycle of quality improvement. This process usually is followed by communicating standards, then monitoring compliance via indicators. Through monitoring, gaps are identified between what is expected to happen in health care, vis-à-vis standards, and what currently is happening. Teams then are assigned to analyze these problems, identify and implement solutions, and make recommendations to the organization for adopting the solutions on a wider basis.

This last part often entails modifying, enhancing, or updating standards so that the organization's expectations for quality are being met. Here again, standards should be periodically assessed for validity, reliability, clarity, and applicability. This can be viewed as a continuous cycle of quality improvement. The next section of this chapter outlines the process of communicating standards to the users.

CONCLUSIONS

Setting standards is a necessary component of defining and improving quality of health care. Through standards an organization defines what it expects for the inputs, processes, and outcomes of the services it provides. Through their indicators, standards are an instrumental part of monitoring the quality of care and identifying problems and measuring improvements in health care service delivery. With periodic updating and modifications, they become a part of an organization's cycle of continuous quality improvement.

Setting standards can be approached using a seven-step methodology: (1) identify a function or system that requires standards, (2) identify a team to address standards, (3) identify the inputs, process, and outcomes of the function or system, (4) define the quality characteristics, (5) develop or adapt standards, (6) develop indicators, and (6) assess the appropriateness of the standards.

COMMUNICATING STANDARDS

The purpose of developing standards is to ensure the delivery of quality patient care. To apply a set of standards successfully, they must be communicated successfully to those who are responsible for their application. Successful communication implies that those who were meant to receive the communication actually did so; that those who received the communication understood it, accepted it, and accurately will implement the necessary tasks.

Communication is the vital link between the development of the standard and the actual application of the standard. Communication of standards needs to be a carefully planned process. Standards that are not communicated in an efficient or effective manner may have many negative effects: dissatisfied patients or staff; wasted time and money used for ineffective communication activities; loss of staff and patient time; and, perhaps most important, diminished quality of care. "For information to become knowledge, it must be received, understood, and then internalized." (Dawkins 1992) This raises issues concerning how an organization designs effective communication approaches and how it measures effectiveness. It affects education, organizational communications, employee training, and new skills development.

Before continuing with a discussion on effective communication of standards, it is useful to discuss the main elements in any system of communication. Communication requires a "sender" — one who initiates the communication; the "message" — whatever the sender wishes to convey; and the "receiver" — the person or group who is the target of communication. In a two-way communication system, the receiver of the information provides feedback to indicate understanding or internalizing of the message. This is a simple model, but the reader should keep it in mind as this section discusses measuring effective communication.

THE ROLE OF COMMUNICATION WITHIN THE MANAGED CARE ORGANIZATION

Effective communication is an essential element for quality management in any organization. William Haney wrote in 1973 that the modern organization requires communication performance at an unprecedented level of excellence in order to survive growing conditions of complexity and demand for efficiency. (Haney, 1973) This excellence in communication applies to all levels of the organization, from the leadership down to care providers, from care providers back up to the leadership, and across divisional lines from manager to manager.

Health care organizations that are NCQA or JCAHO accredited are required to document and communicate continuous quality improvement/performance improvement activities to all those who have an appropriate need to know. Some of those who are appropriate are quality improvement teams, key cross-functional staff, medical staff departments and committees. Not only does certification require showing documentation of communication activities such as meeting notes, communiqués, and bulletins, but also it requires *integrating* the information into the organization-wide quality improvement strategy and other key organizational functions.

In the field of Continuous Quality Improvement (CQI), communicating and sharing experiences and best practices is considered to be fundamental for raising the organizational thresholds of quality. This has been proven successfully in the industrial and service sector, where many organizations pursue ISO 9000 certification to institute quality improvement structures in their company or organization. A large part of ISO 9000 certification is creating a documentation system and a system for disseminating information company-wide and to all customers. This often is done through the quality auditing function of the organization and serves to stimulate change and improvement. Employees are the foundation for gathering data about adherence to company and contractual standards and expectations, and that information is consolidated and disseminated to management and back to the employees. When used well, ISO 9000 certification guides an organization to effectively use formal and informal communication systems to disseminate standards of performance and quality improvement results.

COMMON COMMUNICATION METHODS

Following are some common methods used for effectively communicating standards to workers. An organization must weigh the costs of using these different methods against the importance of the message and need to demonstrate adoption of the standard. A mixture of these methods blended together in a strategic plan helps an organization to maximize more costly methods (such as training) with more inexpensive methods (such as meetings or memos).

Endorsement by Opinion Leaders — While organizational communication flows downward, upward, and horizontally, it also flows through informal channels. These informal channels can be tapped to aid effective communication of standards, sometimes more effectively than formal channels. In all organizations there are professionals at each level who are considered to be opinion leaders by their peers. Most managers know who these people are and certainly peer groups know who they are. Organizations that have involved these opinion leaders in the development and dissemination of standards have found these method to be effective. A communication strategy should include identifying those informal channels and how to best use them to assure effective communication of standards.

In a study of disseminating clinical practice guidelines in the Coronary care Unit of Cedars–Sinai Medical Center in West Los Angeles, researchers found that the process used in their study facilitated adoption of the guidelines by private practitioners. First, the guidelines were derived from literature and modified by local opinion leaders so that the physicians would have ownership of the final guidelines. Data was collected to support the safety and efficacy of the guidelines prior to dissemination. Then the guidelines were communicated to physicians using a system of physicians who were respected by their peers and could offer unsolicited advice to their colleagues. Finally, patient outcomes were measured during periods with and without guideline use to reinforce the safety and effectiveness of the guideline recommendations. (Weingarten, 1992) While the study did not result in quantifiable evidence that this approach was more effective than others, the researchers found that physicians understood and applied the practice guidelines routinely.

Training often is used as one of the first approaches in communicating standards. While this appears to be logical on the surface, it often is misused and leads to ineffectual communication. All health care professionals are trained in some form or capacity in order to be registered in their specialty. Every nurse, doctor, and laboratory technician has been trained to some set of standards to be able to practice his or her profession. Poor performance or inadequate compliance to standards is not due to lack of skills or knowledge, and training is not an effective intervention. Therefore, before beginning long and costly training programs to communicate standards, the organization should conduct an investigation to determine if training is an appropriate method.

An assessment phase is the first step in almost all the training models commonly used. Training is only one of many interventions that can be used to resolve performance problems and it is appropriate only if there is truly a gap between desired and existing skills and knowledge. So the organization must diagnose the "problem," or the existing condition it wants changed. Determine whether it is rooted in lack of knowledge or skill, or rather lack of motivation, supplies, organization support or some environmental factor. Directly asking physicians, nurses, and technical staff who are not following standards helps to determine root causes. If lack of skill or knowledge is the root, then the organization must define appropriate training solutions to address it, including the use of job aids, periodic practice, and adequate feedback. A front-end analysis helps to identified training needs and the expected results, which leads to designing performance-based training objectives and effective training approaches.

Performance-based training is a common term used today. It gained popularity in the military as its training requirements became more focused on effective and safe use of equipment and armaments and performance of tasks. It was less important that an Army mechanic understood the theoretical design of a tank, but more important that he could correctly install a tractor tread or other part. So performance-based training sought the most cost-effective way possible to ensure that he was able to perform this task every time. Performance-based training focuses on the behaviors most important in performing a task. If the trainee already has the necessary skills and knowledge, but does not perform for other reasons, such as lack of motivation or supplies, then training will be a costly failure.

After the assessment stage is concluded and if training is determined to be a cost-effective intervention, trainers are brought in to help analyze the job tasks, the worker characteristics. and specify training requirements, resources available, and any constraints. From this information training developers explore training delivery options and determine the key outcome indicators by which the success of training will be evaluated. Then trainers design and develop the training, the training is delivered, then evaluated to determine if deficiencies are reduced or eliminated.

Meetings — This is a relatively cheap and easy method to communicate standards. Most managers consider this method a basic component to promote communication within and between departments or divisions. Documentation of regular meetings is a requirement for most accrediting agencies especially NCQA and JCAHO, as well as other types of certification, such as ISO 9000. Meetings also can provide an opportunity for workers to give feedback and ask for clarification about standards, both before and after implementation. Quality improvement activities that often lead to changes or modifications of standards can be easily reviewed during regular or special meetings. However, meetings do not provide the supervisor or manager a chance to see how well workers implement standards.

Dissemination Materials. Most organizations use some form of dissemination materials to communicate policies, procedures, or standards. Generally, these can be divided into **regular** and **periodic** dissemination materials. In this age of desktop publishing, many organizations produce low-cost newsletters and bulletins that can be used to update workers about company issues, decisions, or actions. These often are done on a routine basis and provide mangers an avenue of communication to all levels of workers. Other forms of communication may be done periodically as the need arises, such as memos, notices or communiqués.

While these methods are inexpensive and can be done quickly, they do not permit workers to give feedback or clarify any information. Often management officially will communicate some new policy or a procedural change via a newsletter, a memo, or a new procedures manual. If management considers this effective communication, it could be wrong, because the workers may have lingering questions, be confused, or simply not understand the information. Many times these types of official communication ends up in someone's drawer, on a bookshelf, and sometimes in the wastebasket and are never used or referenced. Or worse, they end up in the drawer of the supervisor and never are seen by the target group.

If implementation of standards is important enough, management needs to follow-up through meetings or normal supervisory channels to clarify any questions or confusion. While this does not guarantee effective communication, it will help ensure standards are implemented as necessary. Not all information may warrant this much follow-up, so management must weigh the cost of follow-up against the importance that workers effectively implement standards.

Multimedia and Electronic Methods. Multimedia training and presentations involves several senses and empowers learners to access, express, refresh and review information at their own pace, in their own time, and when they need it. However, these methods can be expensive in terms of hardware, software, and organizational support, although costs are dropping as they gain wider use. Many of the systems needed to support multimedia and electronic methods are being installed in organizations already to carry out all normal business operations. This is one area where an organization really needs to do a thorough cost analysis before investing a lot of capital.

Computer-based learning (CBL) is increasingly popular and has been shown to be cost-effective in communicating and training when well-designed and used properly. (Clark, 1991) New programs are available on CD-ROM that teach appropriate use of certain standard procedures, such as IUD insertion, proper physical examination, and on a number of medical and surgical procedures. There also are numerous programs available on the market that help an organization use ISO 9000 certification processes to improve documentation and dissemination of standards and quality issues.

Many health care organizations have an information system that help to disseminate standards and recommended practices. Short guidelines text appears on the system and references where health workers can access more information. Electronic bulletin boards and networks across multiple sites all serve as a means for easily communicating to large audiences. (Lohr, 1992) The Internet system allows one to access any number of new health care standards and policies via some specific sites.

The Agency for Healthcare Policy and Research (AHCPR) has an Internet site (www.ahcpr.gov) that provides information about standards, clinical practice guidelines, etc. AHCPR-sponsored guidelines are available electronically through the National Library of Medicine's MEDLINE system and the National Technical Information Service. Many of these guidelines now are available on CD-ROM. AHCPR has as a part of its mandate to effectively disseminate clinical practice guidelines, as well as develop and test them. To that end AHCPR has developed a framework for disseminating guidelines to consumers, health care practitioners, the health care industry, policy makers, researchers, and the press. (VanAmringe, 1992)

Supervision — All organizations have some system by which all workers are supervised, from the most basic to the most advanced positions. The supervision system is used to direct and provide support to personnel so they can perform their function effectively. It is used to delegate tasks and responsibilities, to monitor performance, and to make quality improvements. A part of this is effectively communicating standards to personnel, which includes monitoring performance and providing feedback and support as necessary. So any plan to effectively communicate standards should consider how the supervision system can be best used.

Some responsibilities of a supervisor are:

- Help health workers plan, carry out, and evaluate their work.
- Provide technical assistance required at the clinical level and for managing programs.
- Motivate health workers when necessary.
- Deal with work-related complaints and problems of health workers.
- Serve as the liaison between upper and lower management.

In the past, a supervisor's position often was thought of as an enforcer of company policy. Gaps between expected and current performance were handled in a punitive fashion. In today's workplace, the supervisor takes on more the role of a coach, supporting personnel with what they need to do their job and providing corrective feedback. Styles of leadership vary with the ability and willingness of the individual worker to perform his or her job. There is no one right way to supervise personnel and the situational supervisor decides on the style of supervision to use and the timing for using it most effectively. (Hersey, 1984)

Organizational communication that uses formal channels typically happen in a one-way fashion, such as sending out newsletters or memos about new or modified standards without any feedback mechanism from personnel. Two-way communication, which is how we define effective communication, allows for feedback from the receiver of the message. The supervision system is ideal for this type of feedback, because it already is a responsibility of supervisors to take this feedback, clarify any questions or confusion, serve as the liaison between management and personnel, and see to it that personnel properly follow standards. So the supervision system is an integrated part of effective organizational communication. It should play a major role in any plan for effectively communicating standards.

A major role of the supervisor is to provide technical training as needed to personnel. Just-in-time training and on-the-job training are a part of the supervisor's job description. This provides an opportunity for supervisors to communicate organizational standards and to be sure that personnel understand and are able to implement these standards properly. The supervisor's role should be considered when larger training programs are planned and implemented. Whatever type of skills personnel are trained in by the organization should be incorporated into their job description and supervisors should monitor performance of these skills. While this seems obvious, incorporating new skills into the job often is left to the worker and supervisors are left out of the training loop. All this leads to confusion and ineffective communication of organizational performance standards.

Let's take, for example, a managed-care organization that wishes to disseminate new standards for medical records. In this example, these standards identify the way medical records are organized, maintained and filled out. If an organization only disseminates procedural manuals with memos or communiqués explaining the method of the new standards and management's expectations for their use, then it is using one-way communication and risks possible confusion and lack of understanding by the target personnel. Result: Ineffective communication.

The organization could develop and implement a training in the new medical records standards, which would give the users an opportunity to clarify any confusion or misunderstanding about the standards. Developing and implementing the training carries a cost that the organization must consider. Another possibility is to train or inform office administrators about using the new medical records standards and delegate them to communicate this information to personnel This also allows supervisors to build the standards into the job performance expectations of personnel. It puts them in the position of ensuring effective communication of the new standards and building these performance expectations into how they monitor personnel. They can disseminate this information during staff meetings or other regular meetings with personnel.

Developing a Strategy for Communicating Standards

An organization should develop a strategy for communicating standards so it can best use various methods for communicating and avoid potential problems and pitfalls. Usually standards are communicated with background information about why they were developed, why they are important, who they will affect, what tasks will be altered, and any other relevant information that will increase audience understanding, commitment, and adherence. A plan for communicating standards should include the following information:

The intended audience. Different audiences in the organization have different information needs. Define the appropriate audience by considering who carries out the function that the standard is addressing. Consider who will be affected by the standard's implementation. Not all groups of personnel may be affected equally and each group may need different levels of communication or different information. Identify areas of concern that the audience may have and include ways to deal with those concerns.

What needs to be communicated. Once the audience is identified, the information to be communicated must be formulated. This probably is more than just the standards themselves. It most likely will include the background information described above, how and why the standards were developed, who they will affect, what tasks are altered, and any other necessary information. The message should include information to address any concerns that have been identified.

What channels of communication to use. The plan should map out the channels of communication that will be used. This includes the up/down channels and the cross-organizational channels. If informal channels, such as opinion leaders, are to be used, they should be identified here. This is a good time to map out how feedback will occur.

Source of communication. Identify who will communicate the standards to the intended audience. This should be a person or group that the intended audience views as a credible authority. The source person or group should have sufficient information to answer all questions and provide adequate clarification. This source may change for different audiences.

Sequence and coordination of standards. Determine if it is necessary to sequence the dissemination of information or can all audiences receive information at the same time. Based on the information needs for each audience, you may decide to sequence the delivery of information to eliminate any potential confusion.

Methods of Communication. Consider the methods above and any additional methods. Determine which are most cost-effective and decide which to use.

Feedback. Since feedback is essential for effective communication, the plan should include what types of feedback are wanted, who receives the feedback, how they will receive it, and what will happen with this information.

Evaluation. To evaluate the effectiveness of communicating the standards, you will need to answer these questions.

- Did the standard reach the intended audiences and the intended individuals in those groups?
- Was the standard communicated without distortion?
- Was the standard communicated within the time frame that was originally planned?
- Did the audience understand how to implement the standard?
- Did the audience implement the standard?

POTENTIAL COMMUNICATION BARRIERS

Organizations may take care to use well-established methods for effectively communicating standards. However, the organization often unknowingly can create communication barriers, which can be minimized or eliminated if the target audience is consulted while developing the communications strategy for. The following are some situations that create these barriers to communication and some suggestions about how to deal with them:

- The standard contains words, phrases, or terms that are unclear or not easily understood by the target audience. This can be avoided by involving or consulting some personnel from the target audience in the development of the standard. Including a pretest before dissemination also may help overcome this barrier.
- The standard was distorted by modifications, deletions, or additions as it passed through channels of communication. This can be avoided by building in some check points to be sure the integrity of the standard is not altered before it is the hands of those who will use it.
- The standards were communicated at a time when it was difficult for the audience to apply them, for example, laboratory procedures disseminated at a time when the laboratory is shut down and specimens are sent outside the organization.
- The standard does not contain sufficient detailed information to adequately meet the needs of the intended audience. For example, broad national standards that are not specific enough to provide sufficient guidance for work performance. This can be avoided by involving or consulting individuals from the target audience during development of the standard.
- The method of communicating the standard was not appropriate for the target audience, for example, disseminating standards on a CD-ROM to an audience with poor computer skills. This can be avoided by involving

or consulting target personnel during development of the standard, particularly when determining the appropriate format of the standard.

- The method of communicating the standard was not appropriate for the standards, for example, a complex standard, such a new medical or surgical procedure may not be effectively communicated through disseminating information passively, but better through training personnel and supervisors in its use.

The target audience may believe that the application of the standard will result in a change in their status. This can be determined and dealt with by involving or consulting the target audience when developing the communication strategy.

- The target audience may believe that the standard was developed because of their poor job performance. Again this can be determined and dealt with by involving or consulting the target audience when developing the strategy. Also, including respected peers in the plan for communicating can help to reduce or eliminate this barrier.
- The application of the standard requires different groups to cooperate that traditionally have not cooperated in the past. This needs to be considered in the plan and a strategy devised to address it.

REFERENCES

Al-Assaf, A. F. "Quantitative Management in Total Quality." In *The Textbook of Total Quality in Healthcare*, St. Lucie Press, Delary, FL, 1993.

Benson, D. S. and Van Osdol, W. *Quality Audit Systems for Primary care Centers*, Methodist Hospital of Indiana, Inc., 1990.

Berwick, D M. "Controlling Variation in Health Care: A Consultation from Walter Shewhart." *Medical Care*, Vol. 29, No. 12, 1212–1225, December 1991.

Brassard M. *The Memory Jogger Plus.* GOAL/QPC, 1989.

Coffey, R. J, et al. "An Introduction to Critical Pathways." *Quality Management in Health Care*, 1 (1), 45–54, 1992.

Dalkey, N C, et al. *The Quality of Life: Delphi Decision-Making.* Lexington Books, D. C Health & Co., Lexington, MA., 1972.

Dawkins, B. "Hello out there. Is anybody listening?" *CMA, The Management Accounting Magazine,* Vol. 66, No. 6, pg. 29(1), July–August, 1992.

Deming, W. E. *Out of Crisis.* Massachusetts Institute of Technology, Cambridge, MA, 1986.

DiPrete–Brown, L, et al. *Quality Assurance of Health care in Developing Countries.* The Quality Assurance Methodology Refinement Series, The Quality Assurance Project, 1993.

Donabedian A. *Explorations in Quality Assessment and Monitoring, Vol I: The Definition of Quality and Approaches to its Assessment.* Health Administration Press, Ann Arbor, MI, 1980.

Eddy, D. and Couch, J. B. "The Role Clinical Practice Policies in Quality Management." *Health care Quality Management for the 21st Century,* Ed. J. B. Couch. The American College of Physician Executives, Florida, 1991.

Eddy, D M. "Guidelines for Policy Statements," *JAMA.* 263: 2239–2243, 1990.

Eddy, D M. "Practice Policies — Where do They Come From?" *JAMA*. 263 (6): 1265–1275, 1990.

Grossman, J H. "Emerging Medical Quality Management Support Systems for Hospitals." *Healthcare Quality Management for the 21st Century*, Ed. J. B. Couch. The American College of Physician Executives, Florida, 1991.

Hanely, W. V. *Communication and organizational Behavior: Text and Cases*, 3rd ed. Richard D. Irwin, Inc., Homewood, IL, p. 13, 1973.

Hersey, P. *The Situational Leader*. Warner Books, 1984.

Imparato A. and Rites T. "Peripheral Arterial Disease." In *Principles of Surgery*, Chapter 21, Eds, S, Schwartz, G. Shires, and S. Forman. McGraw–Hill, New York, 1989.

Institute of Medicine. *Clinical Practice Guidelines: Direction for a New Program*. Eds. M. J. Field, et al. National Academy Press, Washington, DC ,1990.

Joint Commission on Accreditation of Healthcare Organizations. *1994 Accreditation Manual for Hospitals, Vol I: Standards*. Illinois, 1994

Joint Commission on Accreditation of Healthcare Organizations *Primer on Indicator Development and Application: Measuring Quality in Health Care*. Illinois, 1990.

Lohr, K. N., "Reasonable Expectations; From the Institute of Medicine," interview with Paul M. Schyve. *Quality Review Bulletin*, Vol. 18, No. 12, pg. 393, December 1992.

Mills, D. H. and Lindgren, O. H. "Impact of Liability Litigation on the Quality of Care," *Health care Quality Management for the 21st Century*, Ed. J. B. Couch. The American College of Physician Executives, Florida, 1991.

Scholtes, P. R. *The Team Handbook: How to Use Teams to Improve Quality*. Joiner Associates, 1988.

Watson, G. H. *Strategic Benchmarking*. John Wiley & Sons, New York, 1993.

Williams, W. H. A *Sampler on Sampling*. John Wiley & Sons, New York, 1978.

Weingarten, S. and Ellrodt, A. G. "The Case for Intensive Dissemination: Adoption of Practice Guidelines in the Coronary Care Unit," *Quality Review Bulletin*, Vol. 18, No. 12, pg. 449, December 1992,

7 Monitoring of Quality

Dale W. Bratzler

CONTENTS

INTRODUCTION

Measurements to assess the quality of care have been available to health care professionals for many years. Measures of care, such as mortality rate, and measures of morbidity, such as infection rate or transfusion rate, long have been collected as a part of quality assurance or utilization programs. Most of these programs were designed either to find errors in medical practice or to ensure compliance with accepted standards of care, often as a requirement for accreditation. In general, these programs of quality assurance relied primarily on the professional judgment of clinicians to ensure that patients received high-quality medical care. (Brook, 1996)

More recently, documentation of significant variation in the manner in which health care is provided and variation in outcomes of that care have been the driving forces behind the need to measure performance. Although measuring quality in health care organizations is a significant challenge, numerous systems of measurement and reporting have emerged. In the context of managed health care, there may be unique opportunities to assess quality at multiple levels of care because of the defined patient population base and integrated systems of health care delivery.

Systems to monitor and improve the quality of health care in managed care organizations traditionally have included internal quality assurance programs, external quality review, and published standardized performance reports. It increasingly has become important for health system managers to focus on quality management and to look at other industries for proven quality management techniques that can be applied in the health care setting. Quality management systems based on these industrial models often include features such as customer focus, outcomes measures, process of care measures, and statistical evaluation. (Niles, 1996). In addition to the use of performance data to improve the quality of care, the results of quality measures are being utilized increasingly for other purposes. A number of the administrative functions of health care organizations, such as credentialing and quality-based compensation, increasingly rely on the results of performance measures of indicators of quality. (Blum, 1995; Hanchak, 1996)

The focus of this chapter is monitoring quality by indicators. Its predominant theme will center around measuring performance with respect to processes of health care. This focus is based on the understanding that outcomes in medicine typically result from a sequence or flow of interrelated activities, many of which are measurable. The chapter will begin by reviewing some of the issues related to various customers of information in the health care organization and will review some of the measures of care. After reviewing some key definitions related to measurement of performance, steps in a process of monitoring quality by the development and application of quality indicators will be outlined. Issues related to reporting of performance measures and risk adjustment of those measures will be mentioned. Finally, some of the issues related to quality-of-life measures and the concept of cultural sensitivity will be discussed.

NEED FOR INFORMATION ON QUALITY

The need for information on quality may vary significantly, depending on the customer for the information. Although some performance measures may be useful to all customers, different groups, such as clinicians, consumers, employers or purchasers, and managers, may have needs for information specific to their role in the delivery of health care. (Table 1)

TABLE 1
Examples of Customer Information Needs on Quality

Clinician	Consumers	Employers and Purchasers	Managers
Process measures	*Access*	*Value*	*Financial and Service*
• diabetic eye exams	• primary care doctor	• services	• cost per service
• ER visits for asthma	• hospital affiliation	• benefits/cost	• operating margins
• immunization rates	• office call delays	• access	• utilization
Outcomes	*Service*	*Quality*	• membership
• mortality rates	• office hours	• HEDIS	• access
• morbidity rates	• specialty referrals	• functional outcomes	• waiting times
• functional outcomes	• complaint handling	• network adequacy	*Provider satisfaction*
• overall health	*Outcomes*	*Consumer satisfaction*	• turnover
Access and Service	• preventive service	• problem resolution	• team participation
• office waiting times	• personalized outcomes	• patient satisfaction	*Quality*
• exam room waiting		• community image	• functional outcomes
• subspecialty service			• standards compliance

CLINICIANS

Measurement of health care performance has not been emphasized during the medical education of most clinicians and the language and techniques of quality improvement are not understood by most physicians now in practice. (Blumenthal, 1996) Physicians often see measurement of performance as an unnecessary intrusion into their work and may view some quality improvement efforts as thinly veiled cost containment programs. (Chassin, 1996) As an important and influential member of any team addressing aspects of clinical quality, the physician needs to see the results of a number of performance measures and assist in the interpretation of those measures.

Physicians often are most interested in measures of technical performance. Measures that define aspects or processes of patient care, such as decision making, diagnostic and procedural skill, and timeliness of execution, are useful to improve care. Measures of care processes that are under the control of the clinician also are preferred. Examples of care processes under the control of a clinician might include the percentage of diabetic patients who have seen an ophthalmologist or the number of emergency room visits for a panel of asthmatic patients. Clinicians also may be interested in other more readily available measures, such as mortality rate, though they are unlikely to accept the results of these measures unless the information has been adjusted for risk. Clinicians in managed care settings may be interested in measures of access and service. Information about waiting times for routine office visits and delays in the process of subspecialty referrals may be beneficial to the clinician.

CONSUMERS

Patients often assess the quality of care in ways much different than those of members of the health care community. Patients may be more interested in measures of performance relating to processes of care, such as access and service. Information regarding access to the primary care physician of their choice, office hours, access to specialty care when needed, and hospital affiliations may be most important to the consumer selecting a health plan. Although many health care organizations provide data regarding preventive services and outcomes of care for selected conditions, this information may not be perceived as being particularly important to the consumer who is not seeking care for one of the conditions being profiled.

Recent evidence suggests that consumers are using certain types of procedure specific report cards on health care providers to make important health care decisions, such as the selection of a hospital or surgeon to provide the specific service. Other consumers report that the procedure-specific reports assisted them in asking more informed questions of their doctors and allowed them to increase their general knowledge of the health care being provided. (Isaacson, 1996)

EMPLOYERS AND PURCHASERS

Much of the driving force for the development of standardized data sets, such as HEDIS, has come from the need for information about health plan performance by employers and purchasers of care. The high cost of health care, combined with the knowledge of variation in care processes, have led to the need for standardized measures of quality of care provided by health care organizations. HEDIS 2.5 provides information on performance in five major areas of the health plan: (1) quality of care, (2) member access and satisfaction, (3) membership and utilization, (4) finance, and (5) health plan management activities. At the time of this writing, the final draft of HEDIS 3.0 has been released for health plans. (National Committee for Quality Assurance, 1997) The latest version of HEDIS 3.0 includes a "reporting set" and a "testing set" of indicators. The reporting set includes 75 measures that plans would be expected to report starting in mid 1997. The testing set includes 30 measures included for further evaluation. HEDIS 3.0 would provide information on performance in eight major areas: (1) effectiveness of care, (2) access to/availability of care, (3) satisfaction with the experience of care, (4) health plan stability, (5) use of services, (6) cost of care, (7) informed health care choices, and (8) health plan descriptive information. HEDIS 3.0 includes a standardized patient survey that should allow for comparisons of patient satisfaction across health care plans.

There are other areas of interest to health care purchasers. Information regarding utilization of services, benefit levels, and cost are important to the purchaser. Response to patient complaints and ability to resolve problems are important measures to the purchaser of health care. All of these measures potentially help the employer or purchaser of health care to see value for their purchase and many are now included in HEDIS 3.0.

MANAGERS

Much of the same information described above will be useful to the manager of the health care organization. Information regarding access to care and service provided will be important, especially as it relates to consumer satisfaction. Satisfaction of the providers of care and turnover of staff are important in the management of the health services organization. Information regarding costs associated with care are important to allow the manager to ensure the fiscal viability of the health care organization. Performance measures of quality of care and clinical outcomes are important to the manager to ensure that the organization is effective and to conform to standards of care to assure accreditation. Finally, information regarding the positioning of the organization within the context of the community and measures that reflect overall community health are essential to the manager for the processes of strategic planning and assumption of a leadership position with respect to the public's health.

MEASURES OF CARE

Donnabedian (1988) classified the evaluation of quality of care into measures of structure, process, and outcomes. Structural data include information about the organizational resources, facilities, personnel, equipment, policies, and procedures. Process data include information about what is done to, for, or by patients as part of the encounter between a physician or other health care professional and the patient. Process measures represent intermediate indicators of outcomes. Measures of process evaluate the manner in which health care professionals perform their jobs and evaluate if the work was performed consistent with professional standards. Outcomes data describe a patient's health status which may include clinical (e.g., the proportion of diabetic patients who develop retinopathy) as well as functional outcomes (e.g., ambulation after total hip joint replacement). Outcomes measures evaluate whether the patient regained the maximal functional status and quality of life possible, given the patient's underlying condition and technology available at the time of treatment. Information regarding patient satisfaction with care represents outcomes. (Table 2)

There are three dimensions of measurement that health care organizations may use to measure performance (Cutler, 1995): (1) cost, (2) service, and (3) quality. Cost data refer to measures such as cost per member per month, admission rates,

TABLE 2
Measures of Care

Structure	Process	Outcome
staffing	care plan	clinical
equipment	coordination	functional
physical environment	intervention	utilization
	reassessment	satisfaction

hospital days per 1,000 members per month, and premium revenue per member. Most managed care organizations have information systems capable of closely tracking costs. Examples of service data include member satisfaction rates, waiting times for appointments, turnaround time for lab and radiology reports. Service measures reflect the perceived value that the user of the service receives. Quality measures assess conformance to standards or comparisons to best performances (benchmarks or gold standards).

Each of the measures of care can be evaluated with respect to one or all of the dimensions of measurement. There are costs and service considerations associated with all of the measures of care. Cost measures can be obtained from standard financial information available to virtually all health care organizations. Service measures most readily are obtained by performing customer surveys. Quality measures, though more difficult to identify, can be developed with the participation of clinicians and can be used to evaluate all of the measures of care.

INFORMATION SYSTEMS

Although it is beyond the scope of this chapter to review information management systems comprehensively, discussion of some of the issues is important. In the past, information systems essentially have been transaction processing systems. Particularly in the managed care setting, where clinicians and managers are constantly being asked to justify choices on the basis of eligibility, authorization, and precertification, information systems that support decision making become important. Information systems will allow for both the measurement of performance and the measurement of health outcomes are desirable.

The information systems currently in place in many health care organizations are limited to data derived from the actual claim or transaction. These systems and their use have a number of advantages. (Longo, 1995) The data in these systems usually is extensive and covers a variety of topics, such as diagnoses, procedures, and limited patient demographics. Many organizations have multiple years of data available for review. Informed consent generally is not required to review this information and collection of information from this data is economical since little time is involved in the actual process of collection. There are, however, a number of disadvantages of using claims-based data sets. For the most part, very little information regarding clinical aspects of care can be derived from the data set. Many important aspects of care such as preventive health measures are not likely to be included in the data set and little to no information regarding health outcomes is available.

The challenge to managed care organizations in information management is to go from systems based on claims to comprehensive systems that integrate information on patient care and encounters that support decision analysis and communication between providers. (Kibbe, 1994) A health information network is defined as an integrated system that facilitates the exchange of patient, clinical, and financial information among physicians, hospitals, payers, employers, pharmacies, and related health care entities. (Brennan, 1995) Ideally, information in the network would be stored in relational databases that would allow decision-support analysis. (Brailer,

---

TABLE 3
Desirable Characteristics of an Information System.

- Relational database that can be searched by end users and allows decision-support analysis.
- Allows site-specific customization
- Simple user interface.
- Easy query language.
- Exportable formats for data exchange and compatibility with other software.

Source: Longo, 1995

1996) Characteristics that are desirable in such a system are described in Table 3. Considerations of the capability of the information system will be very important in determining the types of performance measures selected for monitoring and the sources of the data for those measures. The challenge in the use of information systems to support quality measures and improvement is to automate collection, analysis, and reporting of the data.

DEFINITIONS AND TERMINOLOGY

A variety of terms should be defined before discussing the development of monitoring systems based on indicators. Many of the definitions of these terms were developed by the Institute of Medicine and a workgroup assembled by AHCPR that examined ways in which clinical practice guidelines could be used to evaluate quality of care. (Schoenbaum, 1995) Although these terms were described in reference to using clinical practice guidelines to measure care, many of them have relevance to the discussions of performance measurement by indicators in managed care. (Table 4)

DEVELOPING A SYSTEM OF MONITORING BY INDICATORS

The amount of effort involved in developing a system of monitoring quality by indicators will depend on the indicators selected for measurement and the availability of the information sources necessary for the evaluation. Implementation of standardized performance measures such as HEDIS will eliminate much of the development time involved in selecting, defining, and specifying data items and rules. On the other hand, developing a quality indicator based on perceived problems with quality of care or developing new performance measures based on a clinical practice guideline will involve much more time and effort.

In March 1995, AHCPR published a two-volume report that describes the methodologies for translating clinical practice guidelines into review criteria and performance measures. (Schoenbaum, 1995) This report provides detailed information regarding the steps involved in developing and implementing a guideline-derived performance measure. The following discussion presents a successful model that follows some of the key steps defined in the AHCPR publication on the process of

TABLE 4
Definitions

Implicit criteria	Criteria formed by a respected clinician who uses clinical judgment in evaluating performance; these implicit criteria remain concealed in the mind of the reviewer.
Explicit criteria	Objective criteria specified in advance as a basis for making judgments on performance.
Medical review criteria	Systematically developed statements that can be used to assess specific health care decisions, services, and outcomes.
Performance measures	Methods or instruments to estimate or monitor the extent to which the actions of a health care practitioner or provider conform to the clinical practice guideline. These represent quantitative tools that provide an indication of a health care organization's performance in relation to a specified process or outcome.
Clinical indicator	A quantitative measure that can be used as a guide to monitor and evaluate the quality of important patient care and supportive service activities. Clinical indicators may be rate-based when they produce rates for comparing the performance of organizational providers of care, or they may be sentinel event indicators that identify undesired events, such as death, and, therefore trigger a quality review.
Standards of quality	Authoritative statements of (1) minimum levels of acceptable performance or results, (2) excellent levels of performance or results, or (3) the range of acceptable performance or results.
Benchmark	A level of care set as a goal to be attained. Internal benchmarks are derived from similar processes or services within an organization; competitive benchmarks are comparisons with the best external competitors in the field; and generic benchmarks are drawn from the best performance of similar processes in other industries.

Source: Schoenbaum, 1995

developing a system of monitoring by indicators that might apply in a variety of health care settings. The reader is referred to the AHCPR publication for a more complete discussion of developing a new quality indicator, particularly one based on a clinical practice guideline. (Web page: http://www.ahcrp.gov)

IDENTIFYING INDICATORS

The first step in the development of a system of monitoring by indicators is to identify those functions or aspects of patient care that are essential to the quality care of the patient. The availability of the data or the resources required to collect the information may limit selection of some desirable indicators. Putting together a multidisciplinary team of health professionals, quality improvement staff, and administrative personnel is often useful and necessary to successfully identify opportunities for improvement and develop the evaluation tools to measure performance and improve care.

TABLE 5
Desired Attributes of Quality Indicators.

• Relevant and frequent
• Nonobtrusive data collection
• Cost-effective
• Reliable and valid
• Suitable for feedback, profiling, and tracking
• Flexible to allow for continuous adaptation

As discussed in Chapter 6, desirable characteristics of an indicator for monitoring quality of care are described in Table 5. Indicators should be relevant. As discussed above, determining who the customer for the information will be is important in determining the relevance of the indicator. If the performance to be measured is clinical, the indicator should be medically important and should occur frequently enough to allow for meaningful measurement at the plan or provider level.

The indicator should be designed in such a way that it is nonobtrusive to the day-to-day operations of the health care organization. Ideally, the indicator is data driven from sources readily available to the organization. In addition, the data used for quality measurement and management should be the same data routinely used for patient care activities to avoid the development of parallel data sets. If the data required to profile the indicator requires medical record review, then the information needs to be readily identifiable in the medical record and definitions of the data item need to be clear enough to allow objective collection. The indicator should also be cost-effective. Cost-effectiveness is defined as the usefulness of the measure in relation to the cost of its application.

The indicator should be suitable for practice and provider feedback, profiling, and tracking. Clinicians are most likely to respond to measures of care that are under their control. Information on performance that may be profiled over time or comparative information between providers, physicians, or plans often is useful to stimulate behavior changes that lead to improvement in the quality of care.

To be useful in monitoring of quality, the indicator has to be both reliable and valid. Reliability refers to the accuracy and reproducibility of the data over time. When the information is collected from multiple providers, the reliability will depend on the uniformity of data collection across the organizations. The information the indicator measures must be complete. Validity refers to the extent to which the results of a measurement are accurate representations of the care being measured. Outcomes indicators may not be valid, for example, when used to compare providers unless strategies to adjust the data for severity of illness are applied. Validity of an indicator also refers to the process by which the data collected by the indicator is analyzed and interpreted into information about the quality of health care being measured and to the ability to ultimately use the indicator information to make decisions that improve care.

Finally, the indicator should be flexible enough to allow for continuous adaptation. Quality indicators that do not identify opportunities to improve care should be abandoned or revised to focus on areas of greater need. Data regarding indicators may not provide useful information about processes of care that can be improved. Indicators may provide information that results in improved processes, but not improved heath care outcomes. Indicators used to monitor quality should be subjected to the same quality improvement cycle used for other processes of care in the organization. Quality indicators or performance measures need to be periodically reevaluated as to their appropriateness and utility in improving care in the organization.

For the purpose of this discussion of monitoring by indicators, two different indicators that might be measured in a managed care organization will be developed. The first indicator is designed to profile the proportion of diabetic patients who are referred for routine annual ophthalmologic examinations as recommended by the American Diabetes Association. (1995) The second indicator is a service indicator designed to profile delays between specialty referrals and actual appointment times. The following discussion will review some of the issues associated with the development and measurement of an indicator. (Table 6)

IDENTIFYING DATA SOURCE

Many different sources of data are available from which useful information may be obtained in the process of measuring performance on an indicator of care. Information may be collected from patient medical records, records obtained from the pharmacy, laboratory, or radiology department, and administrative data obtained from transaction records. When measuring information known only to the patient, some form of patient survey is necessary. At times, measurement of performance on an indicator of care may require the use of several sources of data.

It also is important to consider the site of care when developing a system of monitoring based on indicators. In the example of measuring performance with respect to the provision of annual eye examinations for diabetic patients, the focus of the review would be the primary care physicians' offices and the administrative data related to the referral process rather than a focus on the ophthalmologists' offices. For any particular indicator, there may be a need to limit the review to certain sites of care or to specific groups of practitioners.

SPECIFY SAMPLING TIME FRAME

Also important in the development of an indicator is determining the time frame from which to sample cases or data. When reviewing performance of practitioners on referral of diabetic patients for their annual eye examination, a logical time frame would be to sample cases for a calendar year. This would allow the managed care organization to establish as the denominator for performance on the indicator all enrolled diabetic patients during the calendar year. Other indicators such as the service indicator of referral delays may be measured over a shorter period of time depending on the availability and timeliness of the administrative data necessary to measure performance. Establishing a time frame for sampling defines the denominator for any indicator.

ESTABLISH INDICATOR CRITERIA

Specific criteria need to be established for case inclusion or exclusion in the sample that is being measured. For example, cases incorrectly coded with a diagnosis of diabetes mellitus should be excluded from the sample and denominator of the indicator measuring annual eye examination referrals. The managed care organization may elect to limit the cases sampled to those diabetic patients who have been enrolled in the plan for at least one full calendar year. Specific circumstances, such as emergency room referrals to specialists, might be excluded from the sample and denominator of the service indicator on referral delays. Specific criteria that define inclusion into the indicator measure must be established before any systematic measurement is begun.

In the development of indicator criteria, acceptable alternatives to an indicator criterion need to be defined. In the case of the diabetic patient, the patient may refuse to see an ophthalmologist. A patient may specifically delay an appointment to a specialist because of personal reasons. In both of these circumstances, the alternatives to compliance with the standards assigned to the indicator are acceptable reasons for not complying with the indicator and these alternatives need to be captured in some way.

The indicator needs to be defined in precise terms so that there is no question about what is being measured. In the example of the diabetic patient, the indicator might simply be that patients without eye disease are referred to an ophthalmologist for an eye examination. The service indicator might be defined as the number of days from the date of the primary care referral to the appointment date with the specialist. The definition of the indicator needs to be defined in such a way to ensure that performance can be measured objectively.

DEVELOP DATA COLLECTION FORMS FOR NECESSARY CHART REVIEWS

Depending on the indicator chosen, the development of the data collection tools or a plan for appropriately identifying and collecting necessary information is the next step in the process. If the indicator requires the review of medical records, a data abstraction form needs to be developed. In the case of a service indicator or financial indicator, it may be possible to collect all of the necessary information from available electronic or administrative sources.

When the development of a data abstraction form is required, careful attention to the details of the form is important. It is important to collect all of the necessary information needed to assess performance with respect to the indicator. On the other hand, it is important to limit the data collection to those items that are important to keep the complexity and cost of the data collection to a minimum. Data items selected for inclusion on the abstraction form should help to assess the indicator criterion, help follow the decision rules for analyzing the data, define exclusions or acceptable alternatives, or identify gaps in knowledge pertaining to the indicator being profiled.

The data collection form should be written in a format that promotes accuracy of the information. This may be facilitated by the development of written instructions or decision rules for abstractors. In addition to the development of decision rules

TABLE 6
Developing a System of Monitoring by Indicator

Annual Diabetic Eye Exam	Identify Indicator	Delays in Specialty Referral
• Primary care medical records of all enrolled diabetic patients • Administrative data on referrals	Identify Data Source	• Referral requests • Claims data on dates of service • Sample of records of patients referred for specialty consultation
• One calendar year	Specify Sampling Time Frame	• All patients referred for specialty consultation for six consecutive months
• Diabetic patients without eye disease referred to ophthalmologist • Acceptable alternatives - patient refuses exam - ophthalmology exam in past year for other reason	Establish Indicator Criteria	• Number of days from the time of the primary care referral to appointment with specialist • Acceptable alternative — patient delays visit for personal reasons
• Patient demographics • Validate diagnosis of diabetes mellitus • Information needed for exclusions or acceptable alternatives • Patient referral and date	Develop Data Collection Forms	• Date referral requested • Date services provided • Information needed for exclusions (such as emergent referral) or acceptable alternatives • Patient questionnaire
• Construct algorithm and flowchart that validates patient inclusion and acceptable alternatives • Design electronic database or analytic program	Design Analysis Plan	• Consider algorithm that specifies acceptable alternatives • Design plan to profile time delays between referral and appointment
• Review sample of medical records of diabetic patients • Clinician validation of the indicator • Assess inter-rater reliability	Pilot Test	• Review sample of medical records if chart review required • Clinician validation of records that are identified as having delays in referral
• Utilize data collection forms to review defined sample of patient charts	Conduct Review	• Review charts if indicated • Review administrative records
•Calculate performance rate • Develop bar graph display • Compare clinics and performance by years • Share information with practitioners	Develop Feedback	• Calculate average number of days consults delayed by month • Plot information on run chart and share with organizational staff
• Investigate observed variation between clinics • Develop standing protocols for ophthalmology referral of diabetic patients	Link Performance Measurement to Quality Improvement	• Apply tools of continuous quality improvement to identify delays in consults • Change systems to address the bottlenecks that cause delays in service

TABLE 6 (continued)
Developing a System of Monitoring by Indicator

Annual Diabetic Eye Exam	Identify Indicator	Delays in Specialty Referral
• Repeat sampling of primary care charts and administrative data on referral of diabetic patients to an ophthalmologist • Profile data annually by clinic	Repeat Measurement to Evaluate Performance	• Continue to monitor number of days from time of referral to date of appointment • Periodically repeat patient survey
• Modify indicator as recommendations from the American Diabetes Association are updated • Utilize automated data from clinical information systems when available	Revise Review Criteria and Indicator	• Revise indicator to address other bottlenecks in the system of consultation referral • Consider other service indicators when desired performance achieved

and instructions, direct entry of data into a interactive computer system or the development of a computerized data entry form can facilitate accuracy of data entry. The development of data entry software can allow for computer prompts for any particular information that can direct the abstractor to collect the correct data. Systems that reject entered data items that are not plausible and systems that prompt for the next data entry item can speed abstraction and increase the accuracy of the data collected. When more than one person or organization is collecting the information, a written set of instructions is essential to ensure consistent data collection across organizations or abstractors. Detailed instructions concerning the use of computerized data entry tools also is important when utilizing multiple abstractors to review records.

In collecting information regarding the provision of diabetic eye examinations, the data collection form might include patient demographic data, information that would allow the reviewer to validate the diagnosis of diabetes mellitus, and questions that would establish the presence or absence of known diabetic eye disease based on medical record documentation. The data collection form would have to identify instances of acceptable alternatives and exclusions such as patient refusal to have an eye examination or current or past treatment of diabetic retinopathy.

Data collection from medical record review may not be necessary to measure performance with respect to delays in specialty referral. Development of a plan of systematic collection of administrative data such as date that a referral record is generated to the date of provided services based on review of paid claims may provide the needed information. A review of a sample of medical records of patients referred for specialty services may provide insight into acceptable alternatives to indicator compliance such as delays in specialty consultation as a result of patient personal reasons. A limited patient survey also may provide useful information regarding delays in specialty referral.

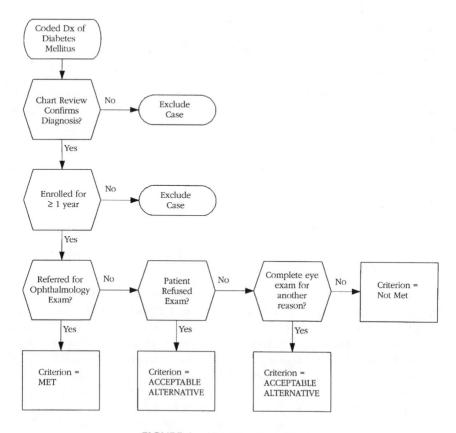

FIGURE 1   Algorithm Flow Chart

DESIGN ANALYSIS PLAN

The complexity of an analysis plan will depend on the indicator chosen for measurement. In the examples used for this discussion, analysis of the time between specialty referral and actual appointment date might be profiled easily. On the other hand, clinical indicators associated with multiple exclusions or acceptable alternatives may require a more detailed plan of analysis.

One of the first steps in the design of an analysis plan is to create an algorithm flowchart. An *algorithm* is defined as a rule of procedure or instructions for solving a problem or accomplishing an objective. Algorithms are built on condition-based (branching) logic, in which the condition encountered at a decision node, or point of branching, determines the next pathway. By expressing a clinical algorithm in flowchart format, the clinical criteria that have been established for the indicator can be communicated and understood more clearly. (Figure 1) Utilization of an algorithm flowchart to design the analysis plan for data collected regarding the indicator ensures that the criteria established for performance on the indicator are applied uniformly to all cases reviewed.

Depending on the complexity of the indicator and the method of data collection, the development of an analytic software program based on the algorithm flowchart may simplify and speed the analysis of the collected data. Linking of database information into a prepared analytic program ensures consistent analysis and allows for the analysis of large and complex data sets. A variety of commercial database programs are available that have integrated analysis packages. Other commercial software packages are available that can link facilitate the linking of information from the collected database into a statistical analysis program.

PILOT TEST

Regardless of the complexity of the indicator or the experience of the team who selects and develops the indicator, pilot testing of the measure is important. Testing of the indicator allows the team to confirm the validity of the measure and test the reliability of the indicator. The pilot test of the quality indicator should be performed by members of the team who are experienced in record review when clinical data is being collected from medical records. The pilot test allows the reviewer to identify problems with the data collection forms, identify ambiguities in the data definitions, and identify problems inherent in the actual collection of the desired data.

As a part of the pilot testing process, clinical validation should be considered. When evaluating performance with respect to clinical indicators, review of a sample of records that have been subjected to the data collection and analysis process should be performed by clinician reviewers. This review allows the team to determine if the criteria utilized to collect and analyze the data appropriately measures the process of care defined by the indicator. Through this process, the indicator, data definitions, data collection forms, and analysis plan can be altered to ensure valid measures of performance.

Finally, the process of pilot testing allows for the initial measurement of inter-rater reliability. *Inter-rater reliability* is a measure of agreement on data collected from the same records by two or more independent abstractors. During the initial phases of testing the indicator, "gold standard" case review can be utilized in the training and reliability testing of independent record abstractors. Typically, a 5% random sample of cases are selected for rereview by a second abstractor and the results of abstraction are compared for the two reviewers. Data items with high degrees of inconsistency between reviewers may need to be modified, abandoned, or redefined to improve the reliability of data collection.

CONDUCT REVIEW

Once the indicators and data definitions have been refined and data collection forms have been tested, the review can be completed. The sample size reviewed will vary, depending on resources and the size of the population of interest. In the event the population of interest is too large to allow for complete review of all records, a random sample or a time-limited sample (e.g., 100% of all records for a specified limited period of time) of records could be reviewed. An ongoing review of a small proportion (e.g., 5%) of the records by a second independent reviewed should be performed to ensure continued data reliability.

Because the referral of diabetic patients for ophthalmology examinations could occur at any time during the year, the best strategy for performance measurement of this indicator would be to review all diabetic cases enrolled in the plan over the designated calendar year or to review a representative random sample of those cases. The sample size would need to be large enough to provide meaningful data to individual practitioners or plan clinics to be useful in assessing care. In the case of review of delays in referral for specialty care, data collection might be limited to a shorter time frame capturing the delay times for all patients (e.g., review the administrative data of approved referrals to date of service provision for all patients referred over a four-month period.)

REPORTING PERFORMANCE

Once the process of data collection and analysis are complete, performance reports are generated that allow customers of the information to link the measures provided to quality improvement efforts. The type of report that is generated will depend on the indicators measured and the planned use and distribution of the information. Performance rates for criterion conformance to guidelines can be calculated by using the following formula:

$$\frac{\text{Criterion Met} + \text{Acceptable Alternatives}}{\text{Criterion Met} + \text{Criterion Not Met} + \text{Acceptable Alternatives}}$$

By including all eligible cases for the indicator in the denominator of the formula, and all cases for which the criterion was met or acceptable alternatives were present in the numerator, a performance rate is generated. The information generated in this way can be displayed in tables, graphs, or charts. The performance rate for diabetic patients referred to an ophthalmologist would be generated as follows:

$$\frac{\text{Referred} + \text{Patients refused exam} + \text{Patients receiving eye care}}{\text{Referred} + \text{Patients refused exam} + \text{Patients receiving eye care} + \text{Patients not referred}}$$

Service or financial indicators may be reported and displayed in different ways. In the example of the service indicator regarding delays in specialty referrals, the unit of analysis might be the average number of days consultations are delayed for each month. This information could then be displayed as a time series or on a run chart.

Reporting of information in a managed care setting can be done for the individual physician or group of physicians, as peer comparison information, or as information aggregated for the entire organization. Reporting individual information without comparative peer data or established standards of care may not be sufficient to stimulate quality improvement. A variety of characteristics of performance reporting are desirable when applied in the managed care setting. The information should be timely and when appropriate, be reported frequently. The indicator being profiled should be evidence-based from scientific literature or have clear relation to quality of care as perceived by the user of the information. The information needs to be

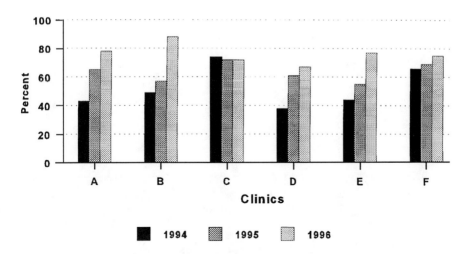

FIGURE 2 Diabetics Referred for Ophthalmology Exam

accurate and reliable and when appropriate should adjust for case-mix (particularly if performance of practitioners or plans is being compared on outcome indicators.) The information must be useful. When providing information to clinicians, the information should be related to processes of care that are under the control of the clinician.

The use of tables, graphs, or charts to display performance on indicators can facilitate the understanding of large amounts of information. Graphical displays of data can be very useful for providing comparison data between individuals, groups, or plans and can allow for the display of information trended over time. Graphic displays tend to engage the reader and communicate information rapidly. The information presented in the graphics should not be threatening or embarrassing. (Mosser, 1995) Feedback that displays threatening or embarrassing information carries the risk of provoking more action focused on attacking the data than on improving care.

Sample performance data on the two indicators profiled in this chapter are demonstrated in Figures 2 and 3. In the first example, comparative data for care provided by six different clinics in a managed care plan on the percentage of diabetic patients referred for ophthalmologic examinations is displayed. This bar graph format has the advantage of providing comparative information between clinics as well as displaying performance at two discreet points in time. The second example demonstrates the average number of days between referral and consultation appointment time by month. This display allows administrative and clinical staff to monitor changes in performance in relation to quality improvement and also to identify special cause variations when they occur.

APPLYING STANDARDS OF QUALITY
TO PERFORMANCE MEASURES

"Standards of quality" are defined by the Institute of Medicine as "authoritative statements of: (1) minimum levels of acceptable performance or results, (2) excellent

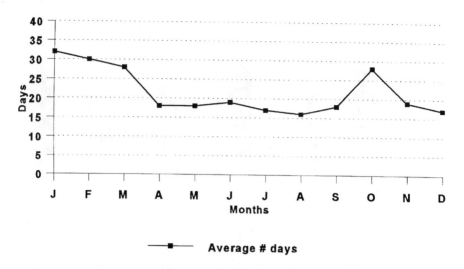

FIGURE 3   Consultation Delays

levels of performance or results, or (3) the range of acceptable performance or results." Measures of performance on indicators are compared to standards of quality to determine if further intervention concerning quality of care is necessary. There are various types of standards that may be used for comparison. (Table 7) Minimum standards may be applied to a performance measure. In this circumstance, measures of performance on the indicator that fall below the level of the minimum standard would require further investigation. "Benchmarks" or comparative standards can be used to identify best practices related to performance on the measured indicator. Clinicians, groups of clinicians, clinics, hospitals, or health care organizations can be compared to benchmark performance. The provision of comparative information between clinicians or organizations can provide strong incentives to improve performance. By profiling information on performance on the indicator over time, improvements related to changes in care or systems of care can be measured.

Other types of standards are commonly in use. Standards for accreditation set expected levels of performance on the indicator measures. Prescriptive standards represent statements of performance level that should be achieved for any particular indicator.

RISK ADJUSTMENT

Because information regarding performance on a variety of indicators often is used to compare physicians, groups, or health care plans, risk adjustment has taken on new importance in monitoring of quality. The goal of risk adjustment is to control for factors that patients independently bring to health care encounters and that can affect their likelihood of experiencing good or bad outcomes. (Iezzoni, 1995) Risk adjustment can be applied to many different types of indicators, including clinical, administrative, and utilization. Risk adjustment may not be necessary when performance

TABLE 7
Standards of Quality

Benchmark	A level of care set as a goal to be attained. (See Table 3)
Comparative standard	A standard derived from a comparison with other performance rates constructed by using exactly the same performance measure, such as the prior performance of a clinician or provider, the observation of the performance of others, or the statistical analysis of group rates.
Prescriptive standard	A statement of what should be achieved rather than a statement of what has been achieved.
Standard for accreditation	A statement of expectation set by competent authority concerning a degree or level of requirement, excellence, or attainment in quality or performance.
Standard of care (legal usage)	In a malpractice case court proceeding there is an attempt to determine whether a patient suffered harm due to negligent violation of a standard of care. The standard of care for the case is elaborated by the questioning of expert witnesses who have studied the facts of the case that are before the court and have relevant knowledge of comparable behavior.
Standard of care (regulatory usage)	Standards for facilities are commonly expressed in terms of a minimal level of policy, equipment, and capacity necessary to achieve licensure or certification.
Threshold	A preestablished level for care. If a desired attribute of care falls below this level or an undesired attribute of care rises above this level, further evaluation or action is triggered.

Source: Schoenbaum, 1995

TABLE 8
Choosing a Risk Adjustment Approach.

- Is the methodology clinically meaningful?
- What is the purpose of the risk adjustment?
- Does the approach capture unique features of the institutions whose outcomes will be evaluated?
- Is the logic available in a way that is easy to understand?
- What data are required to perform the risk assessment?
- Is the system relatively immune to manipulation?
- How much will the risk assessment cost?

Source: Iezzoni, 1995

information is reported for the purpose of identifying opportunities for improvement. If, however, the information is being utilized to compare providers on the basis of outcomes, determine compensation, or make contracting decisions, techniques of risk adjustment are necessary to facilitate comparisons and ensure that performance measures are being applied fairly to each provider.

There are a variety of systems of risk adjustment available on the market. No single risk-adjustment system can apply or provide severity adjustment for all clinical circumstances. The process of developing a risk adjustment strategy includes identifying specific risk factors which may be clinical characteristics or other patient specific characteristics that predict the patients' likelihood of any particular outcome of interest. There are a variety of factors that may influence the patients outcomes. This includes a host of demographic features, specific diagnosis, major surgery or procedures, and a variety of physiologic measures.

Iezzoni (1995) has described a number of questions that should be considered when selecting or designing a risk-adjustment strategy. (Table 8) The purpose of the risk adjustment strategy first must be defined. Risk-adjustment strategies that apply to clinical circumstances may not apply to performance measures related to service indicators. The methodology of the risk-adjustment strategy must be meaningful clinically. It is important to be sure that the strategy is being applied to the circumstances it was designed to be applied to. The risk-adjustment strategy must be sensitive to the special features of the organization to which it is being applied. The logic of the strategy should be made available so that the organization utilizing the risk-adjustment strategy can identify and understand the application of the strategy to the population being served. It is important to understand what types of data will be necessary to apply the risk adjustment strategy. Information that is readily available from sources routinely collected is desirable both in the measurement of performance and in the application of risk adjustment. Data that will have to be collected from medical record review will be subject to documentation issues and the time and expense of data collection. Another issue to consider in the selection or design of risk-adjustment strategies is the ability to manipulate the system, e.g., failure to code or document complications that arise during care. Finally, it is important to consider the costs associated with risk adjustment. Costs may include the direct costs of designing or implementing a system of risk adjustment, or may be associated with the collection of the necessary data for the system. Indirect or hidden costs of a risk adjustment system might include the increased use of diagnostic tests by clinicians to document increased severity of illness of their patients.

LINKING PERFORMANCE DATA TO QUALITY IMPROVEMENT

Linking the results of performance measurement to quality improvement is discussed in detail elsewhere in this book. Observed variation in performance between providers, groups, or clinicians may be due to a variety of factors. Differences in patients populations, errors in measurement, or actual differences in practice or differences in organizational procedures may account for the documented differences. Variations that are identified by performance measurement often require additional investigation to determine the underlying or root causes. The observed variations often can be linked to system errors. Identifying the underlying causes of variation may require individual case review coupled with other techniques of quality management to identify the underlying system errors.

Performance improvement may occur in a variety of ways. Identified system errors can be corrected and systems of ongoing monitoring established. Feedback of performance data can be educational. Providing comparative performance data can function to provide individual groups or clinicians a measure of their performance as compared to others and may allow for comparisons to internal or external benchmarks. Feedback of performance data may serve as a positive incentive when groups or clinicians can see their performance improve over time.

REPEAT MEASUREMENT TO EVALUATE PERFORMANCE

There are two important reasons to repeat measurement of the indicator. The first is to confirm that changes in care or system changes implemented as a result of the baseline performance measures and subsequent investigation are resulting in the desired improvement in care or service. The second is to revalidate the indicator. Failure to document improvement may occur because the changes in care or systems of the organization were not effective in improving the identified quality concern. It also is possible that the changes made in the processes of care or in the service provided did not address the underlying root causes of the quality concern addressed by the baseline measures. Failure to demonstrate improvement may occur because the indicator is not a valid measure of the care being given or service being measured. In any circumstance where performance does not improve in spite of changes in systems of care or service, review findings should be investigated to identify the reasons for lack of improvement in the performance measure.

Remeasurement of indicators can provide important information to the health care organization. Changes in care or provision of services over time can be profiled by remeasurement. When significant improvement is attained for an indicator, remeasurement can define when it is appropriate to identify new areas for quality improvement. Indicators that fail to improve over time will warrant additional investigation as mentioned above.

REVISE REVIEW CRITERIA AND INDICATOR

Indicators and their measurement should be subject to the same cycle of continuous improvement as other organizational processes. Indicators need to be updated with time. New and emerging therapies and technologies need to be addressed in the measurement of care and some indicators will become obsolete as changes in medical care or service provision emerge. Changes in information systems, administrative reporting systems, or clinical care systems may allow for more efficient measurement of performance on indicators and should be utilized when available. Indicators that ultimately fail to identify opportunities for improvement or indicators that do not provide valid measures of care or service should be abandoned.

Some valid indicators deserve refinement over time. Changes in care or service may result in improvements in measures of performance that plateau with time. Refinements in the indicator to measure newly identified areas that present opportunities for continued improvement may allow for even better performance with respect to overall care of the original condition or service being measured. Performance measures need to be linked to outcomes as well as processes. Improvement in performance on an indicator may result in improved processes of care that have little or no impact on the ultimate outcomes of interest for the patient.

INSTRUMENT PANELS AND PERFORMANCE MEASURES

Much of the concern on the part of health care organizations and clinicians has been related to the potential uses of information collected in the measurement of performance. The concept of the "report card" that profiles organizations or clinicians on the basis of performance is one that is common in discussions of performance measurement. Report cards potentially can allow consumers and purchasers of health care to judge providers and make health care decisions based on the data. Report cards are useful in showing trends in health outcomes and costs and can allow consumers and purchasers to identify potential strengths and weaknesses of the health care organization. (Nelson, 1995) Report cards profile information regarding past performance and may not be particularly useful to the health care manager trying to monitor the performance of an organization in a continuous and real time manner.

Instrument panels, sometimes referred to as "dashboard measures." represent dynamic panels of real-time information on a variety of different health services and clinical processes of the organization. Instrument panels need to present ongoing measures of performance about the organization as a whole. Various types of instrument panels can be monitored. In general, the measures that make up the panel should be few enough so that they can be regularly profiled and yet diverse enough to provide an ongoing measure of the actual performance of the organization. Examples of instrument panel measures might include measures of customer satisfaction, utilization and finance measures, health outcomes and clinical care measures, and strategic initiative measures. Instrument panels provide ongoing real-time information about critical processes in the health care organization that allow for ongoing decision making, midcourse corrections in strategy, and ongoing warning systems for problems that may arise. Ongoing measures of performance can identify special cause variations that may affect health outcomes or organizational outcomes that need to be addressed. Information that is routinely collected as part of instrument panel measures may be utilized to generate report card information when required.

OTHER CONSIDERATIONS

Although difficult to collect, quality-of-life measures are important in the measurement of performance in health care. (Testa, 1996) Quality-of-life measures, when accounted for in the measurement of performance with respect to medical treatments or organizational services, may have a substantial effect on the perceived cost effectiveness of the treatment. Quality-of-life measures may allow an organization to determine the effectiveness of a disease-management service or determine the impact of differing forms of medical care or treatment. Measures of process and outcome that go beyond reporting of usual measures, such as morbidity and mortality and also incorporate measures such as day-to-day functionality, daily compliance with medical regimens for chronic disease, and cost of care compared to cost to the purchasing employer for days of lost productivity, are increasingly important. Quality-of-life measures should include objective and subjective components that are important to the members of the patient population to which they are being applied. Ensuring that systems of monitoring by indicator incorporate measures that are relevant to patients such as their ability to function on a daily basis, to work, to socialize, and to have a greater sense of well-being because of improved self-image is becoming increasingly important. There are many different measurement instruments available for measuring quality-of-life such as the SF-36 (Ware, 1992), other generic instruments, and disease-specific instruments.

Finally, in any system of monitoring by indicator, issues of "cultural sensitivity" or "cultural appropriateness" in the delivery of health care will need to be taken into consideration. (Lavizzo–Mourey, 1996) The demographics and ethnic diversity of the population of the United States are changing and the cultures found within the populations of health care organizations are changing too. Cultural competence is conceptualized by Lavizzo–Mourey and Mackenzie as the demonstrated awareness and integration of three population-specific issues: (1) health-related beliefs and cultural values, (2) disease incidence and (3) prevalence, and treatment efficacy. "The belief systems and perspectives of cultural subpopulations, which are equally valid, may give rise to health-related behaviors that clash with the expectations of the health plan. As they penetrate into Medicare, Medicaid, and minority populations, successful managed care organizations will attempt to negotiate these differences respectfully and proactively — while constantly measuring their own performance." The recognition that disease processes vary in different ethnic populations and treatment benefits for some diseases are at population specific make it imperative that these differences are taken into account when monitoring indicators of care. The fact that many of the subpopulations of minorities remain disproportionately represented in low-income socioeconomic categories may create financial barriers to care and access that need to be addressed. Managed care organizations must routinely incorporate epidemiologic information about cultural differences in covered populations into their programs and resource allocation decisions and must hold providers accountable for implementing practice strategies to meet the needs of special populations if they are to maintain acceptable standards of health care quality.

CONCLUSION

Measurement of performance is the driving force behind quality improvement. Performance measures for a variety of indicators provide information about care and services that are already in place within the organization. Performance measures can also guide management in the day-to-day operation of the health care organization. Measuring indicator performance can provide valuable information about changes in care that result from quality improvement efforts.

The process of measuring quality of health care is an evolving one. Health services researchers are continuously developing and validating newer methods for the measurement of quality. There is increasing interest in assessing the quality of decision making that occurs in the management of health care problems. There is also the need to develop methods to make valid comparisons of quality between culturally divergent populations and to correlate clinical performance with measurable processes of care. Because there is increasing need for comparative outcomes data and indicator performance measures, it becomes important for the managed care organization to develop standardized systems for measuring processes and outcomes of care and integrating these measures into everyday clinical and operational practices.

REFERENCES

American Diabetes Association. "Standards of medical care for patients with diabetes mellitus." *Diabetes Care*, 18: 8S–15S, 1995.

Blum, J. D. "Economic credentialing moves from the hospital to managed care." *J. Healthcare Finance*, 22: 60–71, 1995.

Blumenthal, D. "Quality of care — what is it?" *N. Engl. J. Med.* 335: 891–894, 1996.

Brailer, D. J., Goldfarb, S., Horgan, M., Katz, F., Paulus, R.A., and Zakrewski, K. "Improving performance with clinical decision support." *Jt. Comm. J. Qual. Improv.* 22: 443–456, 1996.

Brennan, C. P. "Managed care and health information networks." *J. Healthcare Finance.* 21: 1–5, 1995.

Brook, R. H., McGlynn, E. A., and Cleary, P. D. "Measuring quality of care." *N. Engl. J. Med.*; 335: 966–970, 1996.

Chassin, M. R. "Improving the quality of care." *N. Engl. J. Med.* 335: 1060–1063. 1996.

Cutler, C. M. "What information do managers of health care organizations need to see: a physician manager's perspective?" In *Measuring clinical care — a guide for physician executives.* Schoenbaum, S.C., ed. American College of Physician Executives, Florida, 27–40, 1995.

Donabedian, A. "The quality of care: how can it be assessed?" *JAMA* 260: 1743–1748, 1988.

Hanchak, N. A., Schlackman, N., and Harmon–Weiss, S. "U.S. Healthcare's quality-based compensation model." *Healthcare Financ Rev.* 17: 143–159, 1996.

Iezzoni, L. I. "An introduction to risk adjustment." In *Measuring clinical care — a guide for physician executives.* Schoenbaum. S. C., ed. American College of Physician Executives. Florida, 83–95, 1995.

Isaacson, S. K., Lawes, S., Levie, L., Mandzia, L., and Raynor, J. "Health care: Employers and individual consumers want additional information on quality." *J. Outcomes Management* 3: 4–9, 1996.

Kibbe, D. C. "Designing quality into health care information systems." *Jt. Comm. J. Qual. Improv.* 20: 591–594, 1994.

Lavizzo–Mourey, R. and Mackenzie, E. R. "Cultural competence: essential measurements of quality for managed care organizations." *Ann. Intern. Med.* 124: 919–921, 1996.

Longo, D. R., Daugird, A. J., and Spencer, D. C. "Assessing the quality of primary care: the use and importance of reimbursement data." *J. Healthcare Finance.* 21: 13–30, 1995.

Mosser G. "What information do clinicians need?" In *Measuring clinical care — a guide for physician executives*. Schoenbaum, S. C., ed. American College of Physician Executives, Florida, 63–70, 1995.

Nelson, E. C., Batalden, P. B., Plume, S. K., Mihevc, N. T., and Swartz, W. G. "Report cards or instrument panels: Who needs what?" *Jt. Comm. J. Qual. Improv.* 21: 155–166, 1995.

Niles, N., Tarbox, G., Schults, W, Swartz, W., and Wolf, E. "Using qualitative and quantitative patient satisfaction data to improve the quality of cardiac care." *Jt. Comm. J. Qual. Improv.* 22: 323–335, 1996.

Schoenbaum, S. C., Sundwall, D. N., Bergman, D., Buckle, J. M., and Chernov, A. *Using clinical practice guidelines to evaluate quality of care*. U.S. Department of Health and Human Services. Public Health Service, Agency for Health care Policy and Research, AHCPR Pub. No. 95-0046, March 1995.

Testa, M. A. and Simonson, D. C. "Assessment of quality-of-life outcomes." *N. Engl. J. Med.* 334: 835–840, 1996.

Ware, J. E., Jr. and Sherbourne, C. D. "The MOS 36-item short-form health survey (SF-36). I. Conceptual framework and item selection." *Med. care.* 30: 473–483, 1992.

8 Quality Improvement Activities

Jolee Reinke

CONTENTS

1-57444-073-X/97/$0.00+$.50
© 1998 by CRC Press LLC

INTRODUCTION

Quality improvement activities are conducted in a variety of ways. As mentioned elsewhere in this book, FOCUS-PDCA, the 10-step model, monitoring, supervision, and quality design all can be effective methods for improving quality. The choice of which approach to use sometimes can be confusing. The key is to select an intervention which is appropriate both to the task and resources at hand. Uncomplicated issues may be improved through setting and communicating standards, monitoring, or supervision. More complex processes or problems benefit from a structured, team-based, data-driven approach, directed at making process-level improvements which will be sustained over time. This chapter will propose such an approach which is effective for improving complex processes or problem solving in clinical or support services.

USING TEAMS TO WORK ON QUALITY IMPROVEMENTS

Is a Team Essential?

Many facilities involved in managed care are small, and the staff may be overwhelmed to think it must form teams to work on improving quality. A team might involve every member in a facility. Depending on the topic, a team may or may not be needed.

When considering an **improvement opportunity** (IO), first determine if the situation simply requires a management action, such as effective supervision, policy change or enforcement, or communication of requirements through job aids. If a situation has not improved after initial management interventions, if improvements are not sustained over time, a or the situation is complex, use a team-based approach.

A team is a "high performing task group whose members are interdependent and share a common performance objective." (Francis & Young, 1992) In small practice settings, the team may include the entire staff, while in larger environments, a subset of the staff may be formed. On occasion, a team will include members outside the regularly assigned staff. The key is that all members of a team somehow are involved in the process or problem being studied.

BENEFITS OF WORKING IN TEAMS

Teamwork benefits both the organization and the individual team members. Because a team has more knowledge than any one individual, the organization using a team approach will have a more complete working knowledge of the process to be improved. A team can address larger issues than an individual working alone, and brings wider access to technical knowledge and skills. A well run team will create an open atmosphere, with less blame of individuals and more focus on systems as causes of poor performance. With participation from many people, root causes are more likely to be identified, and a greater number of ideas for solutions will be generated. Because people support what they help to create, teamwork leads to greater acceptance of a solution and a higher probability that improvements will be sustained.

Benefits also accrue to team members. They gain greater understanding of issues impacting their work, and can see how they fit in the larger picture of health care service delivery. Members have an opportunity to share ideas and be creative, while making positive contributions to the workplace. They often develop deeper and stronger working relationships with colleagues, some of whom they may not have routinely encountered. Most team members learn new skills such as team building, problem analysis, or the use of quality improvement tools and techniques. For many members, the most significant benefit is the personal satisfaction that comes from being part of a solution, rather than part of a problem.

TYPES OF TEAMS

There basically are three types of teams: (1) innovative, (2) work, and (3) quality improvement.

Innovative teams explore possibilities and alternatives. They are formed to create something and commonly contribute to quality design of new services. These teams require a high level of autonomy and creativity.

Work teams share common activities and execute a predetermined plan. Examples are a cardiac arrest response team or a surgical team. **Self-directed work groups** are another example, people who commonly work together and are given the responsibility and authority to manage their own practices. These teams need clear performance standards and role assignments. Successful work teams also have high creativity, and are committed to excellence and continuous improvement in their daily assignments.

Quality improvement or **problem resolution teams** work on a specific task directed at improving a particular process or solving a problem. They are usually formed *ad hoc* to address a particular topic. These teams stay focused on the assigned improvement task, and disband after goals are achieved.

Forming a Quality Improvement Team

Quality improvement teams are formed to address opportunities for process improvement or problem solving. In organizations which have Quality Councils, these teams may be chartered after the council does preliminary definition and investigation of an issue. In other cases, an enlightened manager may realize a team is necessary to address an interdisciplinary practice issue, or a topic which has not responded to routine management interventions.

Team membership includes only people involved with the process or topic being examined. If the team is chartered by a larger entity, such as a Quality Council, a leader is usually assigned. If not assigned, the leader usually is a person with authority to act upon results recommended by the team, or is the person with the responsibility to make recommendations to the appropriate authority. Representation should be sought from all groups of people involved, but limited to a size likely to work effectively — usually no more than seven to 10 people. If the issue is multidisciplinary, membership should come from the various clinical and/or management disciplines involved. One person can represent several perspectives, to limit team size. For example, if a manager recognizes an opportunity to improve the at-home follow up of day surgery patients, a team might include a surgical nurse who is also familiar with the educational aspects of pre-surgical patient care, a help-line staff member, a home care staff member, a recently-treated patient, and that patient's family member who assisted with post-operative care.

A quality improvement team should form at a time appropriate to the task. A team formed to select improvement opportunities should expect to change membership or create a new group after the topic is selected. When proceeding through steps of the quality improvement process, teams form as a natural result of defining the improvement opportunity.

Team Building

Teams do not automatically function in an effective manner. Team building is a process of deliberately helping a group evolve into a cohesive and effective unit. This implies a certain level of individual and group learning about both the content and process of team work. Team building may be assisted by an external coach or facilitator, or team building may be done by the group itself with an internal coach, using assessments and exercises to enhance effective team behaviors. Team building also involves learning about quality improvement tools and techniques, and methods to assess and improve group dynamics.

Team building is essential for a new team or one which must achieve results quickly. Team building also is appropriate for a group which wants to achieve more openness, participation, and creativity, or one which needs to improve interpersonal relationships, commitment, or clarity of purpose.

The process of team building starts by determining if an external or internal coach is needed. Inexperienced teams — those with problems in group dynamics or those needing expert help to use QI tools and techniques — benefit most from an external coach. However, this requires that a trained facilitator is available. Alternatively, a team can use the talents of team members to provide internal coaching. Someone with skills in group dynamics, counseling, or human resources training could function as an internal coach. Group process assessment and intervention exercises, and multiple sources to assist learning about QI tools and techniques, are available. (Francis and Young, 1992; GOAL/QPC and Joiner Associates, 1995; Harper and Harper, 1992; Orsburn et al., 1990; Scholtes, 1988; Tague, 1995; Wellins et al., 1991) Often team leaders assume the coaching role, especially when the intervention concentrates on developing clarity about group goals and planning.

STAGES OF TEAM DEVELOPMENT
AND TEAM-BUILDING INTERVENTIONS

A team which is familiar with stages of team development has realistic expectations for team accomplishment and increasingly is able to solve its own group process problems as self-awareness increases. Tuckman (1965) described stages of T-group development which have come to be known as "forming" "storming" "norming," and "performing." When first described, these stages were seen as sequential and required — a team was thought to advance only by completing work in the prior stage. Since then, understanding of these stages has expanded and different nomenclature has been proposed. (Bertcher, 1994, Beck and Yeager, 1996) Now we understand that groups may move between stages and may repeat or skip stages. Changes in team membership, goals, leaders, or individual behaviors may cause the team to repeat stages. In addition, we realize that quality improvement teams working on a specific process or problem will have an additional stage, "closing."

Stage 1   Forming. When a team is forming, members cautiously explore acceptable group behavior. People change roles from "individual" to "member." Members may challenge the authority of the leader, but they also are dependent on the leader for orientation and direction. In this stage, the team needs to focus on its purpose and function. Members generally have these feelings:

- excitement, anticipation, optimism
- pride in being chosen as a member
- tentative initial attachment to the team
- anxiety, fear, or even suspicion about the job ahead (and demonstrate these behaviors)
- polite, rather formal interpersonal relationships
- attempts to define the tasks and decide how they will be accomplished
- definition of further information that needs to be gathered
- discussions about concepts and issues
- discussions about issues not relevant to the task
- confusion related to difficulty identifying relevant problems
- complaining about the organization, barriers to the task, reasons why things related to the reason for team forming are not solved

Useful team leader/coach activities:

- lead and promote introduction and inclusion exercises or activities
- clarify the group task, mission, project, desired accomplishments
- propose task timelines and agendas for initial work
- establish ground rules for team behavior
- provide needed training in necessary topics such as communication skills, planning skills, use of QI tools and techniques, stages of team development

Stage 2   Storming. Not all groups experience storming. At this stage, the task seems more difficult than expected, and members may become impatient and argumentative. They may resist collaboration and be unable to achieve consensus. At the same time, because of the conflicts, individuals establish their own expertise within the group and forge ways of working together which respect each other's point of view. If the team only works together for a short time on a narrow topic, they may not experience the disagreements that characterize this stage. On the other hand a team with persistent internal conflicts may remain in this stage and never reach optimal performance. In the stage members usually have these feelings:

- resistance to the task
- doubt about the appropriateness of goals, agendas, plans
- resistance to QA/QI interventions (and demonstrate these behaviors)
- arguing among members, even when they agree on the real issues
- defensiveness, competition, withdrawal
- withholding information
- questioning the purpose of the work
- unrealistic goal setting and concern of overwork

Useful team leader/coach activities:

- introduce conflict management techniques
- clarify group purpose, goals, agenda, work plan
- clarify or teach about team dynamics, meeting methods, roles, QA concepts

Stage 3   Norming. During this stage, members accept the team, their roles in the team, and the individuality of team members. Conflict is reduced as members are more cooperative, but they also learn how to use conflict for positive results. If the team stalls here, effectiveness may be reduced because of the members' desire to please one another. The team needs to work on group dynamics, such as balanced participation and effective communication. In this stage members usually have these feelings:

- acceptance of membership in the team
- relief that conflicts are past and things will work out
- contentment (and demonstrate these behaviors)
- commitment to working out differences
- giving and receiving feedback constructively

- more expression of feelings
- playful, fun interactions

Useful team leader/coach activities:

- continue to support involvement of the entire group, foster shared responsibility for group progress
- refocus on the agenda or team mission when necessary
- provide group process or QA tools training, as needed
- introduce divergent opinion to limit inappropriate group-think (unchallenged acceptance of views held by influential members, or prevailing group opinion)

Stage 4   Performing. In this stage, the team diagnoses and solves its own problems, uses sound decision making, and effectively plans and copes with change. Members accept each other's strengths and weaknesses, and know their own strong and weak points. They have insight about personal and group process. The team performs more self-evaluation, and members accept more leadership responsibilities. Divergent opinions are considered, yet consensus is achieved.

During this stage, members have these feelings:

- satisfaction with the team's progress
- trust in one another
- responses appropriate to group activity (and exhibit these behaviors)
- ability to anticipate group problems and prevent them, or work through them constructively
- willingness to take risks personally, and as a team
- commitment to team work and goals

Useful team leader/coach activities:

- training in QA tools/techniques as needed
- get out of the way and let the group work

Stage 5   Closing. The work of a quality improvement or problem solving team is intended to end when improvements are in place. The team must deal with either the success or failure of its work, and the disbanding of the team. The leader helps the team to identify lessons learned, and plan how those lessons will be communicated. Any follow up on the group work, such as ongoing monitoring of improvements, must be planned. The team should celebrate its successes, and if they have not reached the desired results should be supported for the good work they did. During this stage, members usually have these feelings:

- if successful: joy, pride, elation, loss (due to dissolution of the team)
- if unsuccessful: frustration, anger, relief at no longer being associated with a losing effort (and demonstrate these behaviors)

- if successful: expressions of appreciation, eagerness to publicize results, avoidance of closure activities
- if unsuccessful: denial, blame, disassociation, relief

Useful team leader/coach activities:

- discussion of next steps, feelings about results
- evaluation of what worked and what didn't work
- assisting with presentations to management, recording team progress

CHARACTERISTICS OF EFFECTIVE TEAMS

Effective teams possess common characteristics. A team can increase its effectiveness by purposefully taking actions which strengthen these behaviors.

Clear role definition refers to the role of the team (its goals, agenda and work plan), formal individual roles such as leader, recorder, time keeper, and coach, and behavioral roles of the members. To achieve this, teams should:

- regularly confirm understandings of the team purpose and expected outcomes
- assign formal roles with clear requirements
- leader — usually a senior person who "owns" the process being addressed; responsible for the results of the group; articulates the group purpose and goal
- coach (internal or external) — helps the leader monitor group process, train in the use of QA tools and techniques, and move the team toward its goals
- timekeeper (may change from meeting to meeting) — tracks progress against predetermined timelines within a meeting; guides the team to start and end on time
- recorder — keeps formal and informal records of team accomplishment, including each step in a process improvement cycle
- balance personality-related roles on the team. This refers to such roles as idea generator, process manager, harmonizer, and so on. An effective team has a variety of these roles, and members can vary their behavior to meet overall team needs. During team building, members may use diagnostic tools to discover the roles they naturally play, which roles are present within the team as a whole, and the roles they need to develop to make a more balanced team. For examples, see the *Team Role Analysis Questionnaire* (Francis and Young, 1992, p. 189) or *Self-Assessment: How do you rate as a Team Member.* (Harper and Harper, 1994, p. 45)

Careful time control and good meeting organization are demonstrated when meetings start and end on time, agendas exist and are followed, members responsibly get work done during meetings, and work required outside of meetings is completed as necessary. To achieve this characteristic, teams should:

- set agendas with internal time limits at the end of the prior meeting, to address pending topics and guide ongoing activities
- identify topics as background, discussion, or decision so members know what the purpose of the topic is, and the agenda can set aside time appropriate to the purpose; then, stay focused and do only what was planned
- provide background information prior to meetings
- post all work during meetings, by using flip charts to record key discussion points and decisions, and using QI tools to display information
- do not unnecessarily create minutes — each member can take notes on the agenda, and a storybook (paper records of team work, including all steps and analysis) or storyboard (displayed summary of team work) can keep team records (Sholtes, 1993); groundrules, and negotiations with the entity that formed the team, should describe what type of formal documentation is required
- seek specific agreement from the team to deviate from the agenda, do not just let internal timelines slip
- be sure members are clear about any work to be accomplished outside of the meeting, and have the resources and time to do so
- check the meeting room prior to the meeting, to ensure necessary equipment, space, tables, chairs, etc. are present and functional

Effective group process skills are demonstrated by members routinely using good interpersonal skills such as active listening, giving and receiving feedback effectively, and seeking clarity in discussions. The team may use meeting time to learn these skills or to do exercises to enhance group communication. Interactions are characterized by respect for others' opinions and a genuine interest in what others say and feel. Differences of opinion are encouraged and freely expressed — the team does not demand narrow conformity or blind adherence to a particular idea. Healthy conflict is welcomed as a way to explore all parts of an issue. The team is responsive to the changing needs of its members, and the environment in which it is working. To achieve these skills, a team should:

- use a coach to monitor group behavior and give feedback, either during the meeting or at the end as a formal evaluation; with practice, team members should become able to self-monitor and provide ongoing process feedback
- set ground rules for desired behavior, and the manner in which feedback on group process will be given
- learn about and use effective conflict management and decision making; encourage appropriate conflict
- do diagnostic exercises and practice skills the team wishes to improve (Francis and Young, 1992; Harper and Harper, 1994; Scholtes, 1993)

An *informal, relaxed atmosphere* helps team members to enjoy their work, identify positively with the team, and consider team work to be a source of professional and personal growth. Members are able to discuss all issues related to the team's work, because confidential discussions and information remain confidential. To achieve this, teams should:

- use good communication and feedback skills
- establish ground rules that allow informal behavior at a level comfortable to members
- set ground rules for confidentiality, both within the team and from the team to outsiders
- do ice-breaking and trust-building exercises early, as the team forms
- purposefully plan the integration of new members
- select a meeting room in a neutral location, with attention to creature comforts
- maintain a stable membership

High levels of interest and commitment are evident in members who are eager to be present and enjoy their work. They are on time for meetings, and are proud to be part of the team. Contributions are recognized and appreciated by both members and senior management. To achieve this, a team should:

- regularly reaffirm clarity of purpose, tasks and timelines
- actively seek members' contributions and incorporate them into team work, with appropriate attribution
- select or appoint members who are available for meetings and have knowledge appropriate to the task; limit membership changes
- if new members are needed, integrate them rapidly, with a clear overview of activities and quick involvement in group work
- use storyboards or other methods are used to inform peers, seniors and clients about team progress; information is posted after each major step in the improvement process
- have senior management or leaders launch the team, receive intermittent reports of both progress and problems, and celebrate team achievements

USING A QUALITY IMPROVEMENT CYCLE

A structured approach to quality improvement is effective when dealing with complex processes or problems. The steps are summarized in Figure 1 in Chapter 3.

Thinking about issues as *improvement opportunities* (IO) is different than thinking about *problems*, which implies something unsatisfactory, resistant to change, or damaging. If *problems* are the only focus, the chance may be lost to make meaningful improvements in things which are satisfactory now, but could be made better — raising the level of excellence yields rewards. The philosophy of looking at IOs might be expressed as "if it's not broke — make it better — don't wait for it to break."

Step 1   Select and Clearly Define
an Improvement Opportunity

Sources of Improvement Opportunities

IOs can come from many sources. Regulatory or accrediting processes may require that certain topics be addressed. A managed care plan's routine monitoring and supervision or client satisfaction information may highlight an area of concern. Topics may be selected because they are important to the clients, a peer group, a work group, or a supervisor. A QM plan will identify important aspects of care which may be appropriate for selection. IOs might be selected because they are related to important organizational goals and objectives. Clinical practices which are high risk, high volume or problem prone may be obvious topics. If other attempts to make improvements have failed, or if a problem is chronic or recurring, those topics might be appropriate IOs. Brainstorming is often used to generate a possible list of IOs.

Who Should Identify and Select IOs?

Traditionally, managers would be expected to identify IOs. However, they may not be aware of topics important to the workers or the clients. While managers should suggest IOs, they are not the only source. A Quality Council or Quality Assurance Committee may identify an IO and later charter a team to do the work. A facility-level or peer group may identify IOs. For topics which involve several groups in a multi-facility managed care setting, the senior-most management, or the first level of integrated management, may recognize appropriate IOs. The important point is that anyone in the health care delivery continuum has the chance to identify opportunities for improvement.

Prioritize IOs and Select One to Work on

There may be overwhelming reasons to select a specific IO. Perhaps the topic must be addressed to meet regulatory or accreditation requirements, or something terrible happened to a client and clinical practices need to be improved. However, in most cases, there will be more IOs than can be addressed at one time, and a decision must be made to select just one or two.

When prioritizing choices, there are several methods that may be used. One option is *executive decision* or *management mandate*. Although this may not reflect a participative management approach, it is a fact of life in some practices. An enlightened manager will "mandate" a topic which is of interest to the involved members. Another method is voting or multivoting. (*see* chapter appendix) While this gives power to each individual's vote, it may create "losers" who resist efforts to work on the selected topic. A third method is to let an expert decide. This may be effective within peer groups when choosing a clinical topic, such as which care guidelines to improve first. Consensus, a choice on which all agree, often is the desired decision method. True consensus, however, may be difficult to achieve. A decision matrix often is helpful. (*see* appendix) This method uses more explicit criteria to force prioritization.

No matter which prioritization method is selected, there are additional considerations when using an improvement cycle for the first time. For initial efforts, choose an IO which is likely to yield success — the team needs to be reinforced for its effort of learning how to use the cycle. This first IO should be: a small but important issue that can be dealt with quickly; a clear process, with beginning and ending points; a frequently used process, so changes can be seen quickly; a topic of interest to both workers and management. Also, be sure there is sufficient time available to follow the quality improvement cycle faithfully.

Some general cautions also apply: Beware of preconceived solutions — do not study a solution, rather study the underlying process. Let the team explore the entire process before reaching a conclusion. For example, instead of addressing "a need to change work hours," the team more appropriately might study the process of scheduling and staffing a particular service. The result might be a change in work hours, but another possible result may be a change in patient flow. Do not select a process that is being changed by other events. For example, studying the medication resupply process while changing pharmaceutical suppliers will be a wasted effort. Beware of trying to improve a whole system. Instead, focus on a process within the system. Rather than working to improve the care of all maternal–child services, efforts may concentrate on the process of antenatal care for teenagers from pregnancy diagnosis to 28 weeks.

Clearly Define the IO

A clear statement describing the IO helps focus remaining work. Some authors call this a *mission statement*, a *task statement*, or *goals of the improvement team*. In any case, if the IO is poorly defined, team members may each work with a different understanding of the issue, and never conduct effective analysis or make recommendations for improvement. The lack of a clear opportunity statement may lead to conflict, confusion, and failure of the improvement effort. When it is difficult to clearly state the IO, examine the topic to see if a system, rather than a process, is being addressed

A QC or management team often is responsible for the first definition of an IO, but the process improvement team must also be allowed to clarify the IO statement. To help craft the statement, consider these questions:

- what is the process, issue, or problem to be studied? (not the cause or solution)
- what is not functioning as desired?
- what are the effects of this process on internal and external customers? on the quality of service delivery? what is the "pain" caused by current practice? is this information available as a quantifiable baseline measure?
- how long have current conditions existed?
- how frequently does the current process not work well?

- what will change to indicate that an improvement has occurred? what will be seen, heard, or measured differently? what dimensions of quality are expected to improve?
- what are the boundaries of the process? when does it start and stop? in what populations does it occur (or not occur)?

A template opportunity statement can help guide this effort:

"An opportunity exists to improve _____(*name the process*), starting with _____, and ending with _____. This is important because current practices cause _____(*the "pain"*). We will know it is improved when _____(*what will change*).

Consider these examples:

An opportunity exists to improve the care of first time mother–baby pairs who leave the hospital after 24 hours or less, starting with antepartum education about post-partum care, and ending with the first postpartum office visit for mother and child. This is important because patients perceive they are at greater risk for going home early and have complained they don't know how to care for the baby at home. This will improve when these patients routinely state they are comfortable going home after short-stay care, and complaints related to lack of knowledge of baby care decrease.

We want to improve the process of using sterile supplies. We occasionally destroy supplies which pass expiration dates, which wastes money, and may prevent us from giving some care if supplies are not available. This will improve when we no longer discard expired supplies.

Either statement would enable a team to start studying the IO, although the second example would require further definition: Is it necessary to consider all supplies, or are only certain ones discarded? Does the process begin with ordering supplies, with restocking, or with daily usage? What is the baseline cost of waste?

The opportunity statement should be posted on the storyboard, representing the first step in the quality improvement cycle.

STEP II   DETERMINE WHO SHOULD WORK ON THE IO

Teamwork is the method of choice for using a quality improvement cycle. The entity which has chosen and defined the IO should select a team, although membership may be readjusted as the team begins its work. To determine membership, review the opportunity statement and identify people involved in the process. A high-level flowchart will help identify the major participants. The appendix includes advice on creating and using this type of flowchart, as well as an example.

Each organization has its own process for appointing team members. Some do this through the QC, others through routine supervisors and managers. Usually the team leader is assigned by the entity forming the team, but some allow the team to choose its own leader, based on who "owns" the process under study. During the first meeting, the team should review the opportunity statement, high level flowchart, and current membership, and recommend any necessary changes to ensure that all members are involved in the process and that all parts of the process are represented by a member.

Set up clear expectations among all parties regarding the amount of authority and responsibility delegated to the team, and the level of assistance available to the team for coaching and training. An organization may have trained coaches/facilitators available, or the leader may need to learn about coaching and QI tools and techniques to train the team. If a QC chartered the team, additional authority might be needed from supervisors or managers to gather data related to the IO, or to seek assistance of staff not assigned to the team.

The team should have a responsible person or group to whom it will report. Guidance should be provided regarding reports of progress and expected time lines. During the first meetings, the team should propose a timeline based on expected steps in the improvement process, and subsequent work should be recorded in storybooks and storyboards. These should be a sufficient report of team work.

In many managed care settings, the "team" may seem to be the entire workforce. Check this assumption against the high level flowchart, before automatically assigning all staff. Also, many managed care processes involve people from multiple facilities, so it may be reasonable to assemble a team from more than one practice site. Occasionally, members are appropriately sought from groups outside the managed care network. For example, if examining prehospital care routines, local ambulance service staff may be needed.

Increasingly, clients and their families are being included in process improvement teams. While staff may be reluctant to involve them in the entire improvement activity, clients nevertheless may be critical in accurately describing the current process. Many are eager to assist, and often have some quality improvement knowledge from business or industry. Be sure to select candidates who have been directly involved in the process under study, who can make a commitment to attend meetings, and participate in the work, and who will be able to understand methods of quality improvement used by the team. Include client members in all training and team building, if they are full-time participants.

Team membership, and perhaps the high level flowchart, should be posted on the storyboard, along with any changes to the opportunity statement. It may also include a group photo and a proposed schedule of work.

STEP III DESCRIBE AND ANALYZE CURRENT PRACTICE RELATED TO THE IO

Clarify What is Known About the IO

The team should examine the opportunity statement and determine what they are really supposed to address. These questions should be answered:

- What process does the IO involve?
- What is our current level of performance related to that process?

If the team cannot identify a process related to the IO, consider another approach: Are there standards, standard operating procedures, policies, or clinical guidelines which relate to the IO? If there truly is no definable process, the opportunity statement has probably not captured the true opportunity for improvement. The team should redefine the IO.

If several processes relating to the IO are identified, the team must clarify which one is the focus for improvement. In this case, the opportunity statement should be redefined, as it probably has captured a system which needs to be improved, not a process. The best action is to prioritize the processes and begin to work on only one at a time.

Quantitative baseline data about current performance related to the process may or may not be available. Error rates, waiting times, or patient satisfaction results could serve this purpose. Often, there is management information which stimulated concern about the topic initially, but this may not be a baseline. The team will use quantitative baseline performance information, both to judge the urgency of the need for improvement and to compare with results to prove things get better. In some cases, qualitative information is available. While this will not be as easy to measure against, it may be the only available information.

There may be a need to collect baseline data. The team should determine if an *ad hoc* data collection should occur now, or if it should wait until later in the analysis phase. If data is easily available, it may be reasonable to collect this data prior to further work. On the other hand, the team will be collecting data after flowchart and cause-effect analysis, and baseline data could be collected concurrently.

Flowchart the Current Process

Working from the opportunity statement, complete a process-level flowchart. This represents the process as it currently happens, not the standard, not the ideal, not a consensus of what is right, but the way it truly happens with all the variations. Consult the appendix for information about construction and an example.

At this point the team may discover it does not really have a process — no two people agree that one step follows another. The lack of a process may be the reason an improvement is needed. The team may be tempted to shortcut the improvement cycle and simply design the process. Although that will likely be part of the solution, the team may miss other issues if further analyses are not done.

After the team has created the flowchart, step back and look at the big picture: Does this chart accurately represent real work? The team may want to wait a day or two and reexamine it to be sure. The flowchart should be posted on the storyboard, in a location where others who work in the process can see it. Their feedback may be valuable in capturing details or variations the team omitted.

Next, begin to look at steps in the process. Ask if each step always happens, or if a step contains hidden decisions that affect the process. The waiting time example in the appendix includes a step for completing insurance paperwork. Is this step needed for each patient? Is there ever a time that insurance paperwork is not done? If so, there may be an additional decision point in this step.

Also look at each step to be sure it records only one step, not many. In the waiting time example it may be satisfactory to call one step *vitals*, but in another situation, separate steps, such as "Is thermometer available?" "Take temperature.", and "Is pediatric blood pressure cuff available?", may be needed. Since the example is a waiting time inquiry, it may not be necessary to detail these steps, unless each nonavailable item creates a separate measurable wait. If, on the other hand, this team was examining the smaller process of taking vitals signs, you would expect this level of detail.

Look at each activity loop, to check that it reenters the process at the correct place and does not skip steps. Loops may go backward in the process, representing re-work or a check step. This usually implies wasted time or repetition. Loops also can go forward, skipping steps, which may be good or bad depending on the situation.

Keep focused on the opportunity statement to determine how many branching arms should be detailed. Look at the example in the appendix again. If this opportunity statement dealt with waiting times for only scheduled patients, this flowchart is appropriate — it does not detail actions taken for patients without appointments. If the opportunity statement dealt with all patients, and one of the complaints was that unscheduled patients waited excessive amounts of time, this team would want to go into detail about the processes for seeing the unscheduled patients.

Use the Flowchart to Analyze Opportunities to Improve Current Practice

Process flowcharts are excellent tools to discover the causes of poor performance or areas to target for improvement. Again using the waiting time flowchart, there are several pieces of information which would help this team evaluate waiting time.

- How long does it take, on average, for patients to go from greeting to exam room?
- How much time do patients wait in each wait step? How frequently do they wait longer than 30 minutes total? (or other time limit indicating "excessive" wait)
- How often is the chart not available? the medical assistant?
- How many unscheduled patients are seen on average each day?

This flowchart could also be used to evaluate whether the current process is the most appropriate one. Examine each step and ask if each is needed; if steps could be re-ordered to achieve greater efficiency; if any steps are redundant. Look at each step which requires input such as equipment or supply — Is there a way to design in a more reliable source of this necessary item? Also consider if any steps could be combined for greater efficiency. In the example, if investigation pointed to unavailable medical assistants as a major contributor to waiting times, perhaps staff cross-training could yield more people capable of taking vitals. Look at decision points to see if any are checks and balances which add value to the process — not all decisions and feedback loops are bad.

Construct a Cause-Effect Diagram

Cause–effect analysis also helps the team understand current practice. Several tools will work, such as *tree diagrams*, *why diagrams*, and *bubble charts*, but one of the easiest and most common tools is the *cause–effect diagram*, also called a *fishbone* or *Ishikawa diagram*. The subject of the improvement opportunity, or the "pain." is the effect, and is written in the "head" of the diagram. The "bones" are filled in with possible causes which lead to the effect. The team must remember that these are hypotheses about the causes, suggestions about what might contribute to improvement. Consult the appendix for details on construction.

Use the Cause-Effect Diagram to Analyze Potential Causes

After the diagram is complete, the team must analyze it in a fashion similar to the flowchart. First, ask people working in the process to validate that all possible causes have been recorded. Then the team should hypothesize about probable root causes.

In a rare case, brainstorming about possible causes uncovers a topic, which, due to the team's expert knowledge about the situation, is recognized as the clear root cause. This can occur when a team realizes that a key contributing factor is missing, which, if supplied, immediately would result in improvement. The absence of agreed upon standards may be one such root cause. If this occurs, the team may want to immediately begin solution development. However, beware of this urge. Is the root cause the absence of standards, or failure to appropriately communicate standards, or lack of job aids, or lack of training, or some other related issue?

More commonly, the team needs to propose hypotheses about the likely root causes. Look at the diagram and ask questions about the most probable causes. Referring again to the diagram in the appendix, the team might ask: "How many times do patients wait because a medical assistant is not available? What are the reasons for that non-availability?" or "How often is delay due to lack of equipment?" or "How many clerks do not know how to use the insurance forms?" Then, in the next step, the team gathers data.

Post the completed process flowchart and cause–effect diagrams on the storyboard. Information questions also may be posted.

STEP IV DETERMINE KEY IMPROVEMENTS NEEDED, OR ROOT CAUSE OF PROBLEMS

The most common error when using a QI cycle is to decide prematurely what improvements are needed or what cause must be addressed. Consider this example: An ambulatory surgery staff notes problems with patients following post-op care instructions — they take pain medicine improperly, return with filthy dressings, and don't return if fever develops. The team might assume there was a problem with patient teaching and expand the current patient education program with more pre-op teaching visits, more detailed home instructions, and home visits the evening of surgery. This intervention might have missed other potential root causes: patients need written instructions in simple language (or in their primary non-English language) to follow at home; or perhaps they don't have money to buy the bandages and supplies to care for themselves — they understand how to do it, but need resources; neither of these would be improved by the first choice of interventions.

This problem can be avoided by using data to drive the decision about which key improvements are needed. The team already posed questions when analyzing the flowchart and cause–effect diagrams. Other questions about baseline performance also may need to be answered.

Determine Data Gathering, Analysis, and Display Needs

Working from the information questions, the team needs to determine:

- What data is needed to answer the questions?
- How should the data be collected? by whom and how often? with what tools?
- How will data be analyzed? with what tools? by whom and how often?

Data needs are determined by asking what would be measured to answer the information questions. Often one data set can be used to answer more than one information question.

Details about data collection and analysis should be based on how the team, or staff, actually will collect data. Determine efficient ways to collect the data. When possible, use existing data sources, but do not hesitate to create *ad hoc* data gathering activities. These activities will be used only to investigate the key improvements needed and the root cause, and automatically should not become long-term monitoring requirements.

Data analysis should be predicted, to allow data collection strategies to match the uses to which the data will be put. For instance, if a histogram is used to display elapsed time, the time will need to be calculated in a way that will allow for creation of time ranges. If ranges on the order of whole minutes are likely, data collection cannot record time estimated to the nearest five minutes. This data might need to be recorded in clock time, and calculations of elapsed time would be made afterward.

A sample *Data Collection Tool* in the appendix suggests a structure for organizing this information. This tool also may help the team realize the amount of work to be done in investigating the opportunity for improvement. If the data collection tasks overwhelm resources, prioritize activities and concentrate on those which most likely are to give critical insights. A clearly defined data collection strategy will reward the team with a bounty of data that can be used in many different ways to confirm root causes or find the key to making improvements. This data collection tool can be posted on the storyboard.

Display and Analyze Data

After data is collected, it needs to be displayed and analyzed to draw conclusions about root causes and key improvements. There are many graphs and charts which

TABLE 1
Common data analysis tools

Tool	Suggested use	Considerations
Pie chart	Display parts of a whole; percents	Difficult to interpret relative values; label with values or percent
Bar chart	Sorts data into categories; compares performance between groups; with continuous data, useful for trending	Effective to compare performance with baseline, or pre- and post-intervention
Run chart	Tracks data over time; can be used to analyze process variation	Makes trends easy to see; effective to compare patterns pre- and post-intervention; use appropriate rules for variation analysis
Histogram	Shows data distribution; sorts data into ranges; skewed distributions suggest characteristic process events	Ranges must be equal for accurate analysis; analysis of distribution patterns can point to potential causes of problems
Pareto chart	Combines bar and run chart to show most significant causes of a given result; helps determine priorities and focus solution development	All "causes" must be related to the same result; may be confusing to learn, but a powerful tool
Scatter diagram	Examine the relationship between two variables	A simple correlation analysis; most helpful when plotting continuous data

might be used. (Tague, 1995; Ishikawa, 1994) Table 1 identifies some of the most commonly used tools and their application. Refer to the appendix for details of construction and interpretation.

Teams will not choose the best data display automatically. In spite of excellent plans, the data may show unanticipated patterns. The team should be prepared to display data in many ways to gain the most knowledge possible. A common example is that data which originally was used in a histogram to show variation over a data set, is put, data point by data point, on a run chart to discover a different pattern of variation over time.

After the data is displayed, the team needs to combine this information with its expert knowledge of the process and draw some conclusions about the key improvements required, or the root cause of a problem. Several things may happen.

One common circumstance is that the team is left with more questions. Perhaps a bar graph comparing several clinics' results of "the percent of women over age 40 who get annual breast exams" shows one clinic has tremendously successful results compared to the others. A reasonable next step would be to ask: "What does that clinic do that is different from the others?" and analyze their process, perhaps with a process flowchart.

Further questions also be may asked when a scatter diagram shows a previously unrecognized correlation, perhaps between long patient waits and the times radiology services are not provided over lunch. This situation might prompt further study of current practices of radiology coverage, or the patterns of referral for radiology services. The team would have narrowed the area of inquiry, but might not yet be prepared to suggest solutions. Scatter diagrams also show what a problem is **not** — for example, patient delays are not longer during the dinner break than the rest of the day; therefore, other causes than dinner staffing need to be considered.

Another possibility is that a clear area for improvement is identified, usually because a root cause is identified. A Pareto chart of reasons for patient dissatisfaction may show the top two complaints relate to hidden costs and lack of courtesy; a bar chart may show that only one surgical procedure routinely is delayed because of incorrect instruments. In these cases, the team could immediately proceed with suggesting interventions to address these causes.

In any case, data displays used to identify key improvements or root causes should be posted on the storyboard, both to tell staff about team progress and engage them in studying the improvement opportunity.

Step V   Select and Implement Improvement Strategies

The key to a structured quality improvement approach is to target interventions at key improvements or root causes. Energy, time and money should not be used haphazardly in addressing all the possible things that could result in improvements, but rather those critical few things which will lead to the largest improvement possible.

Identify the Best Intervention

The team needs to think creatively about interventions, especially if the IO is an issue that repeatedly has been a target of improvement. One intervention is benchmarking — identifying and understanding a highly successful practice and adopting that process. This would be used in the earlier example of studying what made one clinic's breast exam percent so much higher than the others. After that process was understood, other clinics could adapt practices to match this successful clinic.

Another method is brainstorming possible solutions and selecting the one which best meets criteria for improvement. This would be used if the team validated that lack of staff during lunch was the key contributor to patient delays in radiology. They then would brainstorm possible solutions to address the lack of staff, and evaluate the options against criteria using a decision matrix. As an initial screening criterion, the group should validate that the suggested intervention addresses the root cause. Other criteria such as "it is within this team's power to implement," management supports the recommendation," or "low resource commitment" should be applied. The particular situation may lead to other unique criteria such as: acceptable to the union; can be used in all parts of the group practice; fits seamlessly with preceding and follow up care.

As with the other steps, post this solution information. Others may come up with additional suggestions after the team's ideas are posted.

Implement the Improvement Strategy

A team should make only one improvement at a time. After all, if the data analysis points to the key implementation need or root cause, it should be possible to design one correctly targeted intervention to address that issue.

Plan the implementation. One plan step involves change management strategies. Through gap analysis or force field analysis the team should identify those factors which will promote the change, and those which will provide resistance. Steps needed to move from current practice to the new practice should be identified. The implementation plan needs to consider these factors. For instance, management buy-in might be enhanced by a demonstration project, or by seeing a similar process in another location; there may be a key informal leader who needs to be sold on the change; equipment changes may be necessary.

The next plan step involves describing how the solution will be implemented. Who will start it? When, and how? Who will the implementation involve and who will be affected by it? What approvals are needed prior to action, such as new standards or adoption of a benchmarked process? Will it be done as a pilot test, or will all involved parties adopt new practices simultaneously? Create a time line for action, with responsible parties identified. For complex interventions, a team different from the process improvement team may need to be involved, especially if interventions will be implemented by people not currently represented on the team.

Another plan step is to describe the measurements which will document improvements. The strongest support for improvement comes from current, improved results compared to baseline data. However, if baselines are not available, indicators related to data generated during the analysis phase may be helpful. For example, compare waiting time before and after interventions; compare the number of women who get annual breast exams between clinics, and to the baselines within the same clinics. There may be process indicators established to measure performance prior to outcomes, if the outcomes will take a long time to measure. In the breast exam example, it is unlikely that a major portion of a practice's female population will receive exams in any one month, so an indicator might be needed to measure the percent of women coming in (not women in the plan) who receive such an exam. Remember that a plan for data collection during initial implementation may be more complex than the ongoing monitoring which will be done after changes are institutionalized. Also remember that management bases decisions on hard data, not impressions. It will be insufficient to say the staff like a change — the improvement must be documented in some measurable way.

Other indicators may be designed to measure secondary effects of the changes, or unwanted changes feared by detractors. For example, changes in staffing coverage during lunch might cause some people to anticipate increased overtime use. An indicator to detect overtime use is needed.

As indicators are defined, also plan the process for interpreting them. Will results be measured after one month? One week? Select a time period appropriate to the situation, and consider that results should be measured soon enough to encourage continued change but late enough to increase confidence that the change is real. The team may also want to define failure criteria. Although most interventions will have been designed with everyone's best welfare in mind, there may be situations in which process changes have the potential to cause harm. For example, a change of instruments in the standard surgical pack may have been intended to reduce surgical delays, but if the new items are of poor quality, they may cause further delays or patient harm. The plan needs to consider how the team would receive and act upon this type of feedback — would it wait until a whole month went by to measure surgical delay, or is there a method for feedback to reach the team on an informal basis?

Plan for communicating information about these actions to all involved parties: the workers who will be involved in implementation, the responsible management, and clients if they will see the impact. The team will likely have representation from all affected groups, but check that no important participants have been omitted.

Do it — follow the implementation plan. Using the timelines, follow the steps for announcing the changes, implementing the improvements and collecting indicator data. Either the team members or the staff involved in the change should be collecting concurrent monitoring data. Be cautious, however, to not interfere with the implementation prematurely, if data do not seem to be going in the right direction. Stick to your plans for all steps — the doing, the measuring, and the interpreting.

STEP VI   EVALUATE EFFECTIVENESS OF CHOSEN IMPROVEMENTS

Interpret data to evaluate the effectiveness of the improvements. Use data from the planned indicators, and compare actual to expected results. The strongest arguments supporting success will be comparisons of improved performance to baseline data. These should be displayed on graphs to assist interpretation.

Solicit and document feedback about the entire implementation process, to detect unexpected benefits or problems resulting from the change. Anecdotal information provides a helpful background upon which to judge if the improvements are justified by the results. Excellent statistical results might mean less if accompanied by workers unhappy with the changes.

If results were equivocal, try to determine the reason. Perhaps the key area for improvement or root cause was not accurately identified, and further analysis is needed. Perhaps the opportunity statement did not reflect the true problem, but identified a symptom of a related problem. Perhaps the interventions were not honestly implemented, or the post-intervention data was not collected correctly. Decision about further steps require an understanding of why things do not work, as well as successes.

STEP VII   DECIDE ON NEXT STEPS

Make decisions about formalizing the change. Regardless of the success or failure of the effort, the team now must make recommendations about further action. If a pilot was successful, plan for the staged expansion to other areas. Be sure to validate with senior authorities that the team's interpretation of success is agreed upon, and that the expansion will be supported. The goal is to integrate changes into routine work. That may require substantial change in policy, standards, or other major management practices.

Successful implementation must be followed by routine monitoring. The team should recommend a plan for monitoring during the expansion phase of a pilot effort, as well as routine, ongoing measures. Remember that ongoing monitoring should fit seamlessly into routine data gathering for other QA or management purposes — it will not be done by the team. If an elaborate system of indicators is recommended, it will be unwelcome and uncollected. Focus on gathering data on a schedule and intensity appropriate to the topic, and appropriate to detect practices reverting to old behavior. Independent of routine data gathering and analysis, the QC may put this topic on the agenda for discussion in six months, to see that improvements have been sustained.

If results do not justify continuing the change, or if the expense of the change exceeds the benefit, the team may recommend not going forward with planned improvements. They might consider if the subject is worthy of continued study. If so, determine if the same team should do further work. Changes in the wording of the opportunity statement might redirect effort based on lessons learned about the situation during this analysis.

In either case, success or failure, the team must be recognized for its hard work. The QC or senior management formally should acknowledge their efforts. In the case of success, the team should be praised for the contribution to the overall success of the organization. In the case of failure, the team might be recognized for providing an increased understanding of a very difficult problem, or for opening up a discussion about alternative ways to improve practice. Remember that this closing stage of the team requires action.

The storyboard of the entire quality improvement cycle should remain posted for a period of time after the team closes. The team should consider publishing results, successful or not, as many other organizations are interested in quality improvement lessons learned.

Now that the Cycle is Complete

Although this is the last step, it is a step in a cycle. Results from this quality improvement already have directed ongoing monitoring, which in turn may uncover another opportunity to improve. These results also might stimulate the design of new services or standards related to the same topic area, or may cause the redesign of other processes. The skills learned by the team while doing this cycle may be applied in other topic areas, and the QC or responsible management should begin to look for other areas ready for process improvement.

A workforce with the skills of quality improvement will begin to use them in all parts of the job, not just on a process improvement team. Many workers will begin to think about work in terms of processes, and search for ways to make substantive permanent improvements in work by changing the way work is done. Opinions about the goodness of practices will need to be supported by data, not conjecture. The belief that workers have the power to improve their own work will stimulate an interest in making recommendations for improvement, independent of those driven by senior management. All in all, the opportunity to improve processes becomes just a way of doing business.

SUMMARY

How can managed care quality be improved? When routine management actions, such as standard setting, supervision, or monitoring are insufficient or inappropriate, and situations are complex or recurring, managed care staff need more powerful ways to approach quality improvement. This chapter proposed a structured, team-based, data-driven approach to improving quality, using common language to describe a cycle of quality improvement.

REFERENCES

Beck, J. and Yeager, N. "Moving Beyond Team Myths." *Training and Development*, 51–55, March 1996.

Bertcher, H. J., *Group Participation: Techniques for Leaders and Members*. Sage Publications, Thousand Oaks, CA, 1994.

Francis, D. and Young, D. *Improving Work Groups: A Practical Manual for Team Building*. Pfeiffer & Co., San Diego, 1992.

Harper, A. and Harper, B. *Skill-Building for Self-Directed Team Members*. MW Corp., New York, 1994.

Ishikawa, K. *Guide to Quality Control*. Quality Resources, White Plains, NY, 1994.

Orsburn, J. D., Moran, L., Musselwhite, E., and Zenger, J. H. *Self-Directed Work Teams: The New American Challenge*. Business One Irwin, Homewood, IL, 1990.

Scholtes, P. R. *The Team Handbook*. Joiner Associates, Madison, WI, 1993.

Tague, N. R. *The Quality Toolbox*. ASQC Quality Press, Milwaukee, WI, 1995.

The Team Memory Jogger. GOAL/QPC and Joiner Associates, Madison, WI, 1995.

Tuckman, B. J. "Developmental Sequence in Small Groups." *Psychological Bulletin*. 63: 6, 384–399, 1965.

Wellins, R. S., Byham, W. C., and Wilson, J. M. *Empowered Teams: Creating Self-directed Work Groups that Improve Quality, Productivity, and Participation*. Jossey–Bass Publishers, San Francisco, 1991.

Quality Improvement Activities Appendix

DECISION (PRIORITY) MATRIX

This technique evaluates options against criteria. It is effective when options are complex or when multiple criteria should be considered in making a choice. It is commonly used in two steps of the quality improvement cycle: when selecting an IO, or when choosing a solution.

First, choose criteria. Common criteria for selecting IOs include: importance, management support for change, risks if nothing is improved, feasibility of making an improvement, impact on clients or providers, or visibility of the process. Criteria for choosing solutions might include: feasibility, management support for implementation, cost, required staffing, or required time. No minimum or maximum number of criteria exists, but three or four is usually best. More criteria make a matrix cumbersome, and fewer may result in equal scoring. One way to select criteria is to identify any criterion which all options must meet. Use this criterion first to eliminate options through pre-screening. Then use other criteria to select among the remaining options.

Next, determine the rating scale. A simple method is to score based on whether an option meets a given criterion. For example, in a multifacility practice, one criterion might be that the IO occurs in each facility, with scores of $1 =$ yes and $0 =$ no. Another method is to score each option according to how well each meets the criterion, e.g., how much risk is there if no improvement is made? A score of $1 =$ low, $2 =$ medium, $3 =$ high could be used, as Figure A illustrates. Other ranges or scales may be proposed, such as a range from 1–10. Be sure rating scales are used consistently between criteria — that the "best" equals the highest number and "worst" equals the lowest number. This can be confusing when a criterion is met "best" by a "least" measure such as cost. On a scale of 1 (low) to 3 (high), an option with a low cost would be rated 3; an option with high support also would be rated 3.

Finally, taking one option at a time, review each criterion and assign a score. This can be done individually and totaled, or it can be done in group discussion. The option with the highest score is chosen. Table 1 is an example of a matrix using score of 1 (low) to 3 (high).

TABLE 1
Decision Matrix

Options	c #1	c #2	c #3	c #4	Total
Option 1	3	2	2	2	9
Option 2	1	2	2	2	7
Option 3	3	3	2	3	11

(Criteria spans columns c #1–c #4)

VOTING

Voting usually is easy to accomplish, and quick. Each individual has a chance to have a say in a decision. Any number of options can be presented, and criteria can be implicit or explicit. Voting may be used any time a choice is required — selecting IOs, determining which potential causes to investigate, selecting solutions, and so on.

There are three basic ways to structure voting: (1) simple, (2) multi, and (3) weighted.

Simple voting is the "one person–one vote" approach. All options are listed; each person votes once; and the option with the highest total is selected. A disadvantage is that the choice may not be supported by the entire team — someone's choice loses.

Multivoting allows each person to vote more than once. This is very effective when there are many options. A general rule of thumb to determine the number of votes is: up to 10 options = 2 votes, 10–20 options = 3 votes, 20–30 options = 5 votes. All options are listed, and each person selects, for example, the top three choices, one vote for each choice. Votes are tallied, and the high score wins. Although there still are "losers" in this method, there is a higher chance that one of the person's choices was selected.

A slightly more complex type of multivoting can be used to reduce a large number of options to a smaller set. If, for example, you want to choose four things out of a group of 20, begin by letting each voter pick the top five choices, in rank order. (Use one more choice than the result requires.) Assign five points to the top choice, four to the next, and so on. Tally votes by recording the score each person gives to each choice. In this example, the top four results can then be the basis for another vote, or a different type of decision technique, such as consensus or a decision matrix. This method also has a higher likelihood that one of the person's choices is selected, reducing the "loser" effect, but the process of adding the votes can be confusing.

The third type of voting is weighted voting. In this method, each person gets a certain number of points to distribute among the options. The number of points to be distributed should be equal to, or 1.5 times, the number of options. For example, if five options exist, each person might get seven points to distribute among the choices, which might be divided as illustrated in Table 2. This will usually create a clearer difference between choices, and result in fewer ties than other voting methods. A disadvantage is that the distribution of points can be confusing.

TABLE 2
Weighted voting

Options	Team members 1	2	3	4	Score
Option 1	3	2		1	6
Option 2	1	2	7	4	14
Option 3	3	2			5
Option 4				1	1
Option 5		1		1	2

FLOWCHARTS

A flowchart is a graphic representation of a process or system, showing the sequence of steps. Although there are several types of flowcharts, two are most commonly used in the quality improvement cycle: a *high-level flowchart* (or *top-down flowchart*) looks at major steps in a process. A *process flowchart* (or *second-level flowchart*) details each step of a process.

Although many symbols are used in flowcharts, the most common ones are:

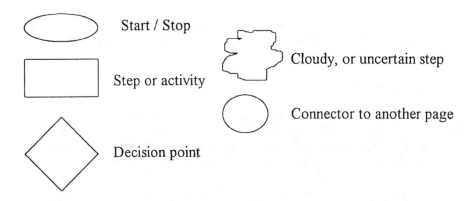

Lines connect symbols, with arrows indicating direction of the process flow. Only one line should be going into or out of a symbol, except for exiting decision points when one direction is "yes" and another "no." All "yes" and "no" lines should point in the same direction, to make the chart easier to follow.

No matter which flowchart is being constructed, the team should start by determining where the process begins and ends. The opportunity statement contains this information, but as the chart is drawn the team may discover that other steps need to precede or follow the stated steps to accurately describe a process. This may result in changes to the opportunity statement.

HIGH-LEVEL FLOWCHART

A *high-level flowchart* shows the major steps of a process. It can help a team get a basic understanding of a process, and is especially useful in determining membership of a quality improvement team. To illustrate, imagine that a staff wants to investigate the pattern of waiting times in an outpatient clinic. They elect to study the process from the time the patient reports to registration to the time the patient is placed in an exam room. Their high level flowchart may look like Figure A.

FIGURE A High-level flowchart.

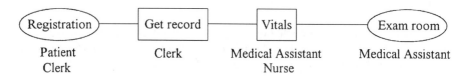

FIGURE B   High level flowchart with participants listed.

To determine team membership, the staff would first list the people involved in each step of this process as shown in Figure B.

Then, a team would be chosen to include all the types of people involved in this process. In this case, a team might include a clerk, a medical assistant, a nurse, and a patient.

PROCESS FLOWCHART

A *process flowchart* details each step in a process, including decision points, waiting time, rework, and feedback loops. When using this tool to describe a current process, it should be drawn to reflect real work, not an ideal situation. If ideas for improvement are generated as the chart is being drawn, they are not included in the chart but are recorded elsewhere for future use. A process flowchart also can be used to develop a new, or ideal, process during the solution phase of an improvement cycle.

Classically, a team starts drawing a process flowchart from the beginning, but some people find it much easier to start at the end and work to the beginning. In either case, it is critical that the people drawing the chart be actually involved in the process. If, during the drawing, a team does not know what happens next, insert a cloud symbol and seek advice from someone who does know. Periodically, review the opportunity statement to make sure the flowchart is addressing the process described by the statement. See Figure C.

CAUSE–EFFECT DIAGRAM

A *cause–effect diagram*, also called an *Ishikawa* or *fishbone diagram*, graphically displays possible causes of a defined effect. The effect, which is the "pain" from the opportunity statement, is placed at the "head" of the chart, and major "bones" reflect categories of possible causes. The example in Figure D gives an abbreviated illustration of possible causes of long waiting times. Some causes may result from others, so subordinate branching is used.

There are two common ways to generate ideas about possible causes. The first is to brainstorm causes, perhaps by following the process flowchart. Causes are then arranged in approximately four–six logical categories. The categories become the labels for the major branches. This method is good if the team finds it easy to think broadly about causes. However, some teams become focused on one topic such as lack of staff and find it difficult to consider other options. In that case, organizing brainstorming by category might be helpful. Some common categories are:

- materials, methods, staffing, measurements and equipment
- clients, staff, supplies, environment and procedures
- what, when, where and how

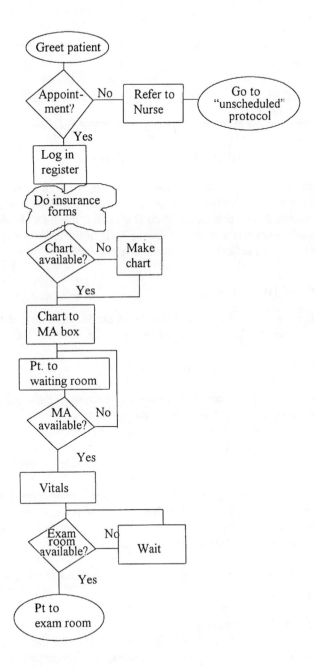

FIGURE C   Process flowchart.

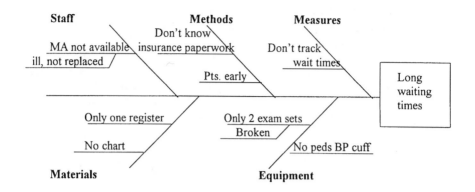

FIGURE D   Cause–effect diagram.

If an idea fits on more than one branch, place it in all locations. Each major branch probably will contain three or four possible causes, which in turn may have subordinate causes. If one category has too few causes, the team should determine if they are missing important items. Check the logic of the causes in reverse order, to see if named causes actually relate to the effect.

DATA COLLECTION TOOL

The *data collection tool* helps a team identify data needs and develop data collection and analysis strategies. Table 3 is based on the prior flowchart and cause–effect diagram.

Information questions" come from analysis of the flowchart and cause-effect diagrams, as well as baseline information needs. It may be necessary to prioritize these questions, focusing on proving hypotheses of root cause and gathering minimum baseline data, to reduce the work of data collection.

"Data needed" should describe exact data to be gathered, and may suggest stratification. Data analysis and data collection methods should be developed concurrently. Knowledge of data tools will help the team select appropriate analysis methods.

Teams often independently propose data collection frequency and responsibility, since members include staff involved in those roles. However, some teams may not have been given that authority, and need to consult a manager or the Quality Council for advice or authority to proceed with data collection.

PIE CHARTS

Pie charts are used to compare parts of a whole. Figure E is an example which displays the marital status of a client population. It allows for instant interpretation of the relative percents, but can be difficult to interpret if unlabeled because the eye has a hard time judging portions which have close values.

TABLE 3
Data Collection Tool

Question	Data needed	Data collection					Data analysis		
		How	Source	Tool	Who	Frequency	How	Who	Frequency
How long do patients wait? (Baseline)	Total wait time per patient	Collect times at selected points in care	Staff record information	Time record on patient chart	Each staff member handling patient	All patients for one week	Histogram; run chart	Team	After one week
What are reasons for waiting?	Reasons for each wait step	Identify why patient waits	Staff record information	Time record	Each staff member	All patients for one week	Pareto	Team	After one week
How long do patients wait at each step?	Wait times by segment	As above	As above	Time record	Each staff member	As above	Histogram	Team	After one week
Do all clerks know how to complete insurance forms?	Number clerks who know/total number	Ask clerks and observe work	Supervisor observation	Checklist of steps	Supervisor	Once per clerk	Pie chart	Supervisor	Once after collection

Percent of Clients by Marital Status

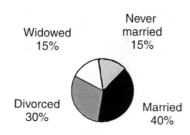

FIGURE E　Pie chart.

Hints:

- segments must add up to 100% of a whole — it cannot compare portions of two different "wholes" e.g., the marital status chart could not also include the percentage of clients with children
- label segments with the percent, not the raw number; unlabeled segments are difficult to interpret
- cannot be used if a segment is zero
- small segments are hard to see — avoid a pie chart if several portions are small, or if there are more than six or seven segments

BAR CHARTS

Bar charts show data in categories. They are helpful when comparing results to a baseline, when comparing the frequency of something between two or more groups, (e.g., number of procedures by provider) and can be used to show parts of a whole.

Simple bar charts sort data into categories. Values are indicated by the length of the bar, and may be oriented along horizontal or vertical axes. Bars may be grouped to enhance understanding of data. Figure F is a simple bar chart; Figure G is a grouped bar chart.

Stacked bar charts show values of subgroups within each bar. They are difficult to interpret, but allow comparison of parts to a whole with many "wholes" displayed in one graph. Therefore, you can compare the relative change in parts over time. Figure H is an example.

Hints:

- Use raw numbers in simple bar charts.
- Use raw numbers to calculate percentages in stacked bar charts, then graph the y-axis according to the percent of each part to the whole.
- Label the x-axis with variable names.

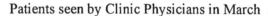
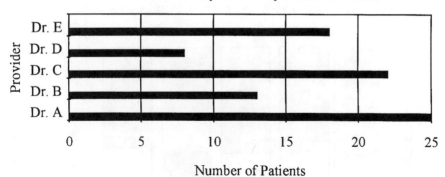

Patients seen by Clinic Physicians in March

FIGURE F   Simple bar chart.

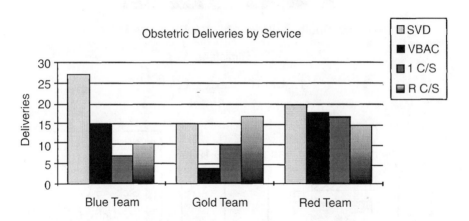

FIGURE G   Grouped bar chart.

- Label the y-axis with values that divide the range into appropriate segments, perhaps single digits for ranges under 15, by multiples of five for ranges up to 40, and by 10 for values up to 100; do not label the y-axis only with the observed values of the variables.
- Determine range of the y-axis by calculating the data range (largest value to be graphed minus smallest), then set the maximum y-value at approximately 1.5 times the range.
- If the y-axis is not long enough, or uses inappropriately-sized range labels, it will be difficult to interpret.
- If values are both positive and negative, a bar graph can be oriented with zero in the center; this is effective when representing gains and losses (see Figure I).

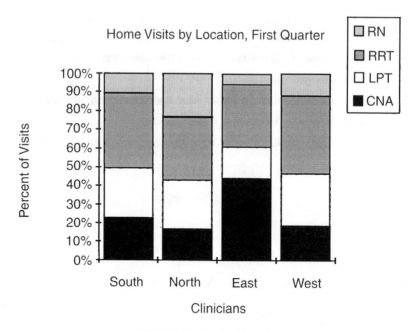

FIGURE H   Stacked bar chart.

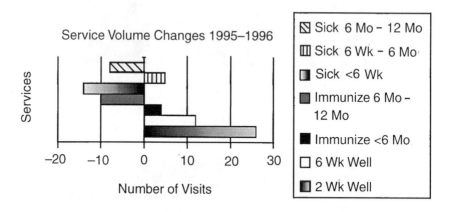

FIGURE I   Bar chart showing positive and negative values.

RUN CHARTS

Run charts track data over time (Figure J). The x-axis plots the sequence of time (by hour, cases in order), the y-axis plots the observations. In the most basic use, run charts show data trends. Data points are actual results, not averages. For best trend analysis, at least 25 data points should be plotted.

When sufficient points exist to calculate a mean, a run chart can be used to analyze process variation as in control or out of control. A process in control exhibits random variation — changes that can be expected as a normal course of events. A process out of control exhibits special cause variation — changes due to unusual circumstances, or changes in the process that affect normal behavior. Control charts offer more sophisticated measures of variation (Ishikawa, 1994; Tague, 1995), but a run chart can begin the analysis. After recognizing an out-of-control pattern, the team should investigate to determine cause.

Hints:

- Collect data in regular intervals, e.g., each event, by shift, hourly. The x-axis records these intervals; if data points are missed the chart will be incorrectly interpreted.
- Calculate y-axis values as for bar charts; if the chart is constructed concurrently (and the data range is not known), base the maximum on expected results.
- As points are plotted, connect them to the prior point with a straight line.
- To interpret variation, calculate the mean of the observed data and draw it on the chart (mean = the total value of the data points, divided by the number of data points).
- Pattern interpretation of variation is based on statistics — the number of observations determines the number of points in the pattern which are needed to draw conclusions about variation; guidance below is based on a universe of 20–50 data points.
- Pattern interpretations do not indicate whether non-random events are desirable or not desirable. For instance, a zigzag pattern could be measuring the difference between two people doing the same activity in different ways even though both are performing acceptably.

Interpreting patterns (*see* Figure J): All these patterns suggest a non-random event (special cause, a process not in control)

- 7–12 consecutive points above or below the mean suggest a shift in the process (1).
- A pattern of 6 consistently increasing or decreasing points suggests a trend (2).
- 7–14 points in a zigzag pattern suggest a cyclical event (3).

HISTOGRAMS

Histograms are bar charts which show distribution. If the process has normal variation, the chart will be similar to a bell-shaped curve (Figure N). Changes from that characteristic appearance indicate variations in the process. Some variations are desirable, so a non-normal variation does not always mean a problem. For example, a graph of processing time for lab results might show a concentration of results at 30–60 minutes. That might reflect normal turnaround time.

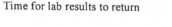

Time for lab results to return

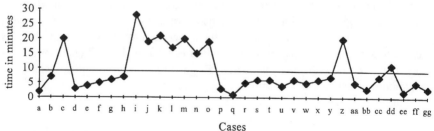

Cases

FIGURE J   Run chart.

Hints:

• With less than 30 data points, there are too few points to accurately judge distribution.

• To construct bars for the graph, first determine the range of the raw data (highest value minus lowest value). To illustrate, imaging a 60 point data set of processing times, from 26 –99 minutes. Range = 73.

• Next, determine the number of bars for the graph. If too few bars are used, the pattern will not be seen; too many bars will flatten the pattern. For less than 50 data points, use five–seven bars; 50–100 points = seven–10 bars. In this example, eight bars is convenient; until the graph is drawn, we cannot tell if it sufficiently displays the data — there is always an option to re-draw with more or fewer bars.

• Now find the value width of the bars: range divided by the number of bars rounded to the next highest number; in the example, the value width of the bars is 10 (73/8 = 9.1).

• Next, pick a starting number convenient to the value of the lowest data point, and set the boundaries of the bars; a convenient low starting point is 26; the first bar will be 26–35 (contains 10 values), the second 35–43, and so on.

• Construct a frequency table to tally the number of observations which fall within each bar, as Table 4 demonstrates.

• Construct the graph by placing the ranges (width values) of the bars on the x-axis, the number of observations on the y-axis.

• This graph is most powerful when using raw data of frequently occurring processes — daily observations often do not give enough information. It is an excellent way to analyze turn-around time, or waiting times. Do not use for data which is previously averaged.

Interpreting patterns:
Bell shaped: normal distribution. (Figure K)

TABLE 4
Frequency table for
histogram construction

26–35	IIII
36–45	IIIIII
46–55	IIIIIIIII
56–65	IIIIIIIIIIIIII
66–75	IIIIIIIIIIIII
76–85	IIIIIII
86–95	IIIII
86–105	III

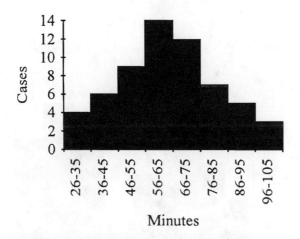

FIGURE K   Histogram showing normal distribution.

Skewed, or *cliff-like*: look for special events at the point of drop-off; short on the left side might happen when there is a baseline wait required for usual processing, such as prep-time for doing a procedure. (Figure L)

Double peaked: two normal distributions; might reflect two processes such as waiting time for lab results when one pattern reflects stat returns and one shows routine processing. (Figure M)

Plateau or *comb-like*: no process going on; also might be observer errors — if measuring elapsed times, one observer rounding values to five minute marks might cause graphed results to peak around these values (Figure N).

PARETO CHART

A *Pareto chart* is a special version of a bar and line chart which is based on the Pareto principle: 80% of results come from 20% of the causes. (Tague, 1995) While

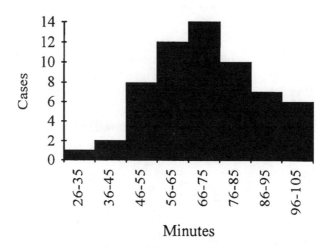

FIGURE L   Histogram showing skewed distribution.

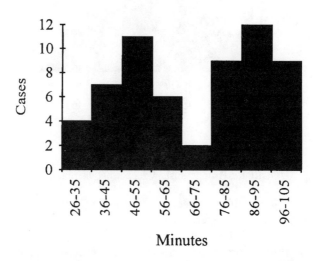

FIGURE M   Histogram showing double peaked distribution.

this may not always be exactly demonstrated, this chart does help to identify the major contributors to an observed effect. The most common use of thePareto chart is to identify root causes. When targeting interventions, the bars on the Pareto which represent approximately 80% of the causes should be addressed.

Refer to Figure O. The left y-axis measures the frequencies, while a right y-axis measures percentage of the total frequencies. The first bar represents 45% of the results, the second 35%, totaling 80% These two bars would be the topics that should be addressed.

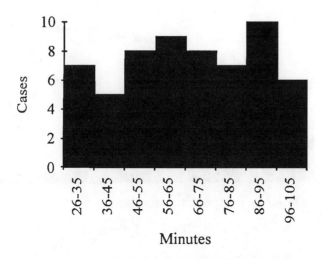

FIGURE N   Histogram showing plateau distribution.

Hints:

- Be sure the topics being graphed logically relate to a common "result." For example, you could graph the topics patient list as dissatisfiers, types of sterile gear missing from instrument packs, or the expenses of equipment related to one type of care.
- The first step is to construct the bar chart, in descending frequencies with the highest on the left.
- Calculate the total number of observations as the y-axis maximum value; this is **not** the highest number on the left bar, but the total of all the bars; this number equals 100% of the observations.
- Calculate the value of 80% of the total; construct the right y-axis with the 100% value as the maximum; place 80% at the point equal to that value on the left y-axis.
- At the right hand corner of the highest bar, place a dot; do the same with all the remaining bars.
- Connect the dots as in a run chart; the final dot should be at a value equal to 100%.
- From the right y-axis, draw an imaginary line from the 80% level to the bars; bars to the left of this intersection create 80% of the total — they are the critical few things which need to be addressed.
- On occasion, some phenomena do not reveal aPareto principle pattern — then the team will have to decide the most important contributors to the effect by another decision method.

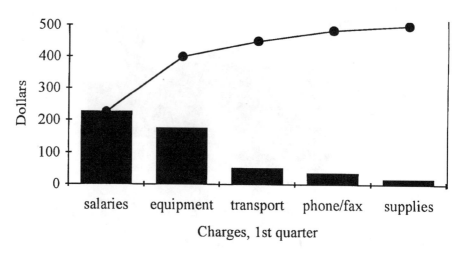

FIGURE O   Pareto Diagram of sources of home care costs

SCATTER DIAGRAM

A scatter diagram shows the relationship between two variables. It does not test or prove causal relationships. While there are correlation analysis tools which are more powerful, this graph is simple and easy to use, and is appropriate for many quality improvement topics. This graph answers questions like: Is there a relationship between the number of admissions and the date of the month? Is there a relationship between the length of time patients wait and the time of day? Is there a relationship between the amount of education a patient receives and the number of calls that patient makes to a help line? Remember that variables must be paired, and must be continuous.

Hints:

- Consider a scatter diagram when trying to relate a cause on a fishbone diagram to the effect; phrase a question about the suspected relationship between the two variables to help determine what to measure.
- Collect paired data and plot them as points on an x-y graph, with largest values to the right and top.
- Look at the pattern the points make; if they form a line, there is a strong correlation; a line sloping up to the right indicates a strong positive relationship — when one variable rises, the other rises, although you cannot tell which is the cause and which the effect (Figure P); a line sloping down to the right indicates an inverse relationship. (Figure Q)
- If no line is formed, there is little or no correlation, but the graph still may give you information (Figure R); for example, an assumption that people wait longer at certain times of day may be disproved by finding this graph does not reflect an increase at the expected times.

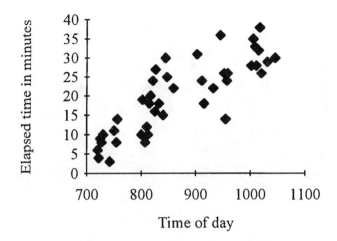

FIGURE P   Scatter diagram, positive relationship.

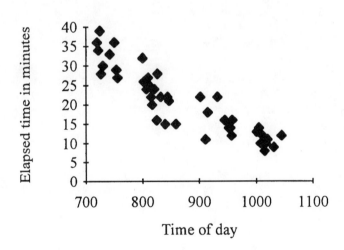

FIGURE Q   Scatter diagram, negative relationship.

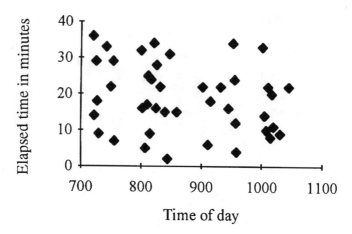

FIGURE R   Scatter diagram, no relationship.

9 Quality Improvement in Managed Care: Using Preventive Medicine Guidelines

Douglas Stewart

CONTENTS

INTRODUCTION

In an ideal world, *managed care* should mean "managing processes of care" rather than managing care providers. Management of a process of care implies that the operators have information that will enable them to reasonably predict the outcome (or output) of the process. Information for management of processes is a goal of physicians and nurses that may be achieved through systematic feedback, scientific evidence, aggregate data from populations, and statistical analysis. Another ambitious goal of many health care providers involves the prevention of disease or injury, rather than merely treatment of disease. Finally, in order to organize for systemness and improvement, all participants should assign priority to the promotion of health and not limit the scope of health care to reaction to the disease state.

The prepayment of health care services through a capitated financing mechanism is a dominant scheme in the managed care environment. A crude reduction of this method, and its effect on the bottom line of the health care organization's balance sheet, involves the pursuit of one of two objectives: (1) deny or defer access to health care services or (2) prevent the need for health care (especially "sickcare") services.

An organization that exists to provide a service to people cannot simultaneously deny access to the offered services; therefore, the latter option emerges as the best strategy where all participants receive maximal benefit.

Several obstacles exist to the wide-spread adoption of a "disease prevention" practice policy in a given practice community. First, the orientation of medical practice continuously has been shaped by the "fee-for-service" method of financing health care services. Technology development, medical education, and public policy have all evolved under the influence of acute care, fee-for-service for many decades. In short, the inertia of health care is against the prevention of disease despite the nobility of that goal. Second, individual and organizational behavior seem to inherently lean toward the short-term over the long-term return on investment. This mindset impedes the investment of today's health care resources in active and passive strategies designed to realize cost savings years to decades into the future. A bias toward short-term gain is very prevalent in the public policy arena. Third, it is difficult to measure an outcome that, in fact, was prevented and establish a causal relationship with an intervention in preventive health services research. This obstacle, coupled with the influence of technology development and medical education, has led to a slow advance in the scientific evidence to support specific preventive medicine interventions. Finally, the population-based perspective has only recently resurfaced as a legitimate lens for scrutinizing groups of people served. This traditional public health point of view has been obscured by the individual or family-centered focus of acute care medicine. The rise of health maintenance organizations and the voice of employers as payers for service has led, in recent years, to the use of population-based data to create useful health care information management systems. Other examples of population-based approaches include the aggregate data from a geographic area of primary care providers, variation in practice patterns between geographic areas or specialty providers, or changes in health status measures for a population of insured people over time. Intermountain Health Care Inc. is an excellent example of an organization with extremely sophisticated health care information management capability that is intimately linked to the management of processes of care through quality improvement.

This chapter attempts to synthesize a unifying framework for understanding and using preventive services guidelines in a system of managed care. Each part of this practice is examined separately; but as is true of most systems, the ideas and actions interact to comprise what should be a basic foundation for pre-paid, managed health care. Some discussion of theory is required in order to develop the practical application. The taxonomy that is borrowed from the fields of economics, policy, and systems theory also will necessitate some treatment in this chapter. This discussion borrows heavily from the collective work of Drs. W. Edwards Deming, David Eddy, Don Berwick, John Wennberg, Steven Woolf, and Brent James, and the U.S. Preventive Services Task Force (USPSTF).

GUIDELINES, GUIDEBOOKS, AND COOKBOOKS

We always have had guidelines and recommendations for practice in medicine. The decision-support tools we have relied upon are called textbooks, the chief of our

teaching service, or a persuasive speaker at a continuing medical education conference. As guideline development has evolved, we saw the use of peer review and
consensus conferences of experts. The approach now considered to be the ideal uses
the principles of evidence-based medical care.

The outstanding archetype for viewing the use of practice guidelines in general
is Dr. David Eddy's *A Manual for Assessing Health Practices and Designing Practice Policies: The Explicit Approach.* (American College of Physicians, Philadelphia,
1992) Dr. Eddy generously has provided us with an opportunity to share a common
understanding of the background for rational, clinical decision-making; as well as
specific definitions for words that have other meanings outside of this important
model. The critical ingredient of evidence is highlighted as it supports the development of a practice policy or guideline. Guidelines have been denounced by some
clinicians who contend that this form of decision-making removes the "art" from
medicine, favors an approach that is rote, and fails to recognize the variation in
individual physician or patient preference among equally effective choices. It is vital
to the understanding and subsequent use of a practice policy to reframe the point
of view along the lines established by this new taxonomy and the defining principles.
The advantages of guidelines include: the routinization of worthy, generic processes
(often involving repetitive human effort, delegation of work, and established role
interdependence); reduction in variation improves quality and prediction; and controlling for variation allows groups to study outcomes. Further, practice guidelines
continuously can be updated and disseminated as new, valid evidence is discovered
that affects the practice policy. (Hayes, 1994) Reliance on diffusion of new scientific
information via textbooks or journals now is being diminished by the increasing
availability of telecommunications in clinical settings. The Agency for Healthcare
Policy and Research has supported for several years the dial-up access and Internet
connection to all of the highly regarded clinical practice guidelines which the agency
has sponsored since its inception.

The notion of a clinical practice guideline must be placed into the context of
our viable alternatives. There are three types of practice policies: (1) standards,
(2) guidelines, and (3) options. There are also four sub-categories of options. The
standards, guidelines, and four sub-categories of options all are considered flexibility
standards.

Standards exist as a *practice policy* when "the health and economic consequences
of a decision are sufficiently well known to permit decisions, and if there is virtual
unanimity among patients about the desirability (or undesirability) of the intervention, and about the proper use (or nonuse) of the intervention." (Eddy, 1992) There
is little room for deviation from the standard due to the strength of the evidence and
agreement among participants. Considerable rationalization is needed to justify the
departure from the policy. Synonyms for a standard include *requirements*, *rules*, or
strict criteria. (Figure 1)

A *practice policy* is considered an option if there is much uncertainty regarding
the outcomes and/or preferences. Options exist in practice policy within four
sub-categories where "(1) the outcomes are not known, (2) the outcomes are known
but patients' preferences are not known, (3) the outcomes are known but the patients'
preferences are indifferent about them, or (4) patients' preferences are evenly

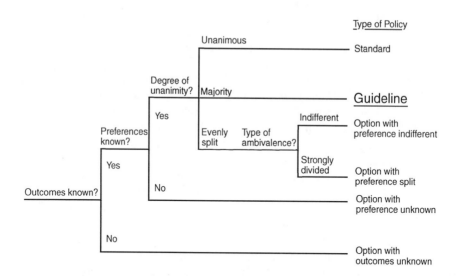

FIGURE 1   A framework for understanding. (From Eddy, 1982)

divided." As opposed to the other two practice policies, options are not concerned with the recommendation of use or non-use of an intervention. An option simply states that the intervention is available, used by some, and there is insufficient evidence to determine appropriateness. Much of what we do in clinical practice is accurately classified as an option. (Williamson, 1979) This is not to say that the majority of clinical practice is bad or not effective, merely that there are large gaps in our prediction of effectiveness causally related to common interventions due to a paucity of valid clinical outcomes research. (Stewart, 1995)

A policy for practice is considered a guideline if "the outcomes of the intervention are well enough understood to permit decisions about its proper use, and if it is preferred (or not preferred) by an appreciable but not unanimous majority of people." A guideline is meant to be flexible since a large minority of patients can differ with the majority about the desirability and use of the intervention. Guidelines should be followed in most cases, but depending on the patient, the setting, and other factors, they can and should be adapted to fit individual requirements. Departures from guidelines will be relatively routine (up to 40% of the time), and are justified by distinctions in individual preferences. (Eddy, 1992) In order to be practical, a guideline must be decidable by having the characteristics of being explicit and easy to follow. (McDonald and Overhage, 1994) Clinical guidelines may vary in their validity ranging from pure "expert" opinion to recommendations based on multiple randomized, controlled trials. The most trustworthy guidelines are based in large measure upon formal processes and are well-grounded in substantial scientific data. Transition from options to guidelines as a practice policy creates a natural by-product in the adherence to evidence-based medicine.

It is important to understand the distinction between boundaries and pathways as they relate to practice policies. Bounding rules are "intended to define the limits of proper practice" while respecting the variation in practice within the limits or parameters. Some have used the analogy of a fence around a field of practice (Eddy, 1992) or guardrails on a wide road. (McDonald and Overhage, 1994) The opposite form used in some practice policies involves the use of pathway guidelines which are designed to direct a clinician along a recommended management track. The pathway guidelines have also been called protocols or algorithms.

An excellent summary of the fundamental concerns surrounding the consideration of a guideline has been written by Dr. Steven Woolf, a science advisor to the USPSTF and practicing family physician. (Woolf, 1995) Dr. Woolf poses 10 questions that should be answered by an individual physician or a group prior to adoption of the guideline as a practice policy. The first issue involves understanding the meaning of practice policies and guidelines specifically. There must be a common understanding of the terminology across roles and disciplines in the clinical setting. The user must be cognizant of the source of the practice guideline and the methodology used to create the recommendation. Dr. Woolf cautions the physician to avoid the perception that a guideline defines the best method of treating a patient. Valid evidence to support an intervention is often imperfect or lacking in medicine. Learning what constitutes best practice may be a long time in coming for some common interventions or conditions. An inadequate guideline may present a barrier to sound clinical decision-making if it does, indeed, represent "cookbook" medicine with rigid language, "if-then" statements, and under-appreciation of the complexity of the intervention or condition. Finally, the inspiration for a guideline created within a group practice may be merely cost containment rather than any clinical orientation. Participating physicians are entitled to know if the guideline in question is supported by a thorough analysis of the relevant scientific literature and if the use of the guideline will lead to an improvement in the health status of the patients served. (Woolf, 1995)

A Madison, Wisconsin-based prepaid insurance plan has developed its own health promotion/disease prevention guidelines. (Mischler, 1995) The internal guidelines have taken form with an eye on HEDIS, several external accrediting organizations, and surveys of enrollees and employers. A primary vehicle used to disseminate the guidelines carries a message that, if effectively communicated to the clinician, may serve to convey the intent and limitation of guidelines better than an entire chapter:

> The guidelines have been developed, critiqued and adopted by [organization names omitted] and are the preferred approach for MOST patients. They are not intended to either replace a clinician's judgment or to establish a protocol for all patients with a particular condition. It is understood that some patients will not fit the clinical conditions contemplated by a guideline and that a guideline will rarely establish the only appropriate approach to a problem.

> — Mischler, 1995, p. 15

PUTTING PREVENTION INTO PRACTICE

The basic strategies of preventive medicine involve the use of screening, immunization/chemoprophylaxis, and counseling or education in order to avert a primary condition or mitigate secondary consequences. Screening, as a clinical process, lends itself to use of guidelines in that the inputs often involve a special population at risk, specific timing or intervals for action, and interdependence with multiple health care workers. The disadvantages of screening include multiple forms of costs and less than perfect technology to support screening tests, i.e., less than 100% sensitivity and specificity. Counseling on preferred health and safety habits is extremely labor intensive as an intervention and evidence to support each counseling intervention is often lacking. Factors such as variation in information presentation, reception by the patient, and exact compliance all contribute to the difficulty in designing controlled trials for counseling interventions. The methods of actual counseling may take several forms including: live dialogue, printed materials, video presentations, and group discussions. Immunizations generally prevent an infection or allay the harmful consequences of an infection. Immunization strategies are easier to test compared to the other preventive services. Costs and benefits are relatively simple to measure when assessing immunizations as an intervention and the outcomes may often be determined after years rather than a life-time.

Curative medicine, as opposed to *preventive medicine,* dominates most aspects of clinical practice. The history of the development of practice guidelines is consistent with the disproportionate attention to curative interventions. There are some outstanding examples of disease and injury prevention strategies that have been incorporated into clinical practice through the use of guidelines. The Canadian Task Force on the Periodic Health Examination led the movement in North America during the late 1970s for the creation of preventive medicine guidelines using a formal process. (Sox and Woolf, 1993) The United States Preventive Services Task Force (USPSTF) was convened in the mid 1980s following the Canadian model to create practice policies for preventive medicine. The first product of the USPSTF was *Guide to Clinical Preventive Services: An Assessment of Effectiveness of 169 Interventions.* (USPSTF, 1989) The explicit method described by Eddy was used to review the evidence and issue the recommendations.

The first task force encountered difficulty with expert consensus opinion, inadequate scientific information to create valid guidelines in many areas, and controversy surrounding conflicting recommendations from other organizations and specialty societies. A new task force was created in 1990 and improvements were made in the process using lessons learned over the previous five years. The second USPSTF consisted of 10 primary care physicians. The work was sponsored by the U.S. Agency for Health care Policy and Research (AHCPR). The task force was augmented by multiple scientific advisors who were employed to search and then analyze the scientific data regarding target interventions. The draft documents from the task force were also made available for review and comment by professional organizations and public health agencies during formulation and prior to finalization. The second edition of the *Guide* (USPSTF, 1996) is an extremely valuable resource for outcomes-based guidelines in preventive medicine (or health maintenance) as well as a practical introduction to outcomes research methodology. The *Guide* is designed to support decisions of primary care providers in office-based settings rendering clinical preventive services to individuals who are asymptomatic. The recommendations do not address the wide range of community-based prevention activities.

Another source for practical information concerning guidelines for preventive medicine is the book, *Clinician's Handbook of Preventive Services: Put Prevention Into Practice*. (DHHS/PHS, 1994) The *Handbook* is a collection of preventive services guidelines from many sources, including the first edition of the *Guide*. It is designed to "provide concise discussions and strategies for brief, targeted preventive interventions." The *Handbook* is more than just a list of recommendations for an intervention, it is a practical reference for implementation into a practice. The disadvantage to the *Handbook* lies with its failure to give weight to evidence-based practice policies vs. "expert" opinion.

By way of example, the USPSTF recommendation for screening for hypertension in asymptomatic children and adults provides an illustration of a guideline and its application. (USPSTF, 1996, p. 39) There is "good" scientific evidence to support periodic screening for hypertension for everyone 21 years of age or older. The optimal interval for this service has not been determined and is left to clinical discretion. The guideline provides some options regarding intervals based on expert opinion. There is a brief listing of the criteria used to decide pass/fail status for a patient who is screened. The link to identification of known risk factors and health promotion (counseling) interventions is also explained in similar detail. The guideline for measurement of blood pressure during office visits for children and adolescents is a weaker recommendation, based on "fair" evidence to support this as a screening test.

The primary care provider in the office-setting is thus equipped with a recommendation that affects the process of care for asymptomatic patients. The services may be provided by adequately trained, nonphysician health care workers who employ the standard methodology using suitable equipment. Information management technology, both simple and complex, may be used to prompt action in the future or stimulate recall for exam. Examples of information management tools include special decals on at-risk patient charts, index card filing systems, or periodic relational database field searches. The criteria for pass or fail can be shared with everyone contributing a role within the process of care. Routine counseling directed toward promoting physical activity and a healthy diet is recommended in addition to the use of the screen for existing hypertension. The counseling intervention is, of course, intended to achieve primary prevention of hypertension. Blood pressure screening is aimed at secondary prevention. Finally, the intervals between screening exams are left to the individual practitioner allowing for individual preference.

CONTINUOUS IMPROVEMENT OF HEALTH CARE

Health care is, in a basic sense, an information science. The system of care includes an input (a patient with a wealth of information from his or her biology, habits, expectations, and social roles) inserted into an operation or a process (involving health care providers, instrumentation, interventions, and transactions), with subsequent outputs (such as health status, adverse effects, neutral effects, costs, and altered expectations). Each component of the system in health care may be accompanied by large quantities of raw data. We constantly are being deluged with great amounts of data, most of which is useless, some is applicable, and very little of which is really consequential. The data placed in context with other data elements and filtered through clinical judgment becomes 'value-added' and subsequently called information.

Richard Saul Wurman describes a four-phase refinement process that is applicable to clinical information (Wurman, 1989). *Data* (the first phase) is that "body of unassimilated observations and objective facts that make up the raw materials knowledge workers form into useful information." *Information* (the next refinement) is nothing more or less than organized data. *Knowledge* (the third phase) is information that "you have managed to integrate with everything else you know." *Wisdom* (the last phase) is "fully-integrated knowledge; bits of knowledge that are even more useful because of the nature of their relationships to other bits of knowledge." Quality improvement theory uses knowledge to build a rational system to manage processes. This knowledge consists of four parts (Deming, 1993) that are quite inseparable: (1) appreciation for a system (or processes interacting together), (2) knowledge of human psychology, (3) knowledge of variation, and (4) a system for ongoing learning (continuously replacing information in order to support new knowledge). Deming referred to the most arcane area, the fourth, as "theory of knowledge." (Deming, 1993; p. 104) Theory of knowledge arose from Deming's reading of a book by C. I. Lewis covering an area of philosophy called epistemology. (Lewis, 1929) Epistemology is essentially "the study of knowing" and helps answer questions such as: "What is the process of gaining knowledge?" and "How do we know that we know?" (Strickland, 1995)

Ultimately, however, data works better than philosophy when working with scientists and physicians. Therefore, beginning with the methodology (evidence-based medicine, practice guidelines, measurement of practice variation, and systematic observations of outcomes) may lead to greater acceptance within health care organizations. The philosophy of quality improvement eventually becomes an innate derivative of using the methodology. For additional information concerning the theory of quality improvement, the reader is earnestly referred to the writings of Drs. W. Edwards Deming and Donald M. Berwick. (*see* References).

MANAGING PROCESSES OF CARE

The key in managing processes of care eventually becomes evident as a matter of how to manage the information and thus avoid chaos. The management of the process requires 'prediction'. Dr. W. Edwards Deming reduced management activity to nothing but prediction. (Deming, 1993; p. 104) In order to achieve the desired output (or outcome), the service provider must be able to reasonably predict that the intervention (process) will act upon the inputs (patient) in a manner that meets or exceeds the expected outcome. The use of evidence-based, preventive services guidelines provides the clinician with that solid predictability which allows one to confidently incorporate the intervention into practice. In addition to prediction, optimal management must utilize feedback from important measures of the processes of care. Measurement of practice attributes, in order to continuously improve them, requires some method for assessing variation in application of the process (i.e., a preventive service) over time and across patients. Another important measurement ingredient would include the quantitative and/or qualitative assessment of outcomes for the population served over time.

There currently are several advanced health maintenance organizations in the United States that have the ability to measure population-based outcomes over the long term. Group Health Cooperative of Puget Sound, Washington, and InterMountain Healthcare (IHC), based in Utah, are two examples of health care organizations that measure variation in important attributes of practice and health status in order to provide meaningful feedback to the physicians and staff who provide care for the patients. This form of measurement is designed for solving problems rather than fixing blame. Issuing "report cards," focusing on outliers, and judging "appropriateness" of care does not contribute to a learning system. (James, 1994) The information collected and used to manage these health systems principally is for improvement. In fact, the stabilization of processes of care within a large group practice, such as Group Health, through use of clinical guidelines effectively has built into daily practice the control arm of a trial. Consequently, reports of population-based outcomes, such as health status of their patients (the "subjects"), is of interest to health care professionals worldwide when the clinicians at Group Health or IHC share their data outside their system.

The clinical information management team at InterMountain strives to provide rapid feedback to physicians in a blinded and adjusted format in order to demonstrate the range of practice patterns at IHC and a quantifiable indication of how the individual physician compares to the group. This ongoing statistical description of the variation in practice throughout the system is always placed in context of outcome whenever possible. Through the use of sophisticated data collection and analysis, IHC is able to create useful information from data by looking for what the late cultural anthropologist Gregory Bateson called "any difference which makes a difference." The questions that they all seek to answer in collaboration are "Why are you different?" and "What represents best practice?" Dr. Brent James views this form of continuous quality improvement theory as nothing less than the "whole idea of the practice of medicine." The IHC information management system enables the physicians as a group to live up to their commitment to (1) observe the treatments they give to patients, (2) along with the outcomes they achieve, and (3) all with an aim to improve treatments and outcomes for future patients. (James, 1994)

Incorporation of the management of a preventive services process might take the form of study, measurement, feedback, analysis, and then informed change (if indicated). For illustration purposes, the measles–mumps–rubella (MMR) vaccination provides an excellent example of a process guided by clear, evidence-based recommendations. This specific process should be disclosed in detail so that the participants can identify and then focus on the key or critical steps. This exercise will lead the group to conclude that the key steps include: (1) identifying a child who has passed his first birthday, (2) having the child physically present somewhere with a skilled provider who is equipped with appropriate supplies, (3) determining that there is no history of anaphylaxis or anaphylactic-like reactions to egg exposure (the absolute contraindication in the guideline), and (4) informed consent or refusal should be obtained from a parent or authorized, surrogate decision-maker prior to immunization. Failure to focus on the key steps will result in the measurement of useless attributes and waste valuable time. Review of the key steps might lead the group to use existing demographic data sources to scan for eligible children on a daily basis or experiment with the setting for the delivery of the vaccine since the specific site where the service is rendered is not critical. Also, the egg allergy warning and the issue of consent may cause the group to focus attention on anticipatory guidance to parents at encounters leading up to the first birthday.

The actual data collection will, at a minimum, involve the systematic recording of missed opportunities over time. This data may be extracted at intervals from chart reviews of representative samples that are selected in a truly random fashion. A better method would involve the maintenance of check or tally sheets on a daily basis at a downstream step in the process of care. The person responsible for patient check out or refiling medical records may be asked to maintain a simple check sheet in addition to his usual roles. The daily collection of data allows the group to present longitudinal data on a daily or weekly basis. A practical consideration surrounds the measuring of defects or missed opportunities which precipitates some degree of fear and mistrust in any setting. The fact remains, however, that more can be learned from failures rather than successes. For optimal use, the data should be adjusted for eligible patient volume and blinded so that the clinician involved in the 'missed opportunity' cannot be identified directly or indirectly. The information should also be displayed using graphical methods and shared with all participants.

The operational version of this process management tool would entail the number of missed opportunities being tallied at the end of each clinic session daily by a designated person fulfilling a role of record clerk or cashier. Another daily data collection task requires a count of the number of children served who were between the ages of one and six and un- or underimmunized with MMR. The number of preschoolers served allows for the adjustment for volume so that "missed opportunities" is the numerator and "total preschoolers served" is the denominator. In a group setting, the measures for the entire clinic or clusters of clinics should be combined in order to blind the data with regard to specific nurses or physicians. The measures should be shared with the workers involved in the process of care at least weekly, a concept known as real-time. An efficient and meaningful method for feedback is accomplished by creating a form of a run chart that can be maintained in a highly visible location in the office such as a charting station, hallway, or staff lounge. This frequently updated 'scoreboard' allows all participants to see the real variation in this service over time as well as trends toward or away from the desired outcome. As stabilization is achieved, new strategies may be selectively inserted into the usual process of care, thereby testing to see if the new process variable has a desired effect on the outcome.

POPULATION-BASED OUTCOME MEASURES

Dr. John Wennberg has been a pioneer in the field of study of medical practice variation. His work with population-based data has caused U.S. physicians to seriously step back and question why we do what we do with such great variation across regions of the country. (Hudson, 1996) Incorporating the use of evidence-based guidelines to address variation plus information management technology to measure key process attributes is only a start in combining quality improvement methodology with management of processes of care. Clinicians must become comfortable with examining their work filtered through the lens of public health. This point of view uses the individual patient, an intervention, or condition as a data element; but adjusts it with the measures of the larger community's health status (i.e., using prevalence or incidence) for a rate. In effect, the rate constitutes an individual as the numerator and the population measurement represents the denominator. (Cole, 1996)

A community is defined as a group of people who share a common interest. If the word *interest* is used in a loose sense, community may then refer to several different kinds of aggregates of patients that are worthy of consideration in managed care. The population-based focus may be applied to the community of people in a service area, employees and dependents of a corporation/employer, or the total group of enrolled patients in a health maintenance organization. Feedback for improvement must originate from the patients served and their relevant 'community'.

THE APPLICATION OF MANAGEMENT INFORMATION SYSTEMS

The history of information management revolving around a defined population and their consumption of health services has traditionally been devoted to the financial accounting perspective. The business of health care services certainly is entitled to effective, dedicated management information systems (MIS). The successful provider or group will endeavor now and in the future to refocus the MIS serving the organization. Brent James describes this shift as a movement from departments (an administrative model) to processes (a clinical model) with a concomitant change in the administrative culture. (James, 1994) An integrated and operational MIS will be characterized by one that supports the capacity to maintain data bases of only the truly important measures, manipulate data elements in order to reveal correlation and trends, combine clinical and nonclinical variables in order to determine cost characteristics, and transform raw data in useful information that is readily comprehensible by the care providers, i.e., through graphical representation of information. In effect, a large managed care organization would be well-served by supporting its own ambulatory care research network for physical and cost outcomes. (Stewart, 1995)

The USPSTF reported several findings based on the five-year process of compiling the second edition of the *Guide*. One of the findings addressed the value of interventions at a community-level rather than in a clinical setting. The nature of some important health problems with a large burden of suffering may be equally or better approached by broader-based action. Examples of these types of interventions include school-based counseling, public policy reforms (both legislative and regulatory), and community programs. (USPSTF, 1996) A managed care organization can be an effective base for a "community" program that may optimize services for enrollees as well as provide spill over into the larger geographic "community." As a civic duty, the managed care organization might subsidize infant car seats or provide low cost rental of same. The organization can enlist the support of public safety officials and partner with automobile dealers or repair businesses. The MIS supporting pediatric services could collect data elements concerning history of car seat use during clinical encounters. This information may be compared with the larger community's measures of use and provided as feedback to clinicians in the organization.

Unintentional injury prevention and control, as a clinical preventive service, provides an illustration of these ideas and the application to the primary care setting. Motor vehicle crashes (MVC) are a significant cause of morbidity and mortality for children and adults in the United States. Injury control professionals measure the frequency, severity, and causal associations with MVC using epidemiological methods. In the absence of a management information system to lend guidance, a primary care physician simply may prescribe the same form of motor vehicle safety counseling to all patients regardless of risk. Limitations in MIS resources ordinarily would preclude any form of observation concerning the outcome except on an anecdotal basis. The clinicians supported by an exceptional MIS will be equipped with measures of compliance for the population served, identification of higher risk patients or families in order to permit specific counseling strategies, and information concerning the cost of the intervention vs. the system outlays for patients who fail to avoid MVC injury.

Tailored strategies may require collecting data on which patients own pick-up trucks (typical low rate of seat belt use) or have air bags in their vehicles (a passive, nondetachable form of restraint that is highly effective, but requires modification of recommendations for infant/child passengers). An understanding of local variation in rate of injury, or even compliance with injury control recommendations, allows the clinician to concentrate on the more common injuries for which there are practical interventions. Finally, actual community-wide cost data for treatment of MVC injuries coupled with expenditures directed toward the promotion and assurance of seat belt/restraint use permits an ongoing analysis of the return on investment of injury prevention services.

CONCLUSION

The goal of this chapter was to integrate evidence-based guidelines, clinical preventive services, quality improvement theory, management of processes of care, and population-based outcomes research into some form of a unifying theory of practice. An attitude of willingness to change, possession of skills in statistical and epidemiological methods, and availability of information management technology are probably requisites for some degree of success in assimilating and applying this knowledge. Cooperation and collaboration, two overused words in general these days, are also key ingredients in seeking systemness for the United States' exorbitantly expensive and fragmented health care service industry. (Berwick, 1992)

The emphasis on preventive services as the intervention of choice was a result of the obvious advantage to provider, payer, and consumer within a pre-paid financing scheme. Preventive medicine is also a practical application that just happens to be served by one of the most comprehensive and authoritative compilations of evidence-based guidelines in existence. (USPSTF, 1996) The reader may substitute most any other clinical intervention for preventive services and still have a useful framework for understanding the interdependence that should exist in health care today, especially between continuous quality improvement and managed care.

REFERENCES

Berwick, D. M. "Continuous Improvement as an Ideal in Health Care." *The New England Journal of Medicine*, 320 (1): 53–56, 1989.

Berwick, D. M. "Controlling Variation in Health Care: A Consultation from Walter Shewhart." *Medical Care*, 29: 1212–1225, 1991.

Berwick, D. M. "Seeking Systemness." *Healthcare Forum Journal*, 22–28, March/April 1992.

Berwick, D. M. "Eleven Worthy Aims for Clinical Leadership of Healthcare System Reform." *Journal of the American Medical Association*, 27210): 797–802, 1994.

Canadian Task Force on the Periodic Health Examination. *Canadian guide to clinical preventive health care*, Canada Communication Group, Ottawa, 1994.

Cole, T. "Medical News & Perspectives: National Public Health Leader Caswell Evans Talks of 'Doing Less With Less'." *Journal of the American Medical Association*, 275 (1): 21–22, 1996.

Deming, W. E. *The New Economics*, Massachusetts Institute of Technology, Center for Advanced Engineering Study, Cambridge, MA, 1993.

Department of Health and Human Services, Public Health Service, Office of Disease Prevention and Health Promotion *Clinician's Handbook of Preventive Services: Putting Prevention Into Practice*, Government Printing Office. Washington, DC, 1994.

Eddy, D. M. *A Manual for Assessing Health Practices & Designing Practice Policies: The Explicit Approach*, American College of Physicians. Philadelphia, PA, 1992.

Hayes, O. "Clinical Practice Guidelines: A Review." *Journal of the American Osteopathic Association*, 94 (9): 732–738, 1994.

Hudson, T. "Mirror, Mirror." *Hospitals & Health Networks*, 24–30, April 5, 1996.

James, B. "Changing Outcomes: Measurement of Clinical Variation Drives Improvement." a presentation at the Sixth Annual Forum on Quality Improvement in Health Care. Institute for Healthcare Improvement, San Diego, CA, Dec. 7, 1994.

Kamerow, D. "Prioritizing Prevention." *The Journal of Family Practice*, 38 (3): 229–230, 1994.

Lewis, C. I. *Mind and the World Order: Outline of a Theory of Knowledge.*, Dover, New York, 1929.

Mischler, N. "Health Promotion/Disease Prevention Guideline Development: Process and Results." *Physician Executive*, 21 (8): 13–17, 1995.

Parmley, W. W. "Clinical Practice Guidelines: Does the Cookbook Have Enough Recipes?" *Journal of the American Medical Association*, 272 (17): 1374–1375, 1994.

Roberts, R., Rosof, B., and Thompson, R. "Practice Guidelines: Coping with information overload." *Patient Care*. 39-57. Feb. 29,1996.

Sox, H. C. and Woolf, S. H. "Evidence-Based Practice Guidelines From the U.S. Preventive Services Task Force." *Journal of the American Medical Association*, 269 (20): 2678, 1993.

Stewart, K. "The Standard of Care No Longer Measures Up." *Family Practice Management*, 42–47, September 1995.

Strickland, R. "C. I. Lewis and Deming's Theory of Knowledge." *Quality Management in Health Care*, 3 (3): 40–49, 1995.

U.S. Preventive Services Task Force *Guide to Clinical Preventive Services: An Assessment of Effectiveness of 169 Interventions*, Williams & Wilkins, Baltimore, MD, 1989.

U.S. Preventive Services Task Force *Guide to Clinical Preventive Services*, 2nd ed. International Medical Publishing. Alexandria, VA, 1996.

Voelker, R. "New Prevention Guidelines Called 'State of the Art'." *Journal of the American Medical Association*, 275 (7): 505, 1996.

Walton, M. *The Deming Management Method.*, The Putnam Publishing Group, New York, 1986.

Wennberg, J. "Unwanted Variations in the Rules of Practice." *Journal of the American Medical Association*, 265: 1306–1307, 1991.

Williamson, J., Goldschmidt, P., and Jillson, *I. Medical Practice Information Demonstration Project: Final Report. Office of the Assistant Secretary of Health*, DHEW, Contract #282-77-0068GS. Policy Research, Baltimore, MD, 1979.

Wilson, M., Berwick, D., and DiGuiseppi, C "The New Edition of the Guide to Clinical Preventive Services." *Pediatrics*, 97 (5): 733–735, 1996.

Woolf, S. "Practice Guidelines: A New Reality in Medicine." *Archives of Internal Medicine*, 150: 1811–1818, 1990.

Woolf, S. "Practice Guidelines: What the Family Physician Should Know." *American Family Physician*, 51: 1455–1463, 1995.

Worral, G. and Chaulk, P. "Hope or Experience? Clinical Practice Guidelines in Family Practice." *The Journal of Family Practice.*, 42 (4): 353–356, 1996.

Wurman, R. S. *Information Anxiety.* Doubleday, New York, 1989.

10 Institutionalization of Health Care Quality

A. F. Al-Assaf

CONTENTS

The process of implementing health care quality is long and intricate. It involves a large number of areas and activities. The organization as a whole usually becomes involved in this process. Whether it is management, staff, providers or consumers, all will be affected by such a process and all will be part of its successes and its failures. That is the reason why health care organizations should plan effectively for the long-term planning of implementation, which should include a plan and a number of processes for sustainability of the quality initiative.

Sustaining health care quality is both an art and a science. It requires leadership skills necessary to keep the momentum of improvements going and the staff morale high, while trying to maximize positive impact and producing actual and measurable improvements in processes and outcomes. (Al-Assaf, 1994) It is a systematic process of continuous employee involvement, empowerment, and teamwork. It is a cultural transformation.

Sustaining health care quality is only the process of the system of institutionalizing quality in an organization. Institutionalization of health care quality involves continuous process improvements, continuous structural improvements, and continuous outcome improvements. (Al-Assaf, 1993) It is a system of true and total quality in an organization.

In this chapter, the system of institutionalization of health care quality and the process of sustainability is presented. The method of presentation will be such that only practical introductory remarks are given on the proper methods of implementing health care quality in an effort to achieve a system or a culture where quality is institutionalized. Remarks presented in this chapter are based on actual experiences of the author gathered from the different health care quality projects implemented nationally and internationally. Every effort has been made to ensure applicability of these remarks and practice tips to managed care plans.

Institutionalization as a system is achieved only after full implementation of quality is completed in an health care organization. Since it is a system, such system must be built gradually at the same time as the processes of implementation are

1-57444-073-X/97/$0.00+$.50
© 1998 by CRC Press LLC

taking place and at the same time as planning activities and improvement strategies are being developed and applied. Therefore, only after the full implementation of health care quality in an organization, that the next expected mile-stone is an established "quality culture." Total health care quality coupled with a quality culture is a status of institutionalization of health care quality. In a system where there is planning for quality, quality assurance (QA), monitoring, quality improvement (QI), and quality management (QM), institutionalization becomes eminent. Therefore, institutionalization is achieved when appropriate health care quality activities are carried out effectively, efficiently, and on routine basis throughout a system, or organization. (Brown, 1995) It is a state of achievement whereby health care quality is practiced and maintained without additional outside resources. In such a state, expertise are available from within and commitment is fully integrated and maintained.

A quality environment or culture is achieved when quality activities become routine activities and happen on daily basis. Such activities are not separate from the normal activities that are carried out daily by the system and its personnel. It is a state where each employee is aware of the quality concept, believes in it, practices its principles, and makes it part of his/her responsibility and not the responsibility of a department or another individual. In such a culture each individual is responsible for his/her tasks. Individuals will then own their quality structure, processes and outcomes. At such a stage, employees will be making every effort to make sure that the processes of QA are maintained, i.e., planning, standard setting, and monitoring. In such a culture, employees are also practicing QI, i.e., they identify opportunities for improvements and set the motion individually or in collaboration with others to make improvements. It is also a situation in which employees are empowered to achieve their goals which are in turn aligned with the organization's mission and vision statements. A quality culture is therefore achieved when individuals carry on "quality" related activities on a routine basis and that working in teams becomes a norm in that organization.

LESSONS IN INSTITUTIONALIZATION

The following are lessons learned in implementing health care quality in health care institutions. If learned well and applied effectively, they may lead this kind of an organization to a system of institutionalization of health care quality. The applicability of each lesson listed may vary from one organization to the next, but generalization has been intended.

- *Effectively plan for the change.* Introducing new concepts and ideas may cause a change or at least a fear of change. Therefore, every effort should be made to plan for this change adequately and effectively. The change process is dramatic. It could be a change from no or little quality to a complete system of quality with all its components and activities. Planning for this change is very important and extremely necessary before actual implementation takes place.

- *Planning for quality* should be done systematically and thoroughly. Delineation of responsibility, identification of scope of involvement, allocation of resources, and the anticipation for the impact of the change on organizational behavior should be completed before activities in QA or QI begin.
- *Priorities* need to be set early in the process with true buy-ins from the key personnel from the organization. Priorities, of course, should be set by these individuals from within the organization not by their consultants. Therefore, a team of key personnel that will be impacted by the change need to discuss, brainstorm, and identify priorities in the change process. Of course priorities should be realistic, feasible, have a high probability of accomplishment, and have the most impact on the bottom line. One method on how to achieve this objective is to conduct a strategic planning workshop and invite all key personnel to attend. This workshop should be held as early as possible in the change process. Also, all resolutions and decisions made at the workshop should be documented and further distributed to all parties involved. A ground rule should be reached that if any change in these decisions is desired in the future, a strict and systematic group decision must be reached before making any amendments. This practice will avert (at least minimize) frequent amendments that potentially may take place in the likely even of changes in personnel or minds.
- *Discuss strategies for implementation.* Methods for implementing the change need to be discussed thoroughly and explicitly with the key individuals in the organization and these indivuals must understand them clearly. Answers to the how, when, who, what, and where should be available early and before implementation starts. All decisions should be documented in writing and agreed upon by all sides. Here a widely used management tool such as a gant chart or development of a workplan with times, tasks to be accomplished and responsible party may prove to be extremely helpful to meet the objectives of specificity and accountability of implementation processes.
- *Securing commitment from management* is helpful and can make the process of implementation move rapidly. The involvement of these top managers in the early activities of planning is essential. Commitment means active participation on teams and tasks as well as the allocation of adequate resources for quality. It involves behavioral change to act as role-models for the rest of the organization to follow and take lead.
- *Develop a mission statement for quality early in the process.* A mission statement that is well prepared and developed in collaboration by senior staff will have a higher chance of survival even, with any turnover of managers and staff. Mission statements should answer the questions of the purpose of the organization, the specific objectives of the organization in quality, the scope of interventions, and the customers of the process of quality. This mission statement must coincide with the organization-wide mission statement. Also, once developed, mission statements should be

communicated effectively to the intended audience internally and externally and should be displayed publically as a constant reminder of the staff regarding their duties and the customers expectations for achievement.

- *Identifying a leader or champion(s)* to lead this movement is highly recommended. A qualified individual with authority, credibility, enthusiasm, and interest can be an asset to the acceleration of health care quality implementation and its institutionalization. This individual can act as facilitator and cheerleader for health care quality initiatives. In managed care plans, this individual traditionally has been a nurse with some background in utilization and case management. With the right qualifications other disciplines can be as good in leading the health care quality process.

- *Consider the pursuit of accreditation* by one of the accrediting agencies, such as NCQA, JCAHO, or AAAHC. Although there is controversy surrounding the issue of accreditation and its impact on quality, there are a number of advantages to an accreditation program. These programs usually are well structured and have specific standards that the organization must adhere to in order to pass the survey and receive accreditation. These standards usually are well written and are valid with benefits of enforcing the establishement and maintaining of a quality structure and may support a number of quality processes and outcomes. A good quality system — structure, processes, and outcomes — is a foundation for a sustainable quality system which in turn is conducive of institutionalization.

- *Organization of a steering committee or council of national representatives* would give the health care quality process credibility, sustainability and momentum. A tasks and duties document of the council or the committee should be prepared and agreed upon by all parties involved, while all members should have a copy of this document and understand it as their charter. It should not be changed without explicit consent of all parties involved. A meeting time and regular schedule should be adhered to (at least once every month) in a regular place during a convenient hour; meetings should not last more than two hours. This group will be responsible for approving implementation strategies, intervention activities, dissemination materials, etc. This committee is important to the sustainability of the implementation process.

- *Forming the structure for health care quality* should be gradual and methodical. It should be based on progress and understanding of the concept and the practice of health care quality. Organizing large structures of committees and councils early on may shift the focus on organization *per se* and away from the actual mission of health care quality, and that is incremental cintinuous improvement. Also, adding structure may require additional resources that may not be necessary at the early stages of implementation.

- *Identify the customer.* An attempt should always be made to identify the customer(s) of both the organization and the health care quality process, but this activity should be done early in the process. Answers should be identified to such questions as: Who is the customer of the quality process?

What are their expectations? How to achieve them? These customers and their expectations needs to be identified and every effort should be made to continuously meet these expectations. Managed care plans should take this issue seriously and start surveying and communicating with their members periodically and frequently. In this way members needs and expectations can be identified, defined and addressed by the appropriate personnel.

- *Staff at the beginning of implementation should be concentrating more on learning and understanding* the concept and principles of health care quality and practice it daily to achieve positive results. Too many committees with too many meetings and too many tasks distract from focusing on expected goals. An important principle of health care quality is design activities as outcome driven but process focused. Thus improvements are targeted and always measured to identify impact.

- *Training.* Deming (1985) suggested, training should be on-the-job and as-needed training. It should be done, however, in a formal and systematic manner where an effective training plan has been developed and would include such issues as number of trainers, type of courses, to whom, by whom, where, and what resources. Every lecture given, every workshop delivered, and every meeting conducted should have as one of its objectives the capability of the participants to duplicate the effort and pass it on to others. Training in quality methods must be stressed, because as you train people you increase their awareness and, as you help them perform the tasks learned in the training, you solidify their learning. Therefore, train people to make them trainers. As more trainers develop, more dissemination of health care quality occurs which leads to more training thus more dissemination will take place and so no. And that is how you sustain a system of profound knowledge and practice.

- *Always have an alternative plan* in case one is slowed down due to the anticipated and frequent staff changes. Make a habit of not relying on one single individual when trying to implement health care quality effectively. Train a number of individuals and prepare several qualified staff simultaneously. This practice will allow for wider selections of coordinators, and will enhance sustainability efforts. Flexibility is expected and desired in change processes and is a signs of cultural maturity.

- *Keep quality activities closely related to the organization's main activities* and its mission without unnecessary change in organizational structure and the allocation of additional resources. At least at the beginning of its implementation, health care quality activities may be delegated to an existing staff member or to an existing department as part of their normal responsibility.

- *Prepare yourself to answer questions related to incentives* for attracting staff to participate in health care quality activities. Staff will ask: "What's in it for me?" or "Why should I do this?" As long as health care quality activities are not required as integral parts of their jobs, employees will question their role in participation. Quality expectations and measurement indicators should be written as part of their performance evaluation and their job descriptions. A system of employee rewards and recognition based on health care quality achievements may be necessary. Therefore, a recognition and reward system for people working for quality outcomes should be designed and instituted by the organization early in the process. This also should include an incentives system that encourages people to be involved in QA/QI activities. As mentioned earlier, answers and mechanisms to these objectives could not be found. The issue of incentives is a sensitive one with differing ideas about the how and the what of the incentives issue. Incentives, however, need not be monetary in nature. Those actually are the worst, but the presence of some incentives will be helpful to health care quality sustainability. There has been several examples on recognizing deserving individuals, such as recognizing teams with plaques, newsletter announcements, letters of gratitude from the organization's CEO, certificates of excellence given to deserving individuals by a special committee, as well as authorship of articles in the local newsletter.

- *Document improvements* by measuring pre- and post-status. Always have quantitative data available for comparisons and for measurements of effectiveness. It also is useful if cost savings are calculated to measure efficiency. These indicators are especially attractive to administrators. Providing measurable parameters gives credibility and sustainability to the process of health care quality.

- *Identify tangible outcomes.* In several projects, it was found that if the final product does not have tangible outcomes, you did not accomplish anything. Therefore, always make sure to identify and look for tangible outcomes early in the game or at least make it as a by-product of the change process. Numbers before and after, dollars saved, measurable outcomes, results achieved all are examples for tangibles. These types of tangibles should be kept in mind during the writings of the workplan and certainly during the course of the project.

- *Actively disseminate achievements and health care quality awareness information* to as many individuals in the system as possible. Make sure that participation is voluntary and is open to everyone as opportunities for improvement are identified. Do not make it a "private club." Keep everybody informed and involved. Quality is everyone's responsibility and it is based on individual responsibility. If everyone becomes involved in improvement activities and in the documantation of outcomes, institutionalization can be achieved easier and faster. Improvement do not have to be big as long as it is continuous.

- *Always use caution in involving everybody in projects that may detract from the main mission* of health care organization, although you may want to involve as many people as possible in health care initiatives. Resist the temptation to involve too many departments and units in too many projects simultaneuously and early. Building an effective process in one area is more important that starting several incomplete processes in different areas. Keep the implementation process focused and desirable. Provide an answer to the "so what?" question to every improvement intervention strategy you are planning to take.

- *Disseminate ideas, standards, improvements, and results.* In dissemination, an active method of communication should be followed, i.e., dissemination is not writing a standard or a guideline and copying it to all concerned. This is passive communication. To make the communication effort more effective, active communication efforts should be targeted, such as focus group meetings, conferences, newsletters, workshops, and direct personal contacts. Therefore, as dissemination is contemplated, one should consider what needs to be disseminated, the methods to be used, the desired target population, the perceived impact, the resources available, and the cost-effectiveness of the activity.

- *Use of consultants and the identification of their roles may be considered.* The organization should ask: What is the objective? Is the consultant the change agent, or is he/she/they the implementor of the plan? What are the objectives of identifying and working with a consultant? Does the consultant agree with the purpose? Weigh the options of full-time vs. short-term consultant with that of periodic long-term consultant. The role of the consultant can change from a starting role as an organizer, a convener, a trainer, an expert, and an initiator to coach, advisor, and strategizer very quickly. This is a good sign and an ideal path for the consultant to be at as long as the momentum of the implementation process is kept at a high level. Still it is found that although dependence on the consultant diminishes soon after the start of the process it never ceases. Consultants, on the other hand, should position themselves as early in the process as possible to act as advisors and mentors and move away from the temptation of participating in each activity.

  Another issue related to consultants is credibility. Both qualifications and experience are needed to earn individual credibility by the host. This is especially important for technical assistance and training capabilities. Consultants should be prepared adequately and have the experience to make appropriate decisions and act on them efficiently. Besides scientific knowledge, desired qualifications of consulting staff are interpersonal skills, sound judgment, organization skills, and crisis management capabilities. On several occasions, any or all of these characteristics proved highly essential for consultants to be able to operate in the field of health care quality. On several other occasions, organizations fall in the trap of agreeing to hire a "qualified" large consulting firm. Soon after that the organization became a field of experiment of newly hired and somewhat inexperienced "consultants" this firm had on its staff. Therefore, it behooves the organization to check and double check the qualification of each individual staff of the consulting firm that will be given the permission to participate in the implementation process.

- *Always have adequate funding available* for the development of new projects and activities not originally planned for. This also will give you the flexibility of shifting additional funds to needed areas where improvements are taking place more effectively. Adequate funds will increase the likelihood of sustainability.

- *Finally, encourage and foster an environment of learning not judgment.* In particular, rely on data and facts in making judgments. Avoid the antiquated disciplinary method of management. Here again, Dr. Deming (1985) suggests in his 14 points of management to "drive out fear" from the organization. Drive out the fear of creativitiy, the fear of speaking up, the fear of correcting processes that do not work, the fear of improvement. Organizations that agree to provide an environment of learning rather than judgment will always succeed in achieving its quality goals faster and more efficiently.

Institutionalizing health care quality is the ultimate goal of the process. The road towards it usually is long and full of obstacles. The objective, however, is to plan for it properly and to move slowly but gradually towards full implementation and sustainability. Institutionalization requires time, aapropriate staff, adequate resources an abondance of patience.

REFERENCES

Al-Assaf, A. F. and Schmele, J, A. *The Textebook of Total Quality in Healthcare*, St. Lucie Press, Delray, FL, 1993.

Al-Assaf, A. F. "Quality Improvement in Healthcare: An Overview." *Journal of the Royal Medical Services*, 1 (2): 44–50, 1994.

Brown, L. and DiPrete–Brown, L. "Lessons Learned in Institutionalization of Quality Assurance Programs: An International Prespective." *International Journal of Quality in Health Care*, 7 (4): 419–425, 1995.

Deming, W. E. *Out of the Crisis*, MIT Press, Cambridge, MA, 1985.

11 Balancing Quality with Costs in Managed Care Settings

James C. Benneyan and Vivian Valdmanis

CONTENTS

This chapter discusses the relationship between the costs and quality of health care and provides an overview of the associated economic issues and cost drivers. These issues are illustrated with two case studies which emphasize the cost savings associated with improved quality.

Historically, the relationship between health care costs and quality has been debated. Some argue that higher costs are related directly to higher levels of quality in that more expensive care leads to better outcomes for the patient engaging in health care services. For example, the quality philosophy advocated by the late quality pioneer, Dr. W. E. Deming, and his contemporaries holds that as process quality improves, costs decrease, and satisfaction increases. The net result on costs, productivity, and profitability of transitioning from traditional quality assurance methods to Deming's approach to quality is captured in the following quote from Dr. Deming (1982):

> "Improve quality, you automatically improve productivity, you capture the market with lower price and better quality. You stay in business, and you provide jobs. So simple."

Under this approach, unnecessary work is removed and hidden costs of rework, waste, and liability are reduced, often said to account for savings of 15 to 25% of total costs in a variety of industries. Further information on total quality management (TQM) in general and Dr. Deming in particular can be found in Deming (1982), Walton (1986), and Neave (1990). More specific to health care, Wilson and Goldschmidt (1995) assert that "the question is not *whether* or not to conduct quality management, but rather how it should be done and how much time and money should be applied." Arguing that costs are far outweighed by the potential benefits of reduced financial loss due to reduced iatrogenesis, preventable errors and complications, unnecessary tests, poor treatment selection, liability and malpractice litigation, and inefficient use of resources:

> "Certainly, quality management bears a cost; but administrators must weigh this cost against the cost of needless deaths, iatrogenic illness, extra days in the hospital, and defending and paying malpractice claims … Managing quality costs money. But the *lack of quality* can be, and invariably is, even more costly."

On the other hand, it also may be argued that more health care may not necessarily be better since it may lead to a higher probability of iatrogenic diseases and that excessive care and services do not lead to better health outcomes. For example, longer hospital stays have been correlated with higher rates of nosocomial infection and other adverse events. (Martone, et al., 1991) Several others also have suggested that greater attention to quality control programs only will further increase health care costs. This view tends to reflect a traditional quality assurance approach to health care management, rather than a quality management orientation. In clinical laboratories, for example, contrary to Deming's philosophy above, Dr. Inhorn (1995) recently stated:

> "The reality is that (quality control procedures) increase the workload of the laboratory and the cost of cytologic analysis. Many studies have shown that Total Quality Management systems *add* at least 25% to overall laboratory costs."

Many others also have echoed this viewpoint that higher quality can be achieved only via additional costly quality assurance programs. For example, Mango (1995) stated:

> "In my opinion, there are no known quality control procedures that do not impact workload or costs."

Note that this general reasoning reflects a traditional "pre-TQM" viewpoint (based, for example, on audits to screen and correct problems) which is contrary to that suggested above under the "modern" approach to quality management, which focuses on improving process quality to the point where fewer total costs of poor quality (CPQ) are incurred. This cost-versus-quality debate has become more intensified due to the proliferation of managed care systems, including health maintenance organizations (HMOs) and preferred provider organizations (PPOs), and to the changing economic incentives under managed care reimbursement policies.

Therefore, it is useful to review briefly the relationship between costs and service delivery as a function of the types of reimbursement methodology used. Under historical fee-for-service reimbursement systems, physicians had economic incentives to provide all the care available irrespective of medical benefits. For example, in economic jargon, this meant that physicians might treat patients until no further benefit is accrued without regards to the cost of resources used for this treatment. Hence, the costs of providing the last unit of care could be much greater than the benefit of that care for the patient. However, physicians were paid for all services rendered and patients who were insured faced little or no out-of-pocket costs. Both parties, therefore, had little financial incentive to decrease the use of unnecessary health care services and, aside from ethics and a professional concern for patients' well-being, its critics have argued are strong incentives to increase this use.

Under managed care, conversely, the payment scheme is capitated or pre-determined. In other words, the physician gets a set fee per patient who is enrolled with the managed care system regardless of the costs for treating this patient. A presumed benefit of capitation reimbursement systems is that the physician can have a financial incentive to limit the amount of unnecessary care provided. A potential drawback and criticism of capitation, however, is that physicians and case managers also may have incentives to limit care which otherwise would be advisable. Returning to the question posed above, therefore, does this effect of capitation to "limit" the amount of care necessarily mean lower quality?

Although it is important not to extrapolate beyond their specific context, the media has reported anecdotal evidence that the quality of care is indeed poorer under managed care systems. For example, *The New York Times* (May 19, 1996) reported that several states are taking aim at how HMOs do business, inferring that capitation payment schemes lead to denied access to necessary care and, hence, lower quality. A related story which aired on the CBS Evening News on June 3, 1996, reported that the managed care system operating the Tennessee Medicaid program (TennCare) has established prescription formularies that allow only certain drugs be used on TennCare patients. This led to two women being denied the preferred medication (not on the formulary's list) that increased their health care problems, including increased stays in the hospital and prolonged treatment for an ailment that could have been treated less expensively had a freedom of choice remained for prescription drugs.

These anecdotes suggest that managed care can be too concerned with cost minimization and profit maximization to the point of being at the expense of the patient's health and well-being. While there may be nothing wrong in itself with cost minimization or profit maximization, these incidents underscore the legitimate concern about the effect of over-emphasis on patient well-being and access to care. (It also is important to consider a possible "publication effect" — that is, it is well-known that the media is more likely to pick up stories which suggest something interesting than those which find nothing conclusive.) But it also begs the real question: Does there have to be a tradeoff between costs and quality? One way to ascertain whether this tradeoff arises and to what degree is to approach the issue from a total quality management (TQM) perspective. TQM is based on the concept of continuously seeking improvements in quality and eliminating all activities that add costs but do not add value to the process of providing quality. For example, the average cost of poor quality of Japanese manufacturers is about 5% of the cost of operation, whereas in the U.S., an average of 25% of the cost of operation can be attributable to scrap alone. In a health care facility, these non-value activities include checking, filing, sorting, moving, copying, waiting, reworking, retesting, etc. (Suver, et al., 1992) Inherent in the TQM approach is the identification of necessary and unnecessary "cost drivers" — activities that cause costs to be incurred. For example, the unnecessary costs of the above non-value added activities would not be incurred if all processes functioned perfectly all of the time. Some primary cost driving activities include (Suver, et al. 1992):

- the complexity of the service performed
- the equipment that is used for service (both medical and managerial)
- the number of services that are repeated
- the number of bad outputs due to poor quality
- the number of vendors that are used in the delivery of services
- the number of staff members that are needed for direct medical services
- the number of staff members that are needed for the indirect services provided by the managed care system
- the number of schedule changes

Some of these cost driving activities may add to the costs of services at a managed care system but do nothing to add to the quality of care (and in some cases detract from quality). By improving process quality through TQM these unnecessary cost driving activities should be eliminated.

A related aspect of the managerial approach to quality of care is total cost management (TCM), which includes both the financial and non-financial indicators that support decision making. TCM integrates management and health systems and reflects the *total* life cycle of the organization's provision of health care services.

By using TQM and TCM, improvements in quality can improve revenues and decrease costs, which improve the bottom line. In other words, high quality care costs less than poor quality of care, since costs of nonconformance and costs of poor quality are reduced, clients needs are better satisfied (Suver et al., 1992), and a link between profits and quality of care can be made. (Waress, et al., 1994) This chapter aims at providing some evidence to address this issue. More specifically, we provide some economic reasoning behind why quality of care and measuring quality of care and cost minimization can be directly related as well as provide a case study to show how gauging quality of care can lead to both higher quality and lower costs. The chapter is organized as follows. In the next section, the variety of economic issues in the quality of care — cost of care relationship are defined. The costs of monitoring quality and the associated information costs are described in Section III. The chapter concludes with two case studies which illustrate these economic concepts.

ECONOMIC ISSUES FOR QUALITY OF CARE AND MEASUREMENT

Two of the most common types of measurement of a minimum acceptable level of quality of care are (1) the licensure and certification of providers by federal and states governments as well as other governing bodies, i.e., medical associations, and (2) the monitoring and accrediting of health care organizations by various accrediting groups. The government oversees the licensure and certification process to ensure a certain level of quality of health care services provided. One reason the government is involved in licensure and certification is due to "asymmetric information," which means that providers typically have much more information than patients ever could regarding the prescribed medical treatment regimen. As a consequence, patients are unable to determine the quality of providers or of the services they provide. With licensure, the patient is at least assured that the provider has a certain level of competence, i.e., attendance to a medical school, completion of a residency program, etc.

Hospitals and other health care organizations likewise are monitored by JCAHO, NCQA, HCFA, and others to ensure the public that facilities are up to at least a minimum standard of care. Both providers and health care organizations are subjected to periodic review to ensure a maintenance of some level of quality of care and to guarantee to the public that standards are met. However, these quality of care issues are basic and interorganizational differences may exist in quality and costs even though the organizations and/or providers meet certain regulatory standards. Conformance to minimum standards of quality also should not be confused with excellence nor with the optimal quality cost level which minimizes the total of all economic issues associated with achieving any given level of quality. In this section, we describe some of the more germane economic issues as they relate to quality of care.

DEFINITION OF QUALITY COSTS

The American Society for Quality Control (ASQC) defines quality costs as:

> "A measure of costs specifically associated with the achievement or non-achievement of product or service quality — as defined by all product or service requirements established by the company and its contracts with customers. More specifically, quality costs are the total of the costs incurred through (a) investing in the prevention of non-conformance to requirements; (b) appraising a product or service for conformance to requirements; and (c) failure to meet requirements."

Suver et al. (1992) reword this definition of quality costs as "all costs incurred to help the employee do the right job every time and the cost of determining if the output is acceptable, plus any cost incurred by the organization and the customer because the output does not meet specifications and/or customer expectations." While these definitions are good starting points regarding the discussion between costs and quality, more precise definitions of specific types of costs and associated performance measures are discussed below.

EFFECTIVENESS AND EFFICIENCY

Effectiveness is defined as the appropriateness of the medical care regimen chosen to treat a certain illness or condition. Hence, effectiveness is concerned with making the right choices from a medical standpoint. Conversely, efficiency may be defined either as the amount of medical care for a given cost (where more is better) or similarly as the lowest costs incurred to provide a given level of medical care (where less is better). These efficiency definitions may be extended to the concepts of a desired quality of care at the lowest possible cost or the highest possible quality for a given cost.

By incorporating quality into these definitions, effectiveness and efficiency can be determined together. For example, a treatment is effective in treating an ailment; therefore, the quality objective is met because there has been a positive outcome. By pursuing the efficiency objective in this course of treatment, costs are minimized because extraneous treatments were not used which would not have altered the outcome in any way. Hence, effective and efficient treatment leads to lower overall costs while maintaining a desired quality of care. (Mone, 1994)

Whereas this may appear to be a relatively simple relationship, the real economic challenge is to define costs that are relevant. It often is a helpful and informative means of analysis to identify and classify costs into different categories. Some relevant types of costs associated with quality of care include:

- immediate vs. subsequent costs
- direct and indirect costs
- opportunity costs
- non-achievement costs
- costs of poor quality (CPQ).

The costs of poor quality include all current and future costs incurred by the system and the patient as a result of poor quality. Note that these costs are referred to as poor quality costs, rather than simply as quality costs, because none of them would be incurred if high quality were known to always exist. In quality management, these CPQ costs classically are categorized into the following areas (for example, see Juran and Gryna, 1988, Montgomery, 1991, Evans and Lindsay, 1995):

- appraisal and inspection costs
- defect prevention costs
- internal failure costs
- external failure costs.

Similarly, in a health care context Suver et al. (1992) define internal and external costs as prevention costs, appraisal costs, and failure costs. Each of the above types of costs are described in greater detail below.

IMMEDIATE VS. SUBSEQUENT COSTS

Immediate costs are the costs or cost savings that are evident right after a course of action is taken. For example, if unnecessary care is reduced or eliminated then the cost savings are evident in terms of reduced laboratory costs, X-ray costs, etc. This is particularly true for unnecessary care that is largely harmless. (Palmer, Donabedian, and Povar, 1991) However, if potentially harmful care is provided less often, then there will exist both immediate and subsequent cost savings. The immediate cost savings will result due to the fact that the cost for the treatment no longer exists, whereas subsequent cost savings will result from the fact that any costs for treating the harm done to the patient from this treatment also no longer will exist. In this regard the benefits of less treatment far outweigh the costs, and quality of care is achieved in an efficient and effective manner. Hence, the strategy to lower costs and maintain quality involves discouraging the use of interventions that provide little or no value and encouraging the use of interventions that provide high value. (Eddy, 1996)

It also has been suggested that one way to pursue only effective and efficient medical regimens that would result in both immediate and subsequent cost savings would be through protocols or predesigned treatments. The potential value of such practice guidelines lie in the premise that deviations could be measured together with their resulting costs (or cost-savings). (Pryor and Fortin, 1995) The ability to increase quality of care delivered also will increase cost management in both the short and in the long run. That is, use of the protocols can make explicit which treatments are not quality enhancing but rather are wasteful uses of resources. (Pryor and Fortin, 1995) It can be argued further that by following protocols, certain harmful treatments also may be avoided.

In cases where protocols do not exist, the managed care system may incorporate coverage criteria. The basic premise behind these criteria is to discourage the use of interventions that provide little or no value and encourage the use of interventions that have high values. In other words, managed care systems provide services that are medically necessary or medically appropriate. (Eddy, 1996) The issues that are germane in determining medical necessity or medical appropriateness include (ibid.):

- General statements regarding the scope of services
- Detail in the description of what services are medically necessary
- Specification of the managed care system's responsibility
- Identification of the patient's medical condition
- Indication of the appropriate health intervention
- Description of the indications for a medical intervention
- Presence of sufficient evidence of the intervention's efficacy
- Definition of health outcomes from the medical intervention.

The necessity for these criteria arises because resources are limited. In other words, if resources and financing were unlimited, then interventions that lead to even the least bit of benefits would be permissible. In reality, managed care systems and health plans need to determine ways that ensure that the limited resources for which their patients, members, and purchasers are willing to pay are used efficiently to optimize the quality of care received. (Eddy, 1996) The use of criteria such as those defined above is similar to the use of protocols in the sense that inefficiencies from medical or managerial misuse can be identified and eliminated, especially if there is no commensurate value in quality of care or health outcomes.

If, on the other hand, managed care systems only pursue health care delivery costs without regards to long term quality, total costs will increase (Weinstein, 1990), as suggested by the media anecdotes presented in the introduction of this chapter. By allowing bad quality of care, costs for caring for the patient will increase due to future treatments for these patients, resulting in higher premiums for insurance due to an expected increase in benefits that will have to be paid. Further, costs to the managed care system may result due to a diminished reputation, such as if patients dis-enroll, thereby reducing the patient base and, subsequently revenues.

DIRECT AND INDIRECT COSTS

Costs also can be defined as either direct costs or indirect costs. Whereas the immediate vs. subsequent costs were based on when the costs arose in time, direct and indirect costs are based on who bears them. Direct costs are those costs which are borne by an individual or organization. For example, the direct health care costs include:

- Technology necessary for treatment
- Tests and Procedures used for treatment
- Costs associated with any side-effects
- Health care resources (physicians, nurses, technicians, other personnel as well as capital) to provide treatment.

Under capitation, these costs initially are created by the provider, but ultimately paid for by the consumer (either the employer or patient) through membership fees. Therefore, if excessive and unnecessary resources are used by the provider, some of the increase in direct costs also is passed to the consumer, who has to pay for it without any type of additional health benefit. Conversely, if fewer unnecessary resources are used, providers can decrease their membership fees and increase their profit margin and market share. Thus both parties — the purchaser and the provider — benefit if direct costs can be reduced.

However, minimizing direct costs should not be pursued if it means an increase in indirect costs. Indirect costs include:

- Loss of the patient's productivity due to increased illness due to low quality care
- Increased opportunity costs (defined below)
- Costs borne by society due to having individuals sicker for a longer period of time

The loss of a patient's productivity will lead the patient to work less thereby lowering his/her standard of living. Although these costs are not borne by the managed care system, the repercussions may be. For example, a patient who has to bear the brunt of poor quality of care may reduce his/her regard for the managed care system and may disenroll and encourage others to do the same. Similarly, employer groups may be dissatisfied with the managed care system's poor quality of care and disenroll all of their employees. This can lead to a significant reduction in market share and hence revenues and profits.

OPPORTUNITY COSTS

Additionally, the costs borne by society for sicker individuals include the value of their work in the production of goods and services, as well as possibly having to expand public and private resources for these individuals' care. Hence, if poor quality translates into higher governmental expenditures, increased regulations may result, possibly affecting the managed care system's operations and increasing their costs. Therefore, costs related to quality include both the costs incurred in achieving and maintaining quality and the costs resulting from not achieving or maintaining quality. (Waress, et al., 1994)

Another related economic concept is that of opportunity costs, which are defined as the value of alternative uses for resources. For example, the patient's opportunity costs for being sicker for a longer period of time is the value associated with an alternate use for that time, e.g., the wages lost due to an inability to work or an increase in indirect costs. The opportunity costs for the managed care system include the use of resources or an increase in direct costs to treat a patient who received poor quality of care rather than using the resources for investments or expanding benefits to attract a larger market share and hence increase revenues and profits.

PREVENTION COSTS

Failure in providing quality of care can be minimized by investing in quality improvement methods that prevent failures from occurring. In other words, spending money early in a service delivery process may prevent costly mistakes from being made later on in the health care delivery process. (Waress, et al., 1994)

Prevention costs are incurred at the beginning of the process to protect an organization against errors. These include:

- identification of the client's needs
- education and training of employees
- development of quality monitoring and reporting systems, i.e., TQM
- institution of quality administration
- planning and design of the system
- quality control systems
- supplier quality evaluation
- improvement projects.

APPRAISAL AND INSPECTION COSTS

Appraisal costs are defined as the costs associated with inspecting and evaluating the extent to which service delivery meets the patient's requirements in terms of both medical service and overall patient satisfaction.

These costs include:

- quality audits, accreditation and state surveys, licensure, and certification reviews
- maintenance of equipment
- inspecting and testing purchased items
- quality data acquisition and analysis
- documentation of services and processes
- inspection or evaluation of services and processes.

INTERNAL AND EXTERNAL FAILURE COSTS

Failure costs can be defined as costs due to either internal or external failures. Costs due to internal failure are incurred when poor quality is discovered prior to its external impact (that is, the failure occurs internally), including:

- waste
- investigation of defective tests or other errors
- rework and unnecessary repetition of activities
- idle time and lost time
- reinspection and/or corrections
- failure analysis
- reduced capacity to treat as many patients.

The costs of external failures arise after defective services have been delivered to the clients and are discovered by the clients. In addition to the above examples, external failure costs also include:

- responding to patient complaints
- additional health care services to treat and induced medical condition
- insuring against liability or exposure to malpractice
- loss of client goodwill
- lost revenue due to dis-satisfaction and disenrollment

Note that prevention and appraisal costs are inversely related to failure costs — the more prevention, for example, the fewer failures. However, in many organizations the costs of failure far outweigh the other costs of quality. For example, one health care organization estimated the cost of external failure at 30%; internal failure at 45%, appraisal at 20% and prevention at 5% of total quality costs. (Suver et al., 1992) This serves as an example of an organization not paying heed to the notion that engaging in certain immediate and less costly activities may reduce subsequent costs over time. Even though these preventative activities also may incur higher direct costs, they must be compared with the subsequent cost savings that can be achieved. These activities are the internal aspect of cost reductions; i.e., identifying and correcting failures in the organization before the patient enters into the system for care. (Waress, et al., 1994) Direct costs in prevention activities may include the labor involved with improving operations of the managed care system and raising quality.

EXPECTATION AND NONACHIEVEMENT COSTS

External failures also arise if the external expectations; i.e., the type of care patients expect to receive before entering the system are not met. If the patients are the first to notice and identify problem areas in the organization, such as poor quality of care, there may be serious repercussions, including increased dissatisfaction with the managed care system that would lead to dis-enrollments and subsequent lower revenues. By reducing errors, patient satisfaction with the health care services provided also may increase.

The failure to meet these expectations may be due to what are referred to as "non-achievement costs." (Waress, et al., 1994) Included in these non-achievement costs are:

- Mistakes
- Having to repeat procedures
- Inefficiencies
- Poor planning

The managed care system may have to pay for these mistakes via higher malpractice insurance, higher reimbursement premiums, labor costs associated with handling patient complaints, and the opportunity costs of the lost profits. (Waress, et al., 1994) As a reminder, however, if there is no breakdown in the managed care system due to early detection and correction, then there would be no resources expended on addressing the patients' complaints. (Waress, et al., 1994) Hence, the inverse relationship between preventive and appraisal costs and failure costs.

COSTS OF MEASURING QUALITY OF CARE IN MANAGED CARE SYSTEMS

From the preceeding discussion, it becomes apparent that there are many types of costs to be considered in the delivery and measurement of quality of care in managed health care systems. Paying attention only to the short-term bottomline may be costly in the long run, with insufficient attention to the measurement and improvement of quality may lead to lower profits, a reduction in membership, and competitive position.

In this section, therefore, we discuss methods for measuring quality costs and assessing the economics of engaging in projects that enhance quality, as well as the relevance of data and information, patient satisfaction, and the physician as an input to the quality enhancing process.

Measuring quality costs can be a useful tool in the process of quality improvement. (Waress, et al., 1994) Further, monitoring quality of care costs can serve as a method for determining what factors in the system are highest priorities as well as for identifying specific opportunities for quality improvements. (ibid.)

For example, the Lovelace Health Systems in New Mexico developed a model that distinguishes between activities considered to be investments in quality from the costs associated with not achieving quality. (ibid.) The basic premise of their model is to identify the returns on a quality investment. This included the following steps:

1. Determine whether an investment in quality is in line with the organization's definition of quality
2. Collect a longitudinal profile of quality documents including all quality outlays and investments, and determine how quality improvement impacts the costs of service delivery
3. Assemble the organization's investment in quality and examine the costs of not achieving quality
4. Compare the investment in quality with any savings achieved in quality management
5. Align the quality management changes with external accrediting bodies such as the JCAHO.

It should be noted that these steps involve the internal working of the managed care system and the organization aiming to relate these prevention costs — investments in quality that prevent problems from occurring — with the benefits or the cost savings of improved quality due to a reduction in failure costs. By spending money early in the service delivery process, costly mistakes can be avoided later on.

In order to determine whether or not an investment is valuable to an organization, it is necessary to compare costs expended in the present with benefits realized in the future. Two methods for doing this are cost-effectiveness analysis and net present value (NPV) analysis.

Cost-effectiveness analysis compares the dollar value spent to achieve an outcome; for example, the dollar value per immunization. The objective is to determine the least costly way of providing immunizations to a patient base. This analysis is relevant in meeting an objective with the lowest cost. The essential features of a cost-effectiveness analysis are that (1) the objective is pre-specified, (2) the organization is committed to meeting this objective, and (3) the organization compares the intervention with its next best alternative. (Eddy, 1996)

Net present value analysis converts costs and benefits to dollars and compares the current costs with all present and future benefits. If these future benefits are greater than the costs incurred, then the project is worth pursuing; if not, then the project should be abandoned. However, comparing future benefits with current costs requires discounting in order to account for the fact that dollars in the future are worth less than the same amount of dollars in the present. The formula for the net present value of a project is given as:

$$NPV = B_0 - C_0 + \sum_{t=1}^{T} \frac{B_t - C_t}{(1+i)^t}$$

where: C = costs
   B = benefits
   i = the discount rate,
   t = the time period in the same time units as the discount rate
     (e.g., t = 0 represents now and t = 1 might represent one year from now).

These types of analyses are particularly relevant when comparing immediate cost with subsequent costs and benefits. For example, it always is the case that positive net present values of projects always adds value to the organization. Therefore, if an improvement in quality is associated with lower future costs and more patients remaining in the managed care system then profits will rise. Conversely, if quality improvements are not made, quality of care may not be acceptable and the managed care system could lose market share incur higher subsequent costs with fewer benefits, and hence lose net income. (Weinstein, 1990)

These analyses also can be used in determining whether quality measurement methods themselves are effective. For example, engaging in a study to determine whether data errors exist in coding patient's data may cost more than allowing data errors to persist. An "opportunity cost" rationale for not pursuing such a study could be because the managed care system might be able to use the money allocated for the study to some other activity that would lead to better outcomes for patients and the organization.*

From the previous discussion, it is evident that in order to monitor an activity of quality improvement and to make rational decisions, data-derived information is essential. However, increasing the capacity of an information system also may increase costs due to increased labor costs for oversight, increased management information system costs, increased computer costs, and the increased use of care plans and protocols. (Pryor and Fortin, 1995) Nonetheless, these costs may be well worth the investment, especially if increasing data and information likewise decrease the potential for poor quality. In other words, and in the above terminology and concepts, increasing the information base (preventative costs) may decrease subsequent costs due to internal and external failures if potential quality problems can identified and removed. This is relevant because the performance of a managed care organization is a function of access to care for patients, decreased costs, increased quality of care, and increased patient satisfaction. (Rosenstein, 1991) Hence, managed care organizations need to actively measure and improve outcomes through data-driven internal analysis, of identifying critical issues early and having the ability to either improve or justify results and to advertise successes to potential clients.

---

* An example of this technique will be presented in the case studies section of this chapter.

Some data items that are necessary for this data-driven internal analysis include indicators for increased quality of care such as disease specific morbidity/mortality, infection rates, and surgical complications. Other relevant data items include indicators for utilization defined as length of stay and the number of denied days and indicators for resource management i.e., ancillary services. With better and more real-time data, evaluation of high volume — high cost — high risk procedures can be identified and remedied. (ibid.) Further, if the managed care organization is pursuing quality because of demands by companies who contract with them, then quality and the ability to demonstrate quality, is critical to competitive success. Hence, other data sources include claims data screening, medical record analysis, and quality improvement due to changes in organizational behavior. (Heinen et al., 1993) Note again that this identification can lead to the organization's ability to gauge immediate and subsequent costs and savings.

In order to assess quality performance, the managed care organization, for example, needs to evaluate ambulatory care patterns for evidence of regular monitoring of severity of illness, patient education regarding compliance with medical treatment, patient knowledge of warning signs of disease, as well as provider education on the benefits of cost-effective care. Note that in this sense, quality of care responsibility rests with both providers and patients.

Another type of quality assessment that has been effective is onsite concurrent review rather than simple pre-admission review or utilization review. Onsite concurrent review consists of daily review of a patient while in the hospital to ensure that effective quality care is being provided. Smith and Gotowka (1991) found that this type of review was most effective for more "expensive patient groups" (i.e., patients that require costly care) and that admission rates declined more for patients concurrently reviewed than patients not reviewed, as well as a lower rate of complications for reviewed patients.

Patient satisfaction with managed care systems is becoming a critical measure of quality of care as managed care systems increasingly find themselves competing against each other. (Rice and Gabel, 1996) Ninety-seven percent of all managed care systems undertake patient satisfaction surveys and 97% use these surveys for continuous quality improvement. Issues that have been found to affect patient satisfaction include the amount of out-of-pocket payments a patient must make at the time of service, the appropriateness of the service provided, medical outcomes as well as other service oriented benefits the managed care system provides. (ibid) While quality and satisfaction should not be confused as synonymous, gauging patient satisfaction can help identify problem areas that can be improved, as well as help identify processes which should be monitored to ensure quality does not deteriorate. For example, it has been found that there is a greater burden of illness and greater dissatisfaction in an elderly population that did not receive an influenza vaccine as compared to an elderly population that did receive an influenza vaccine (36.9/1000 vs. 26.3/1000, respectively). (Murray et al., 1996) It also was found that mailing postcard reminders to patients improved their compliance with the vaccine schedules, demonstrating that knowing patient nonmedical data, such as the accuracy of postal addresses, is important. (ibid.)

Expending costs to determine if errors exist in the patient data files, therefore, could result in medical cost savings by increasing patient awareness and preventive treatment which often is less costly than curative care. Because patients spend less money to get the vaccine rather than if they contract the disease, they would be more satisfied with the care provided. This is an example of preventative costs, since the postcard reminders incurred an added cost, but decreased internal failure costs (because there would have been excess costs incurred for treating the illness) and external failure costs because there would have been a loss of client satisfaction. Therefore, if fewer breakdowns in the service delivery process occur, fewer patients would complain and thus fewer resources would be expended addressing these complaints.

Physicians also are important inputs into the quality measurement process. With managed care systems interested in pursuing failure prevention, appraisal and detection activities, getting insights from physicians is important, because they are in the closest contact with the patients. As such, physicians can be valuable both in conveying to patients the notion that quality care and cost containment are possible simultaneously and in determining the effectiveness of medical treatment. This additional responsibility of physicians might be achieved by increasing physician education. For example, in some instances physicians who were educated reduced the use of ancillary services by 10–20%, indicating that costs and quality can be inversely related. (Rosenstein, 1991)

By aligning provider incentives across the entire system, providers have an incentive to provide cost-effective care but under the constraint of quality of care. This change in incentives arises due to changes in the financial risk borne by the provider, thereby increasing accountability, performance documentation, and outcome measurement (Rosenstein, 1994). Hence, with managed care systems, physicians have to become more accountable as well as place a greater emphasis on performance criteria, with providers being held responsible for documenting the outcomes of the health care intervention. Therefore, the economic efficiency gained by capitated payments will determine the total costs involved in patient care, with providers sharing the responsibility to manage patients as efficiently and effectively as possible. (ibid.)

The preceding section discussed the types of costs and benefits of measuring and improving managed care quality. In particular, the facts that pursuing quality may lead to lower rather than higher total costs and that only paying attention to short run accounting costs will not be in the managed care system's best interest were emphasized. In the next section, two case studies illustrate how pursuing a cohesive quality enhancement program will lead to benefits in real dollar terms for managed care systems.

CASE STUDIES*

These case studies illustrate the general application of quality management methods to improve health care processes. The approach of both cases is based on the TQM philosophy of developing an understanding of a system, statistically and otherwise

---

* Various portions of the first case study originally appeared in Benneyan (1996a) and Sloan (1995).

in order to improve quality and reduce costs. In both cases, cost analysis methods are used to help health care managers determine when and where it is — and where it is not — cost effective to inspect or audit in order to reduce internal and external failure costs. While the studies illustrate particular applications, note that these types of problems can arise in virtually any clinical or nonclinical health care process where any type of quality inspection activity — be it a financial audit, medication check, peer review, laboratory screening, or otherwise — does or could exist. In fact, improper quality and inspection methods often can account for as much as 5% of net operating costs and significantly increase clinical liability. For example, considerable savings often are possible by changing from relying on exhaustive reviews and inspections to a quality control philosophy based on statistical analysis. Note that this concept of "inspection" is very broad, and thus the general approach illustrated below is widely applicable for helping health care managers minimize total inspection, appraisal, and failure costs. After some background and a brief review of this method, case studies in a managed care Enrollment and Billing department, laboratories, and other examples illustrate a range of administrative and clinical applications of these concepts. Several additional applications also are suggested below.

INSPECTION COST-EFFECTIVENESS ANALYSIS

One of the fundamental tenets of quality management is to achieve such high quality processes that costly exhaustive reviews and inspections are unnecessary. In fact, one of Deming's key concepts is to build quality into a process in the first place rather than to try to inspect it in after the fact (Deming, 1982):

> "Cease dependence on inspection to achieve quality. Eliminate the need for inspection on a mass basis by building quality into the product in the first place."

While this quote represents an ideal objective, two very important practical questions are

- When should one inspect or not inspect?
- At what point can one cease inspecting?

Fortunately, a simple method exists to help determine where it is and is not cost effective to inspect or audit a process in order to minimize total costs of poor quality (CPQ). This cost-analysis method helps to balance internal appraisal and inspection costs with internal and external failure costs. In many cases, considerable savings are possible by changing from an inspection-oriented mentality to a quality control philosophy based on statistical process control.

This method helps determine the appropriate inspection policy in order to minimize the total expected costs of poor quality. This model also illustrates that anything but 0 or 100% inspection never results in a lower cost policy, despite continued widespread partial sampling practice to the contrary.

ENROLLMENT/BILLING CASE STUDY

Deming's k1/k2 cost minimum method (Deming, 1982) helps determine where inspection steps should and should not exist in any process, based on the costs of poor quality the cost of appraisal, and the impact of failures on the patient. The method selects the least expensive inspection policy between the three general approaches:

- 100% Inspection: Inspect every case for being nonconforming in order to try to ensure that no errors are passed on to an external or internal customer.
- 0% Inspection: Inspect *no* cases in order to save inspection time and money.
- Partial Sampling: Inspect a partial and random sample in order to balance between the above costs.

In many processes, either adding or eliminating inspection steps can result in significant savings. Without going into mathematical detail (*see* Anscome, 1958, Papadakis, 1985, Gitlow et al., 1989, and Benneyan, 1994), another very important result is that, given certain reasonable assumptions, either 0 or 100% inspection always will be optimal. For this reason, the rule sometimes also is referred to as the "all-or-nothing" quality inspection rule. Partial sampling, while intuitively very appealing, never will have a lower total longterm expected cost than the optimal policy. One reason is that historical quality control sampling plans are mostly based on appraisal costs and do not account for the total costs, including the impact of failures on the customer, i.e., direct and indirect external failure costs.

Although this result may be counter-intuitive, it is nonetheless a statistical fact which in some cases can significantly reduce costs and liability. This result is based on several general assumptions and is fairly robust and applicable in a wide range of settings. The expected costs of the three general policies are based on the following inputs and notation:

p: Process fraction nonconforming (assumed stable over time)
k1: The average cost to inspect a single case
k2: The average cost of not detecting a problem
N: The total number of items under consideration in the given time period.

Note that the cost to inspect each case can include labor, time, equipment, overhead, amortization, etc., whereas the cost of not detecting a problem can include the direct internal and external failure costs, rework, scrap, dissatisfied customers, liability, lost market share, etc.

Using this notation, the minimal expected cost inspection policy then easily is determined by comparing the ratio of k1/k2 to p as follows. If,

- k1/k2 ≤ p, then inspect 100% of the cases
- k1/k2 > p, then inspect 0% of the cases.

Additionally, the expected long-term costs of 0% inspection is:

$$\frac{N * k1}{1 - p}$$

and the expected long-term cost of 100% inspection is:

$$\frac{N * p * k2}{1 - p}$$

The following case study illustrates a straight-forward application of the above cost minimization method to a typical managed health care administration process, and the second case study extends these concepts to clinical applications, namely laboratory screening for cervical and breast cancer.

When new members join or leave a particular managed care system, all member applications, terminations, and reenrollments are entered into a computer system manually in an enrollment and billing department. Due to a high rate of data entry errors, all work traditionally then was 100% checked for data entry errors. This end-of-the-line inspection activity consumes time and delays the process until a newly enrolled member can book an appointment in the computer appointment system. This resulted in additional prevention, internal failure, and non-achievement costs and in low satisfaction with the enrollment process by patients and major employer groups. In other words, the managed care system incurs non-achievement costs due to internal failure. (Figure 1)

By using quality management and various basic statistical quality control tools described in other chapters and elsewhere (Montgomery, 1991, Duncan, 1986, Benneyan, 1996b, Benneyan and Kaminsky, 1995, Laffel and Blumenthal, 1989, and Sloan, 1995), data entry accuracy was improved from approximately 8% error to less than 0.5%. For example, Pareto and control charts helped identify and quantify causes of keying errors, and scatter plots and regression analysis were used to investigate possible causes of these errors. (Benneyan, 1996b) As a result of these improvements, additionally, the end-of-the-line quality control inspection now probably was less justified by its time, expenses, and questionable effectiveness.

Deming's "k1/k2" inspection cost analysis method, described above, therefore, was used to determine if the end-of-the-line inspection was no longer cost-effective. That is, given the reduced error rate, what now is the best inspection policy to minimize the overall cost of poor quality? As shown below, this cost-effectiveness analysis revealed that significant savings now were possible by eliminating this costly end-of-the-line inspection activity altogether. As a result of the process improvements and the k1/k2 cost analysis, this step was removed, together saving approximately $120,000 per year and helping to significantly reduce turn-around-time.

Using the above notation, the following figures were estimated and entered into the k1/k2 formulas. The fraction of data entry errors had decreased to approximately

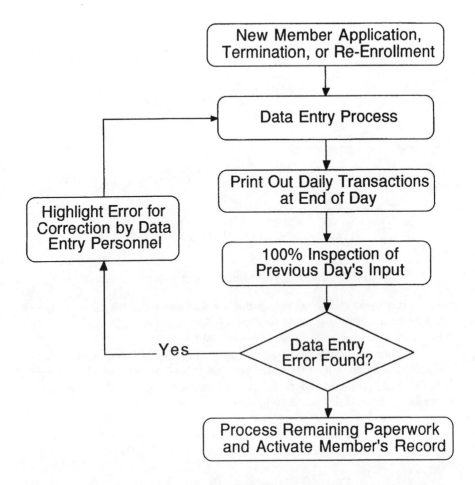

FIGURE 1   Flow diagram of an enrollment data entry process wtih end-of-the-line inspection.

$p = 0.005$ and the average cost to inspect a single involve was estimated at $k1 = \$0.52$. Due to a recent merger, approximately 12,500 transactions may be processed monthly, or approximately $N = 150,000$ per year. Note that the exact cost of not detecting a data entry error is tougher to estimate due to intangible external failure costs such as customer inconvenience and dissatisfaction (i.e., intangible costs). However, a lower bound on the tangible rework costs (e.g., reprocessing time, postage, materials) was estimated at $k2 \geq \$0.58$. Using these estimates, then

$$k1/k2 = \$0.52/\$0.58 = 0.897 \geq p = 0.0005.$$

The criteria given above therefore indicates that 0% inspection is the optimal policy. Given that, the k2 cost of a data entry error is not known with certainty, Figure 2 plots the annual cost of each of the three inspection policies (0% inspection, 100% inspection, and partial sampling) in order to examine a range of possible k2

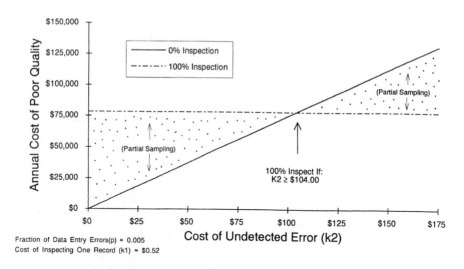

FIGURE 2   Graphic representation of three inspection policies.

costs. As this figure shows, supposing that a reasonable range for k2, — including customer dissatisfaction — might be anywhere less than $104, eliminating the end-of-line inspection clearly could save considerable costs.

In fact, the possible savings achieved by switching policies quickly can be obtained by computing the differences between these cost functions. For example, using the above estimates and the formulas given above, the annual cost of keeping vs. removing the end-of-line 100% inspection are:

$$\text{Cost of 100\% Inspection} = (N*k1)/(1-p)$$
$$= (150,000*\$0.52)/(1-0.005) = \$78,391.60$$

$$\text{Cost of 0\% Inspection} = (N*p*k2)/(1-p)$$
$$= (150,000*0.005*\$0.58)/(1-0.005) = \$437.19$$

The annual savings which would be possible by removing this inspection step therefore is:

$$\text{Savings by Switching Inspection Policies}$$
$$= 100\% \text{ Inspection Cost} - 0\% \text{ Inspection Cost}$$
$$= \$78,391.60 - \$437.19$$
$$= \$77,954.77 \text{ per year.}$$

In other words, the end-of-the-line inspection can be viewed as a nonvalue activity that if eliminated reduced costs with no discernible effect on the quality of care provided by this managed care system. In this case, the immediate savings of almost $78,000 annually equates to approximately 5% of the net operating cost of

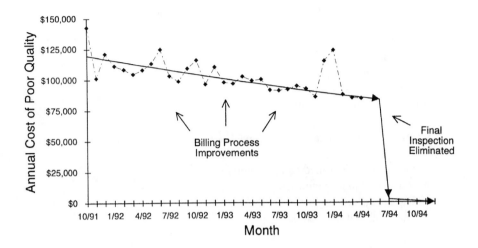

FIGURE 3

the process, which is not uncommon in a variety settings and industries. Figure 3 summarizes the annualized combined savings of approximately $120,000 due to a combination of incremental process and the later elimination of the costly-end-of-the-line inspection. Note that even before removing the 100% inspection, an investment in quality resulted in approximately $42,000 savings per year, demonstrating that incremental continual improvement increased quality and reduced costs as Deming theorized. Moreover, recent dramatic increases in membership and market share, as well as the increased capacity now to handle volumes from other divisions of the health care network, suggest that the eventual annual savings could more than double.

FINANCIAL CONTROL CHARTS

It is important to note that the selection of 0 or 100% inspection is for the purpose of minimizing total costs given current quality levels. Even if 100% inspection is eliminated, periodic small random samples still should be plotted on a statistical control chart in order to detect if the process deteriorates and to ensure that 0% inspection remains the minimum cost policy. Note that, as shown below, this approach incurs a small amount of appraisal and prevention costs in order to avoid larger future failure costs.

OTHER HEALTHCARE AND LABORATORY APPLICATIONS: PAP SMEARS AND MAMMOGRAPHY

This success led to the identification of similar possible administrative and clinical applications in several other departments, within the same managed care organization, with the total potential annual savings simply by switching to the most cost-effective inspection policy exceeding $600,000 per year.

Some of the potential administrative applications include:

- Medical records
- Internal Audit
- Cash Handling
- Accounts receivable
- Outside utilization authorization.

Several clinical applications also have been identified, including the accuracy of:

- Prescription and medication accuracy
- Radiology and mammography
- Pap smear reading
- Other laboratory results.

In clinical applications, the cost of an error includes patient health and liability, with savings including significant reductions in unnecessarily lost lives. This is especially true in clinical laboratories, where ensuring the earliest detection of disease, both at minimum possible costs and accounting for the possibility of human error, is critical. For example, all of these laboratory or diagnostic procedures can be thought of as inspection-type of activities which could question when, and how may many times, to review ("inspect") a specimen for indications of a particular medical condition. As one example, mammograms sometimes are screened by a technician with subsequent radiologist verification of results. Additional possible diagnostic applications include screening for colorectal cancer, prostate cancer, breast cancer, and others.

Another important example is the reading of Pap smears to detect cervical cancer. Although the cure rates for cervical and breast cancer generally are high if detected in early stages, treatment is considerably less successful when allowed to progress undetected. For example, breast cancer is the number one cancer-related cause of death among females in the U.S., and over 200,000 preventable cervical cancer related deaths occur per year worldwide.

Benneyan and Kaminsky (1996), therefore, recently developed similar methods to that described in the preceding section (although somewhat more complicated mathematically) in order to help identify the most cost-effective number of screenings and re-screening rate in these laboratory settings. Using these results, analysis somewhat similar in concept to that above recently has shown that significant improvements are possible via alternative quality policies than those currently mandated by the Clinical Laboratory Improvement Amendments Act (CLIA) of 1988. For example, Figure 4 illustrates one situation where four multiple evaluations of every Pap smear actually results in the minimal total cost, due to a high cost of not detecting cervical cancer (i.e., high external failure costs).

Similar to the k1/k2 analysis method, these results also show that the optimal policy always will employ either 0 or 100% re-screening by one or more lab technicians. That is, in no case will any amount of partial laboratory rescreening

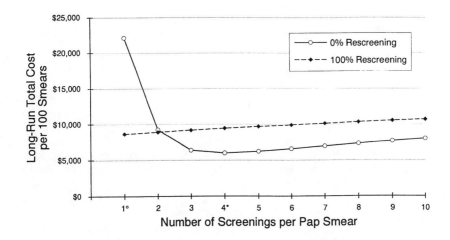

FIGURE 4

result in the most cost-effective nor the most efficient laboratory policy, with other options always producing more accurate and less costly results. This is a very significant result in light of current practices and requirements to the contrary. Related methods also are being used to identify the most effective and efficient mammography policies and to determine optimal cutoff points in testing for HIV and hepatitis.

COSTS VS. BENEFITS

It is important to note that in each of the above examples, the benefits of improving quality easily justified the costs of collecting data, conducting analysis, designing prevention systems, etc. In the enrollment process, for example, the estimated total expenses were approximately $2,600 per year in current and future costs for the work team to improve the process and collect and review data, monitor the process over time. In the laboratory applications, although developing the cost analysis methodology took over a year of research, collecting, and analyzing the data necessary to apply this method in any particular application now can be conducted within one–four weeks, with demonstrated results-to-date ranging from several hundred thousand dollars to several million in annual savings, dependent on case-specific estimates the size of the particular facility.

In order to account for the time value of money, the costs vs. benefits of these quality projects also can be evaluated by applying the earlier net present value formula. For example, in the enrollment process assuming the end-of-year costs and benefits shown in Table 1 and an annual discount rate of $i = 0.05$, then at the start of this project in July 1991 the NPV (in 1991 dollars) over the first five years was approximately $266,606.15.

TABLE 1
Approximate Costs and Benefits of Enrollment Quality Improvement Project

$$NPV = B_0 - C_0 + \sum_{t=1}^{4} \frac{(B_t - C_t)}{(1+i)^t} \approx \$266,606.15$$

Year	Time Period	t	Cost (C$_t$)*	Benefit (B$_t$)*	C$_t$–B$_t$	(1 + i)^t	Present Value (in 1991 $$)
1	7/91–6/92	0	$2,600	$14,000	$11,400	1	$11,400
2	7/92–6/93	1	$2,600	$28,000	$25,400	1.05	$24.190.48
3	7/93–6/94	2	$5,600 ($2,600 + $3,000)	$42,000	$36,400	1.1025	$33,015.87
4	7/94–6/95	3	$2,600	$120,000 ($42,000+$78,000	$117,400	1.1576	$101,414.53
5	7/95–6/96	4	$2,600	$120,000	$117,400	1.2155	$96,585,27

* Assuming costs remain the same over time.

5 Year NPV ≈ $266,606.15 (in 1991 dollars)

Similarly, McGuckin and Abrutyn (1979) found that collecting, measuring, maintaining, and analyzing quality control data for infection control "required less than one hour per day for 700 beds, and permitted prompt recognition of two outbreaks" (i.e., appraisal and prevention costs), whereas Evans (1991) estimated that "the average 250 bed hospital loses $1 million a year because of nosocomial infections ... on average, a surgical wound infection adds a week to the patient's hospital stay," i.e., external failure costs. Other estimates have suggested an average increase in hospital costs of approximately $14,000 per surgical wound infection, not to mention the pain, suffering, and occasional deaths that result. (Koska, 1992) Clearly, in this case the external failure costs far outweigh the appraisal and detection costs. Benneyan (1996b) further discusses the application of quality control methods to infection control and other epidemiology concerns, as well as a (more complex) method for identifying the minimum total cost quality measurement and control charting system to use in any given infection control application.

SUMMARY

Total quality management and total cost management are effective techniques which should be used in managed care to balance and reduce long-term total costs of quality. Sound cost-effective methods should be designed and implemented which ensure the ability to efficiently prevent or detect quality problems, of any kind, at overall minimum cost. As shown by the precedding examples, use of these methods can result in significant reductions in total costs and increases in overall quality. For example, the enrollment and billing department has eliminated unnecessary work, streamlined key processes, replaced frustrating work with more meaningful work, and significantly reduced cost and turn-around-time with fewer resources. Similarly, significant improvements in ability to detect cervical cancer and reductions in total costs are possible by changing the current mandated Pap smear inspection policy.

As seen by the above discussion and case-study example, it is possible to reduce costs without compromising quality of care. However, this endeavor involves several parties — the managed care organization's management, physicians, medical and other personnel, and patients. It also involves gathering information and designing plans and strategies that encompass the totality of care and costs, not just short run or internal accounting costs. TQM and TCM, as illustrated herein, is a much sounder approach to managing health care quality and costs, be it for administrative, clinical, nonclinical, or laboratory processes. This framework can be used to make rational decisions and to illustrate that the objectives of quality of care and cost containment are not particularly at odds.

REFERENCES

Anscombe, F. J. "Rectifying Inspection of a Continuous Output*" Journal of the American Statistical Association* 53, 702–719, 1958.

Benneyan, J. C. and Kaminsky, F. C. "Another View on How to Measure Healthcare Quality," *Quality Process*, 18 (2): 120–124, 1995.

Benneyan, J. C. *Applying Deming's k1/k2 Inspection Cost Minimization Rule: A Tutorial*, Technical paper, IE94-14C, Industrial Engineering and Operations Research, University of Massachusetts, Amherst, MA, 1994.

Benneyan, J. C. "Improving Healthcare Using SPC and Quality Engineering: Billing Laboratory Case Studies" *Healthcare Information and Management Systems Society Conf. Trans.*, 1996a.

Benneyan, J. C. "Statistical Quality Control in Infection Control and Hospital Epidemiology." Two-part series, *Infection Control and Hospital Epidemiology*, 1996b.

Benneyan, J. C. and Kaminsky, F. C. "Statistical and Economic Models for Analysis and Optimal Design of Laboratory Screening Policies for Cervical Cancer" *Annals of Operations Research*, in press.

Deming, W. E., *Quality, Productivity, and Competitive Position*. MIT Center for Advanced Engineering Study, Cambridge, MA, 1982.

Duncan, A. J. *Quality Control and Industrial Statistics*, fifth edition, Irwin, Homewood, IL, 1986.

Eddy, D. "Benefit Language — Criteria That Will Improve Quality While Reducing Costs." *Journal of the American Medical Association*, 275 (8): 650–657,1996.

Evans, G. "Infection Control Staffing: Is One ICP for 250 beds Enough?" *Hospital Infection Control*, 18 (16): 17–79, 1991.

Evans, J. G. and Lindsay, W. M. *The Management and Control of Quality*, second edition. Est Publishing Co., Minneapolis, MN, 1993.

Heinen, L., Peterson, E., Pion, K., and S. Leatherman. "Quality Evaluation in a Managed Care System: Comparative Data to Assess Health Plan Performance" *Managed Care Quarterly*, I (l) 62–76, 1993.

Inhorn, S. "Quality Assurance and Quality Control in Clinical Cytology... 11." *Compendium on Quality Assurance, Proficiency Testing and Workload Limitations in Clinical Cytology* 1995

Juran, J. M. and Gryna, F. M. *Juran's Quality Control Handbook*, fourth edition, McGraw–Hill, New York, 1988.

Koska, M.T. "Using CQI Methods to Lower Post-Surgical Wound Infection Rate," *Hospitals*, 66 (9): 62–64, 1992.

Laffel, G. and Blumenthal, D. "The Case of Using Industrial Quality Management Science in Healthcare Organizations." *Journal of the American Medical Association*, 262 (20): 2869–2873, 1989.

Mango, L. "Quality Assurance and Quality Control in Clinical Cytology... 11." *Compendium on Quality Assurance, Proficiency Testing and Workload Limitations in Clinical Cytology* 1995.

Marone, W.J., et al. "Nosocomial Infection Rates for Interhospital Comparison: Limitations and Possible Solutions." *Infection Control and Hospital Epidemiology*, 12 (10): 609–621, 1991.

McGuckin, M. B. and Abrutyn, E. "A Surveillance Method for Early Detection of Nosocomial Outbreaks." *American Journal of Infection Control*, 7: 18–21, 1979.

Mone, L. "Managed Care Cost Effectiveness: Fantasy or Reality?" *International Journal of Group Psychotherapy*, 44 (4): 437–448, 1994.

Montgomery, D. C. *Introduction to Statistical Quality Control*, second edition. Wiley, New York, 1991.

Murray, J., Hanchak, N., and Schlackman, N. "Health Services Research at U.S. Quality Algorithms" *Medical Care Research and Review* 53 (Supplemental) S104-Sl17, March, 1996.

Neave, H.R. *The Deming Dimension*. SPC Press, Knoxville, TN, 1990.

Palmer, R., Donabedian, A., and Povar G. *Striving for Quality in Healthcare*. Health Administration Press, Ann Arbor, MI, 1991,

Papadakis, E. "The Deming Inspection Criterion for Choosing Between Zero or 100 Percent Inspection." *Journal of Quality Technology*, 17 (3): 121–127, 1985.

Pryor, D. and Fortin. D. "Managing the Delivery of Health Care: Care-Plans/Managed Care/Practice Guidelines" *International Journal of Bio-Medical Computing*, 39: 105–109, 1995.

Rice, T. and Gabel, J. "The Internal Economics of HMOs: A Research Agenda,." *Medical Care Research and Review*, 53 (Supplemental) S104-Sl17, March, 1996.

Rosenstein, A. "Financial Risk, Accountability, and Outcome Management: Using Data to Manage and Measure Clinical Performance. *America Journal of Medical Quality*, 9 (3): 116–121, 1994.

Rosenstein, A. "Utilization Review Health Economics and Cost-Effective Resource Management." *American Journal of Medical Quality*, 6 (3): (85–90, 1991.

Sloan, M. D., ed. *Success Stories on Lowering Healthcare Costs by Improving Healthcare Quality*. APPC Press, Milwaukee, WI. 1995.

Smith, D. and Fortin, D. "Managing the Delivery of Health Care: Care-Plans/Managed Care/Practice Guidelines" *International Journal of Bio-medical Computing*, 39: 105–109, 1995.

Suver, J., Neumann, B., and Boles, K. "Accounting for the Costs of Quality" *Healthcare Financial Management*, 46 (9): 29–37.

Walton, M. *The Deming Management Method*. Pedigree Books, New York, 1986.

Waress, B., Pasternak, D., and Smith, H. "Determining Costs Associated with Quality in Healthcare Delivery" *Healthcare Management Review*, 19 (3): 52–63, 1994.

Weinstein, M. "Principles of Cost-Effective Resource Allocation in Healthcare Organizations." *International Journal of Technical Assessment in Healthcare*, 6: 93–103, 1990.

Wilson, L. and Goldschmidt, P. *Quality Management in Health Care*. McGraw–Hill, Sydney, 1995.

12 Managed Care Accreditations and Certifications

William P. Gideon

CONTENTS

INTRODUCTION

Managed care accreditations and certifications are the first major steps in addressing the current public perceptions concerning managed care ethics and economics. The rise of managed care has signaled the beginning of a period of profound transformation in the health care delivery system. The changes raise many ethical questions regarding the values that should guide the broad formulation of health policy. A major question concerns the conflict between the traditional values of patient benefit and autonomy and the values of economic self-interest, profit-taking, and economic efficiency. It often is perceived that the contract of primacy is the one between the employer and the managed care organization, not the contract between patient and physician. *Chicago Tribune* reporters, Ronald Kotulak and Peter Gorner wrote about a HMO that approved amputation of a patient's infected leg instead of skin grafts and antibiotics based on the least cost option. Business-related goals, such as shareholder profit, physician bonuses, and extravagant executive or physician salaries, find little basis within the ethics of health care delivery. (ACOG, 1996) The public is troubled by stories of the chairman of U.S. Healthcare reaping $1 billion in stock and cash from a buy out by Aetna Life & Casualty Co. (*Chicago Tribune*, 1996).

1-57444-073-X/97/$0.00+$.50
© 1998 by CRC Press LLC

Currently there are few outcomes-oriented or quality assessment data available on managed care organizations. Managed care organizations are beginning to report on their care to employers and payers. A major method is through HEDIS. This process involves in-depth data collection on the association between specific practices and outcomes. Managed care organizations will produce these only for compelling reasons, such as continuous quality improvement initiatives or for accreditation requirements imposed internally or externally. (*Women's Health Issues*, 1996) The Joint Commission on the Accreditation of Health care Organizations (JCAHO) announced plans to release the National Library of Healthcare Indicators (NLHI) in late 1997. These performance indicators will be in three categories: (1) clinical conditions arrayed against performance, (2) functional health status arrayed against performance, (3) and satisfaction of patients/enrollees, practitioners, and purchasers. A national panel of individuals with expertise in managed care narrowed the initial indicator group from 900 to about 200 indicators having face validity. The first publication will include measures from the Agency for Health care Policy and Research, the National Committee for Quality Assurance, Northwestern University, the Primary care Outcomes Research Institute, Kaiser Permanente, and others. (*Network News*, Issue Two, 1996)

ACCREDITATION AND CERTIFICATION STRUCTURES

Large organizations currently providing managed care accreditation and certification include the National Committee for Quality Assurance (NCQA), the Accreditation Association for Ambulatory Health care (AAAHC), JCAHO, the Healthcare Financing Administration (HCFA), and the International Organization for Standardization (ISO-9000). Several regional bodies with less comprehensive and costly review also have appeared. A late entry in the race is the Utilization Review Accreditation Commission (URAC) are currently beta-testing newly adopted network standards. The general processes for the accrediting organizations involved include multiple variations on guidelines, planning, self-study tools, presurvey format, survey format and reporting of results. An entity's specific accreditation and certification process reveals their focus and scope with respect to the elements and features of a managed care program. Each individual standards define performance levels and provide a measurement for the weight a review entity places on any given element.

NATIONAL COMMITTEE FOR QUALITY ASSURANCE

The NCQA is a Washington-based private, not-for-profit organization that assesses and reports on the quality of managed care plans. It is governed by a board of directors that includes representatives from organized medicine (AMA), health plans, quality experts, regulators, employers, consumers, and labor. The mission statement emphasizes the provision of information that enables purchasers and consumers of managed health care to rank plans based on quality. Typically HMOs, including POS plans and some PHOs and PPOs, also may qualify.

NCQA accreditation evaluates how well a health plan manages both providers (e.g., physicians, hospitals, carve outs) and administrative services. It is a process-oriented approach with an emphasis on governance and procedures. Accreditation standards address practice in six different areas: (1) quality improvement, (2) physician credentialling, (3) members' rights and responsibilities, (4) preventive health services, (5) utilization management, and (6) medical records. A weighted scoring system recognizes that certain standards are more important than others.

NCQA has several process indicators relating to women's health care: first-trimester care, regular mammography screening for women 40 and older, Pap tests for women 18 and older, and low birthweight. (NCQA, 1993 draft) A need for process indicators is well illustrated in a Twin Cities HMO study. A study of the mammography and the Pap indicators showed that ob–gyn physicians were more likely to do preventive gynecological services than were internist and family practitioners combined. (Laurie et al., 1993) Rates for female practitioners were higher than those of male colleagues but below the rates for ob–gyn physicians of either sex. The value of the indicators is not controversial. Specialty difference in their provision is troubling. (Burg and Lane, 1992)

An accreditation review is a voluntary process requested by an employer. The health plan submits to an offsite and an onsite review by a team of surveyors consisting of physicians and quality experts. These reviews consist of: review of written documentation from the health plan, site observation of two to four days, health plan employee interviews by the surveyors, a medical record review and assessment of patients complaints, education and services. Surveyors perform a multiday site visit at the health plan's headquarters. The review consists of staff interviews, record review and consultation with employees. The team prepares a written report with recommendations for the NCQA's Review Oversight Committee. As the final step, the committee reviews the reports and makes an accreditation determination — full, one-year, provisional, or denial.

The other side of the NCQA coin is performance measurement. To fulfill the measurement need, NCQA has developed a standard performance measurement set (HEDIS), and an audit process to assure HEDIS credibility. The HEDIS measures will be collected into a national database called Quality Compass to allow bench-marking, comparison, and analysis by users. For the time being it should be noted that the Quality Compass database is from unaudited HEDIS data. Unaudited data is the usual basis of report cards that individual plans have released. Currently more than 330 health plans are producing some HEDIS statistics. The lessons learned from implementation include the need for auditing, benchmarking and analysis of HEDIS data. HEDIS 2.0/2.5 includes 60 standard statistics focusing on clinical quality, access and satisfaction, plan financial performance, general plan manage-ment, membership and utilization. Plan performance measurement such as average obstetrical hospital stays, immunization rates, and medical loss ratios are included. A version of HEDIS for Medicaid has been released and a HEDIS 3.0 draft was completed by the end of 1996. The developers of HEDIS 3.0 are including public purchasers and consumer representatives. HEDIS 3.0 includes both a reporting set of measures and a testing set. Health plans were expected to report data for measures in the reporting set by 1997. It also includes a description of a set of issues needing further research. NCQA also plans to use a standardized survey of members health care that incorporates the best questions from existing satisfaction surveys. The survey requires a random sample of plan members adjusted for differences in population health. NCQA has released draft accreditation standards for managed behavioral managed care organizations (MBHOs) and began reviewing MBHOs in early 1997

The national NCQA Oversight Committee may award one of the four accreditation decisions to a health plan. Full accreditation is for three years and is synonymous with excellent continuous quality improvement. One-year accreditation is given to those plans that meet most of NCQA standards. Recommendations are provided to the plan and a review is conducted after a year to determine if adequate progress has been made to move to a full accreditation status. Provisional accreditation is granted for one year with adequate quality improvement. These plans must demonstrate progress before qualifying for a higher level of accreditation. Denial is given to plans with significant noncompliance with NCQA standards and in which NCQA identifies a risk to quality of care.

NCQA Accreditation Summary Reports (ASRs) are available on each health plan with a full review as of July 1, 1995, and any rereview that results from those full reviews. The first page of the ASR will describe the specific plan, the type of delivery system (e.g., staff model or IPO, the type of business (e.g., for -profit), the number of enrollees, and the year established. The back page of the ASR will show the specific plan score as compared to an overall plan average in each of the six standard categories. A pilot report card from the NCQA on 21 managed-care plans in 1995 uncovered wide ranges of performances. For example, the average hospital days per 1,000 enrollees varied among the plans from 140 to 814 for enrollees ages 44–65. For the first time HEDIS results were compared with a benchmark figure. (Gardner, 1995) NCQA accreditation is sought for a variety of reasons. Some are seeking a competitive edge; many want independent confirmation of the adequacy of their quality improvement systems. Other plans are mandated by major purchasers (GE, IBM, PepsiCo, UPS, Xerox), by states (Pennsylvania, Florida, South Carolina), or by the plan's corporate offices to seek accreditation

There has been criticism of the NCQA relating to cost, administrative burden relating to the paper trail for each of the six areas of standards. Individual provider with several different health plans must respond to credentialling requirements and documentation for each health plan. Criticism also centers on possible hindering of competition. Only well established HMOs can comply easily with NCQA standards. Do NCQA standards drive some HMOs out of business and hinder the development of new ones? NCQA's high cost and new market opportunities are allowing the growth of other accreditation body competitors.

In summary, as of early 1997 close to half of the nation's 636 HMOs had been reviewed by NCQA. It now is receiving approximately 5,000 requests per month for the free accreditation status list, which shows plans alphabetically and by state. The Accreditation Summary Reports provide even more detailed information by illustrating how an individual plan scores against a plan average in each category of standards. Detailed information is available from:

NCQA
2000 L Street, NW, Suite 500
Washington, DC 20036
Telehone; 202/955-3530
Fax: 202/955-3531
Web page: http://www.ncqa.org.

THE ACCREDITATION ASSOCIATION
FOR AMBULATORY HEALTH CARE

The Accreditation Association for Ambulatory Health Care, Inc. (AAAHC) of Skokie, Illinois, was established in 1979. It is a not-for-profit nongovernmental national accrediting organization for ambulatory health care organization that has accredited more than 450 ambulatory health care organizations, including single, and multspecialty group practices, imaging centers, radiation oncology centers, ambulatory and office-based surgery centers, college and university health services, health maintenance organization and other managed care systems, dental group practitioners, community health centers, and occupational health centers. It receives professional guidance and financial support form the American Academy of Facial Plastic and Reconstructive Surgery, American College of Occupational and Environmental Medicine. American Society for Dermatologic Surgery, American Society of Outpatient Surgeons, Association of Freestanding Radiation Oncology Centers, Federated Ambulatory Surgery Association, the Outpatient Ophthalmic Surgery Society, American Academy of Dental Group Practice, American College Health Association, Medical Group Management Association, and the National Association of Community Health Centers.

An organization is eligible for an accreditation survey if it meets nine criteria outlined in the accreditation handbook. If a survey is conducted and it is found the standards do not apply, the survey will be deemed a consultation. Most standards are written in general terms unless the acceptable methods of achieving compliance are limited. The core standards are entitled: Rights of Patients, Governance, Administration, Quality of Care Provided, Quality Management and Improvement, Clinical Records, Professional Improvement, and Facilities and Environment. The core standards apply to all organizations desiring a survey. The adjunct chapters are applied as appropriate to the services provided by the organization. Reference is often made in the handbook to specific standards or documents of other organizations.

AAAHC expects substantial compliance with applicable standards. Compliance is assessed through at least one of the following means: documented evidence, answers concerning implementation or onsite observations and interviews by surveyors. Use of nonphysician health practitioners does not result in noncompliance if the activities specifically are authorized or mandated by state law. The survey process is a combination of evaluation, education, and consultation. Health care practitioners and administrators used as surveyors are in active practice in ambulatory care settings. Surveyors are physicians, nurses, dentists, and administrators selected and trained by AAAHC. Extensive preparation prior to the survey allows the surveyors to gather information with minimal disruption of clinical and administrative duties. The surveyors hold a summation conference for the governing body, medical staff, and administration to allow comment on or to rebut findings, as well as comment on their perception of the survey. The length of the onsite visit and the numbers of surveyors is determined by the type, size and range of services offered by the organization. The final accreditation decision is made by the Accreditation Committee of the Board of Directors. The degree and number of standard noncompliance as well as the weight of the deficiency are considered.

Organizations or individuals may obtain free survey forms by writing to Accreditation Association for Ambulatory Health Care, Inc., 993 Lawler Ave., Skokie, IL 60077-3708. There is a fee for the *Self-Assessment Manual* and *Presurvey Questionnaire*, as well as for the *Handbook. The Application for Accreditation Survey* requires an organization to certify its compliance with survey eligibility criteria and its willingness to comply with AAAHC policies and procedures. The *Self-Assessment Manual* is an optional tool that follows the same format used by AAAHC surveyors in completing a *Survey Report Form*. It allows a staff to go through a mock type survey and to identify potential weaknesses. The *Presurvey Questionnaire* allows AAAHC to assess the governing structure, the scope of health care services offered and to request clarification if needed prior to survey. The *Survey Report Form* contains the survey finding, recommendations, and consultative comments. The organization surveyed also completes a survey evaluation form to evaluate the survey, the fairness of the standards and the value of the consultation.

The fee is based on the onsite number of surveyors and the number of days required to complete the survey. The survey fee must be paid 30 days prior to survey, unless prohibited by law. With cancellation less than eight weeks prior to survey, the requesting organization will be billed for cost in preparing for the survey along with a cancellation fee. After a mutually agreeable survey date is determined, AAAHC will send the confirmation date(s) of the survey, the names(s) of the surveyors, and other information including the survey schedule.

The accreditation survey includes a review of all aspects of the organization, any subunit seeking accreditation or any closely related separate patient care organization(s) as determined by the AAAHC staff. For example, when an ambulatory surgical center is surveyed, a related medical practice medical records would be reviewed, but accreditation would be conferred on the ambulatory surgical center. AAAHC will review a subunit when the subunit exhibits autonomous characteristics. A surgical unit might be part of a larger health clinic legal entity, then either the entire entity or the surgical unit might seek accreditation if it exhibits autonomous characteristics.

Organizations with multiple service sites may elect to have all service sites visited or to have a representative sampling in order to control costs. IPA and network model HMOs are surveyed using a sampling methodology that combines visitations to selected primary care provider sites with a review of a sampling of the HMO enrollees medical records. The sample selection is made by the AAAHC staff in consultation with the HMO. AAAHC requires that a notice of the date(s) of survey be posted four weeks prior to the visit to allow interested individuals or groups to comment. Unintentional failure to post the notice will result in a survey without an accreditation decision. The organization has three months in which to post the notice. If interested individuals request the opportunity to comment, a surveyor will be sent at the surveyed organization's expense to receive the information. Comments are taken verbally at the time of survey in a session chaired by an AAAHC surveyor and attended by at least one representative of the surveyed organization. A request for presenting information during the onsite survey must be made at least two weeks before the survey date(s) Comments also can be made by writing or by telephone to the AAAHC's headquarters.

After the onsite survey, the AAAHC staff members review the survey report, overall recommendations, and any other relevant information and make a recommendation to the Accreditation Committee of the AAAHC. The Accreditation Committee reviews each survey report, surveyor and staff recommendations and other relevant information. The decision of the Accreditation Committee is the final step. A three-year accreditation is awarded if an organization is in substantial compliance with the standards. A one-year accreditation is awarded when the organization's commitment to compliance with the standards does not have an established track record. In some instances, AAAHC may conclude that the surveyed organization may request a special onsite review within one year without payment of an additional application fee. A deferred accreditation decision occurs when an organization is in less than substantial compliance with one or more standards, but has the resources to correct the deficiencies within six months. In such cases the organization my request another onsite survey. This request must be made within six months of the deferral decision, otherwise the organization will be deemed nonaccredited.

Denial of accreditation results when an organization is not in substantial compliance with the standards. Organizations denied accreditation or whose accreditation is revoked, may apply at the time of such decision for resurvey. An appeals procedure is outlined in Appendix B, "Appeal of Accreditation Decision" in the *Handbook*. Notification of the accreditation decision is by mail to the chief medical executive and the administrator of the organization.

An accredited organization is subject to resurvey with or without advance notice at the discretion of the AAAHC at no cost to the surveyed organization. Lack of substantial compliance will result in revocation of accreditation. To maintain accreditation, an organization must undergo a regular survey at least once every three years. The accreditation survey application and the presurvey questionnaire must be completed again four months in advance of the expiration date to allow the survey to occur within three months of the expiration date. In some instances a modified survey smaller in scope may be performed if there has been little change in the physical plant or in the scope of services. Transfer of accreditation does not occur automatically when the organization changes ownership or control. It is a mandatory requirement that the AAAHC must be advised within 30 days of such change to allow the Accreditation Committee to review the circumstances; otherwise accreditation will be lost.

The AAAHC will publish lists of accredited organizations periodically. Information relating to receipt of application for survey, the status of the decision process or the final decision is available on request. Unless required by law, the AAAHC will not release information on organizations without the written authorization of the surveyed organization.

Consultative nonaccreditation surveys are available to organizations seeking assistance in standards interpretation, preparing for accreditation, or in achieving compliance with specific standards. The organization must be in current operation, consultation cannot be part of a preconstruction or preopening planning. Fees for consultative visits are based on the number days onsite and the number of surveyors. A survey variation is found in California. All AAAHC surveys are performed in cooperation with the California Medical Association (CMA). The surveys are part of the CMA–AAAHC Ambulatory Review Program. One of the member of the AAAHC team will be CMA physician trained by the AAAHC. There is also a significant educational and consultative component that allow compliance with the *CMA Guidelines for Ambulatory care Review.* For further information about the California guidelines, call the CMA at 415/882-5168.

The AAAHC has applied to the Health care Financing Administration (HCFA) to be granted deemed status for accreditation of ambulatory surgery centers (ASCs). Deemed status would allow organizations with AAAHC–Medicare survey to meet Medicare conditions of participation without further inspection by the state health agency. The additional Medicare standards can be found at the end of certain specific chapters in the *Handbook.* The additional standards relate to facilities and environment, surgical services, pharmaceutical services, diagnostic imaging services and compliance with the provisions of the 1985 NFPA Life Safety Code applicable to ambulatory surgery centers. The Medicare-AAAHC survey will be an *unannounced* survey. The regular AAAHC surveys will be on an announced basis. (*Accreditation Handbook*, 1996–1997 Edition).

THE JOINT COMMISSION ON ACCREDITATION OF HEALTHCARE ORGANIZATIONS

In the early 1990s, JCAHO initially had a small response to its initial offering in managed care accreditation. The response probably was based on a business world assumption that JCAHO, an accreditation organization founded in the 1950s by health care providers, was dominated by health care providers. JCAHO had left the field to NCQA, but has returned. The new Joint Commission network accreditation standards, released in 1994, were developed in collaboration with more than 100 health care professionals and managed care experts. The program is supported by the Professional and Technical Advisory Committee (PTAC), composed of 20 experts in the managed care field representing health care professional organizations, consumer organizations, business groups, government entities and insurance companies.

The standards measure quality of patient care at the headquarters level, at the component level and at the health care practitioner level. General accreditation areas of concern reflect on: the continuum of care, the management of doctors, nurses and other staff, preventive care, the rights of patients, and the procedures for measuring and improving the quality of care. The network standards focus on seven functional areas: (1) rights, responsibilities, and ethics, (2) continuum of care, (3) education and communication, (4) leadership, (5) management of human resources, (6) management of information, and (7) improving network performance. *Rights, responsibilities, and ethics* addresses ethical issues arising at the network, components and practitioner levels. *Continuum of care* emphasizes services and service delivery linkage that is accessible and member-centered It also includes the impact of financial performance on the provision of services. *Education and communication* relates to patient participation in their health care. *Leadership* areas include: planning, directing, providing and improving health services in a cost-effective responsive way. *Management of human services* covers the provision of adequate number of qualified, competent and motivated providers. *Management of information* applies to both individual and network-wide performance of member care, governance, management and support processes. *Improving network performance* covers the methods used for establishing priorities for measurement and assessment activities.

Surveys are scheduled within 30–60 days of receipt of an application, and reports are delivered 60–90 days after the survey. The accreditation decision rules are published in *the Making Accreditation Decisions for Healthcare Networks* book. Accreditation decisions are disclosable. The individual performance reports and the health care network reports are available for purchase for all types of organizations surveyed since Jan. 1, 1994. The base fee for accreditation is $10,000. In addition, a fee of $2,390 per surveyor per day is charged for components and high risk practitioner sites selected for survey. The team of two surveyors will spend from three to five days. Each performance report includes a brief overview of the report with the accreditation decision and identified deficiency areas for which recommendations for improvement were made. The overall evaluation score, and the individual or grouped accreditation grid element scores also are compared to other organizations surveyed.

The Joint Commission defines a network as an entity that provides or provides for integrated health care services to a defined population of individuals. A network offers comprehensive or specialty services and is characterized by a centralized structure that coordinates and integrates services provided by component organizations and practitioners participating in the network. Some delivery systems subject to survey under the tailored survey policy may be included in the definition. Multiorganizational systems are included if the system is serving a defined population. Individual component entities in such systems are not granted separate accreditation status of as result of network accreditation. Components are accredited individually only if they have undergone a successful full accreditation survey. A network is eligible for a review by the JCAHO if it meets four criteria: (1) the Joint Commission standard should be applicable to the network services, (2) the network must be U.S.-based or operated by a U.S. governmental or nongovernmental entity, (3) there should be a process for assessing quality of services which involves review of care by clinicians, and (4) the network needs to identify all services provided directly, through contracts, or by other means. The network is awarded a category of accreditation status based on compliance with JCAHO standards.

An accreditation decision is not made for any of the surveyed components when the network is surveyed unless the component has been accredited separately.

All component entities within the network are eligible for accreditation under the multiple JCAHO accreditation manuals for hospitals, home care, long-term care, mental health, chemical dependency, and mental retardation/developmental disabilities services, ambulatory health care, pathology and clinical laboratory services. An application form for survey can be obtained from:

Joint Commission on Accreditation of Healthcare Organizations
Network Application Requests
One Renaissance Blvd.
Oakbrook Terrace, IL 60181
Telephone: 630/916-5970
Web page: http://www.jcaho.org

There are three phases to network accreditation: (1) survey preparation, (2) onsite survey, and (3) the accreditation decision. The networks survey preparation work begins with a review of the standards, scoring guidelines and accreditation decision rules. This may necessitate seminars and custom education by the Joint Commission. These sessions can provide specific information on the standards and teach quality concepts unique to networks. The Joint Commission organizes a network compatible team of surveyors and assigns an organizational liaison to facilitate communication. The six weeks prior to review are concerned with development creation of a survey agenda including appropriate network staff needed during the survey. Logistics for the onsite activities and required documents are determined jointly. The liaison will brief the network and component survey team(s) assigned to the network and its component and practitioner sites about the networks structure.

The onsite survey assess network compliance with applicable Joint Commission standards. Compliance is assess through several means: evaluation of verbal information, examples of implementation of standards, onsite observation by surveyors, and review of documents. The four basic elements of the survey process are: (1) survey of the network central office, (2) survey of components, (3) survey of practitioner site(s), and (4) a leadership briefing at the central office to review accreditation findings. The manual used for the survey is the Accreditation Manual for Health care Networks (AMHCN).

The second element of the onsite survey is a survey of a sample of unaccredited components of the network providing high-risk and low-risk services. Component high risk services include anesthesia, overnight patients, dialysis, emergency/urgent care, infusion therapy, ventilator care, contrast imaging other than gastrointestinal, radiation oncology, birthing centers and sites that provide 24-hour recovery services. The high-risk service will be surveyed if the component is a hospital, or if the network enrollees served are greater than 15% of the population served at the site. A third type surveyed applies if network enrollees are less than 15% of the population served at the site, at least 2 or 15% of sites, whichever is greater. For low-risk components, a statistically significant sample of each setting/type/service (e.g., physical rehabilitation services, hospice) is surveyed. Standard selected are taken from the Accreditation Manual for Health care Networks (AMHCN) and focus on several performance areas. The areas included are: competency of providers, patient safety, patient rights, and patient care management. The components also are surveyed using Appendix G of AMHCN to determine the performance of the component as measured against the expectation of the network. Survey length and surveyor number usually are based upon the complexity of the organizations. Survey length ranges from one to two days and the number of surveyors ranges from one to three.

Practitioner site survey, the third major element of the process, validates network oversight of practitioner sites. Documentation concerning oversight is reviewed during the central office survey as well as leadership interview. A maximum of eight practitioner sites are selected for survey. The sampling criteria is based on the number of practitioners in the network. The two network central office surveyors will have an additional day added to the three-day network central office survey for every two practitioner sites selected for survey. Practitioner sites represent the network as a whole. Variable used in this process include a selection of both primary and specialty practitioner sites. The number of members receiving primary care at a site is the second factor. The actual onsite survey of practitioner sites includes: document review, medical records review, practitioner and staff interviews, and observation of the office operations and environment.

A leadership briefing highlighting strengths and weaknesses is held with the network central office at the completion of the network, practitioner sites and component site reviews. Preliminary findings are presented with an emphasis on network implementation in the components and whether or not the components are acceptable parts of the network.

Phase three of the accreditation process is the accreditation decision. An organization will receive one of the five categories of accreditation: (1) accreditation with commendation, (2) accreditation, (3) conditional accreditation, (4) provisional accreditation, or (5) not accredited. Accreditation with commendation necessitates: a summary grid score of 90 or higher, an acceptable survey of components, no type I recommendations on any component data sheet(s), and that components survey by other accrediting entities were accredited successfully.

Accreditation indicates substantial compliance with standards either with or without type I recommendations. A type I recommendations must be resolved within a specified period of time and in most cases improvement is monitored through a focused survey or written progress report (WPR).

Conditional accreditation indicates substantial compliance deficiencies. Correction of the deficiencies must be demonstrated at follow-up survey to serve as a basis for further consideration. Conditional accreditation results with the assignment of follow-up monitoring for many areas or when one specific issue is serious enough to require closer monitoring. Lack of correction of a type I recommendations in the time frame required also results in conditional accreditation. The organization must develop a plan of correction and demonstrate adequate improvement in a follow-up-survey. The organization may be accredited with or without type I recommendations or denied accreditation.

Provisional accreditation results from substantial compliance with the provisional accreditation survey (PAS) This option consisting of two separate surveys conducted six to 12 months apart is for networks not quite ready for full evaluation.

The initial survey is a get acquainted survey, while the second survey is a more comprehensive evaluation and determines the three-year accreditation status. The first survey assess the network main site and any component or practitioner sites desired by the network. The second survey is a full accreditation survey that addresses the central operation of the network, all unaccredited components and practitioner sites selected using the sampling criteria. A network's accreditation status is the determined by the approved decision rules of the JCAHO. The network is charged a regular fee for both the first and second surveys.

A not accredited decision can occur under three circumstances. (1) Accreditation can be denied or withdrawn by the Joint Commission. (2) An organization may also withdraw from the accreditation process. (3) Not accredited also describes any organization that has not applied for accreditation during the past two years. (*Survey Preparation Guide*, 1996)

A pilot project by CIGNA HealthCare will be comparing accreditation through JCAHO and NCQA. CIGNA currently has more than four million HMO network participants serving all or part of 43 states, including Washington, DC, and Puerto Rico. More than 15 million Americans receive medical or dental benefits though their combined managed care and indemnity plans. The health plans chosen are CIGNA HealthCare of Louisiana, CIGNA HealthCare of Florida/Jacksonville, and Lovelace Health Systems in New Mexico. Louisiana represents a statewide plan where three networks (Baton Rouge, New Orleans, and Shreveport) can be accredited as a unit. Florida/Jacksonville is part of a statewide plan with full three-year accreditation by NCQA in Tampa and South Florida. Lovelace represents an integrated delivery system owned and operated by CIGNA. Cited as strong points are the more than 40 years experience of JCAHO in accreditation of health care entities, the comprehensive nature of the audit, and the opportunity to streamline their credentialling process by consolidating accreditation of physicians, hospitals and ancillary personnel. (*Network News* Issue One, 1996)

JOINT COMMISSION INTERNATIONAL

Historically, JCAHO has worked with the International Hospital Federation and the International Society for Quality Assurance in sponsoring symposia and other activities concerning health care quality issues. In 1986, JCAHO formed a not-for-profit consulting subsidiary, Quality Healthcare Resources Inc. (QHR), with responsibility for negotiating and providing international education and consultation services. The two entities, JCAHO and QHR, formed a partnership named the Joint Commission International (JCI) to work with countries to develop and introduce culturally sensitive performance measurement methods that would meet the need of the requesting country. The performance standards would include development of standards, indicators and appropriate evaluation tools. The four major areas of JCI assistance are: (1) operations improvement, (2) evaluation system development, (3) custom-designed evaluations, and (4) quality improvement assistance. Operations improvement relates to development or enhancement of clinical pathways and clinical guidelines: physician and managerial leadership, quality improvement systems, and information systems, including medical records and management systems. Evaluation system development assists organizations in country-specific evaluation systems for health care providers that can be used for: licensure, credentialling, accreditation, and monitoring and regulatory systems. National policy development is another facet of consultation. Technical assistance, education and hands-on experience is provided to assist in the development of standards, performance outcome indicators, evaluation methodologies, surveyor selection and training, accreditation decision methodology, and communication programs to facilitate system utilization. Custom designed evaluation allow use of Joint Commission standards adapted to the local culture and conditions. The consultants, which include a hospital administrator, physician, and nurse, will provide an onsite assessment, an evaluation report, and an action plan. Under quality improvement assistance JCI provides consultation and education to organizations covering quality improvement concepts, techniques and leadership skills. A continuous quality improvement (CQI) methodology based on a scientific approach and the needs of the requesting organization is used(JCI-Statement).

JCI has provided training and technical assistance to public and private clients in more than 21 countries. In 1993, QHR subcontracted on an Agency for International Development (A.I.D.) contract to provide quality related assistance as it related to health care financing and delivery system reform in the independent States of the former Soviet Union. As of mid 1994 JCAHO was working with the U.S. Department of the Treasury in Saudi Arabia and with the Agency for International Development (A.I.D.) in 10 Eastern European hospitals. The Saudi Arabian project was designed to establish a nationwide program to monitor and evaluate hospital quality of care. The 10 Eastern European hospitals project involved a partnership with 10 U.S. hospitals to evaluate patient outcomes. Initial measures will be those for which data is readily available and usable. (Donahue & Gilmore, 1994)

HEALTHCARE FINANCING ADMINISTRATION

The Healthcare Financing Administration (HCFA) has a threefold approach to managed care certifications: (1) federal qualification, (2) Medicare, and (3) Medicaid. Each has its own rules, regulations, and guidelines necessitating a comparison of organization, process, and operations. Federal qualification requirements cover legal/state licensure, fiscal soundness as well as all aspects of operations. With Medicare contracting, HMOs/CMPs must provide the entire range of Part A and Part B services to beneficiaries who are enrolled with the HMO or CMP. There are other requirements concerning administration, fiscal soundness, marketing, enrollment, claims processing and HCFA payments to risk-and cost-based contractors. Managed care plans wishing to provide care to Medicaid recipients must contract with the state agency. State Medicaid agencies or other state offices may develop a state specific monitoring strategy following guidelines established by HCFA. Plans remain federally qualified indefinitely unless relinquished by the plan or revoked by HCFA. Medicare has a biennial review of plans through inspection or other means [42 CFR 417.482(a)]. For Medicaid the state establishes a system of annual periodic medical audits which at a minimum collect data on the reasons for enrollment and termination and the use of services [42 CFR 434.53].

Review team requirements are significantly different. The HCFA Office of Managed care conducts the federal qualification application review and the ongoing monitoring. After an in-house analysis, an onsite visit is performed. Deficiencies found must be corrected prior to qualification. Medicare uses a team from the Office of Managed Care, Regional Offices and HCFA consultants and follows the same format as used for federal qualification. Once awarded, there are biennial onsite and ongoing monitoring of plan activities. Under Medicaid the state agency monitors directly or they may use a contractor. States use a variety of monitoring approaches, including submission to the state of specific data on a periodic basis, onsite inspections, or a combination of both. (A Health Care, 1993)

In determining certification as a federally qualified health maintenance organization, HCFA makes one of three determinations: (1) An organization is defined as an operational qualified HMO if it provides basic and supplemental services in accordance with all requirements. (2) It receives the designation of preoperational qualified HMO if it can be in compliance within 60 days. (3) A transitionally qualified HMO designation applies when the delivery systems meets all requirements other than benefits and premium rating in force for group policies [42 CFR 417.14.]. The release of information on reviews and application materials is subject to the Freedom of Information Act unless portions are deemed privileged. [42 CFR 417.406(a)(2)(i)] and 42 CFR 417.143(h)]. The HCFA fees are $3,100 for a CMP seeking federal qualification, $6,900 for an HMO seeking expansion of services, and $18,400 for seeking qualification as an HMO or qualification as a regional component of an HMO. If there is no site visit, $8,000 is returned.) [42 CFR 417.143(c)]. There is no charge for entering into a Medicare or Medicaid contract.

HCFA has two application processes for managed care organizations leading to certification: the qualification application and the Medicare contract application for Federally Qualified Health Maintenance Organizations. All applicants for qualification may concurrently apply for a contract with the HCFA under Section 1876 of the Social Security Act, as amended by the Tax Equity and Fiscal Responsibility Act of 1982 (TERRA), using the qualification application.

The qualification application covers three categories. A prepaid health plan seeking federal qualification as a health maintenance organization (HMO) under Title XIII of the Public Health Service Act is the first category. An applicant may request one for more regional components in its initial application. Each regional component must provide substantially the full range of basic health services and may establish a separate community rate for each component based on the different costs of providing health services. The second category includes federally qualified HMOs seeking to expand qualified service areas or to establish one or more additional regional components. The third category included federally approved Competitive Medical Plans seeking federal qualification. (*Qualification Application,* 1993)

The Medicare contract application for HMOs covers three categories. The first relates to a federally qualified health maintenance organization seeking an initial Medicare risk-based or cost-based contract. The second covers a Medicare contract service area expansion into an area already federally qualified. The third covers any additional Medicare risk based or cost-based contract for a qualified regional component. (*Medicare Contract Application*, 1993)

To be eligible for a Medicare risk-based contract, the HMO must have at least 5,000 prepaid members, or at least 1,500 if rural. If the HMO does not have this enrollment, it may be eligible to contract if it is a subdivision or subsidiary of an organization with such prepaid enrollment. The organization meeting the 5,000 enrollees requirement must assume responsibility for the financial risk, and adequate management and supervision of health care services furnished by its subsidiary. The HMO applying for a cost-based Medicare contract must have a total enrollment of least 1,500 commercial enrollees prior to signing a Medicare cost-based contract.

At the time of application submission each HMO and each contract area should have at least 1,000 prepaid commercial (non-Medicare, non-Medicaid) enrollees, or 500 if rural, This minimal membership will demonstrate the health plan's operational experience.

Each HMO and contract service area must adhere to the "50/50" rule enrollment requirement. At no time may the Medicare/Medicaid enrollees, exceed 50% of the enrollment in the contract area. A waiver may be granted to a governmental entity or an organization which serves an area in which more than 50% of the population is Medicare/Medicaid.

A risk-based contract may not be granted to an organization which has terminated or nonrenewed a prior risk-based contract within the last five years unless HCFA determines that circumstances warrant special consideration.

The HMO applying for a risk-based Medicare contract must have its adjusted community rate (ACR) approved by the Division of Finance (DOF) within the Office of Managed care (OMC) before signing the Medicare contract. As part of the ACR approval HCFA approves premiums and benefit packages for basic and high option plans. The HMO applying for a Medicare cost-based contract must complete a cost budget for DOF reviews.

Information requested in the application is based on Title XIII of the Public Health Services Act and applicable regulation and Section 1876 of Title XVIII of the Social Security Act and the applicable regulations. The applicant should be familiar with the following materials, which are available from the OMC upon request:

1. The HMO Act (Public Law 93-222) as amended in 1976, 1978 1981 and 1988
2. Other Federal Register publication including interpretive ruling and approved exclusions
3. Section 1876 of the Social Security Act, as amended — Payments to Health Maintenance Organizations and Competitive Medical Plans
4. Updated applicable implementing regulations at 42 CFR Part 417
5. Medicare HMO/CMP Manual
6. Financial Guidelines
7. Insolvency protection for members
8. Highlights of Medicare Claims Reconsideration Appeals Process

HMO National Data Reporting Requirements are available from the National Association of Insurance Commissioners, 120 W. 12th St., Kansas City, MO 64105, telephone: 816/842-3600.

There must be evidence of arrangements for basic health services in the requested service areas at the time the application is submitted. If applying for a Medicare contract, evidence may be the explicit inclusion of service to Medicare members and/or specific payment arrangement for services to Medicare members in provider contracts. Assistance is available to all qualification applicants in the preparation of the application from the staff of the Office of Managed care at telephone 202/619-2911. If also applying for a Medicare contact, the appropriate HCFA regional office can provide assistance relating to health services delivery and Medicare.

There is a special clause pertaining to establishment of regional components. A regional component is defined as geographically distinct and separate from any other regional components, [which] provides substantially the full range of basic health services to its members, and without extensive referral between components of the organization for these services." A HMO may establish a separate community rate for separate regional components. When applying for two or more regional components specific information must be provided for each component. When the information is the same through out all components, it should be stated as such.

Applicants for federal qualification only need to send four hard copies and two disk copies to:

Office of Managed Care
Operations and Oversight
Room 4406, Wilbur J. Cohen Building
330 Independence Ave., SW
Washington, DC 20201

Applicants for federal qualification and a Medicare contract, need to send three hard copies of the application and two disk copies to the address above. Also two hard copies of the application need to be forwarded to the appropriate regional office.

To receive budgetary assistance, the organization should contact the Division of Finance (telehone 410/966-7635) to request the ACRP or cost budget materials and instructions. The organization must send two hard copies and one disk copy of the completed ACRP to:

Healthcare Financing Administration
Office of Managed Care
Operations and Oversight
Division of Finance
6340 Security Blvd.
Oak Meadows Bldg. 1-B-2
Baltimore, MD 21207

Application fees for qualification application are:

1. $18,400 for an HMO
2. $18,400 for each regional component
3. $6,900 for a service area expansion that is not a regional component This maybe an expansion of a qualified HMO or regional component. There is a separate fee for each component being expanded.
4. $3,100 for a federally approved Competitive Medical Plan seeking federal qualification.

Payment is due at the time of submission. The check is payable to the HCFA HMO Application Fee, and a copy of the application cover sheet should be sent as follows:

If through U.S. Postal Service:

Healthcare Financing Administration
Division of Accounting
PO Box 7520
Baltimore, MD 21207-0520

If through delivery service:

Healthcare Financing Administration
Division of Accounting
6325 Security Blvd.
East Low Rise Building 2-C-4
Baltimore, MD 21207

The Division of Accounting will notify the Office of Managed care when the check has been received. Applications will not be reviewed until this notification is received (*Qualifications Application*).

If a health plan is a separate legal entity, then it is the applicant. If the health plan is a line of business of a legal entity, then the legal entity is the applicant.

Several categories of documents must be available for inspection at the site visit.

1. State license
2. Evidence of HMO marketing licenses or approvals
3. Insurance and other arrangement for malpractice, general liability, casualty losses, fidelity bonds
4. Copy of incorporation, partnership or other State required organizational documents and bylaws of each IPA and medical group with which the HMO contacts for the delivery of services in the proposed area
5. Executed physician, hospital, and other provider contracts
6. Internal Revenue Service Letter for nonprofit status, if applicable

7. Policy making body and committee minutes
8. Administrative policy and procedure manual
9. Authorization/Referral Forms
10. Encounter forms
11. Policy manual of procedures for health professionals
12. Minutes of Utilization Review and Quality Assurance Committees for the proposed area and currently qualified areas, if applicable
13. Evidence that institutional providers are certified under titles XVIII or XIX of the Social Security Act
14. Quality Assurance Plan for the HMO
15. Management information system reports
16. The most recent financial statement to update those submitted with the application, using the same format.
17. Actuarial analysis prepared by independent actuaries if used in developing the financial assumptions.
18. Underwriting guidelines
19. Account files for groups included in he enrollment projections
20. A list of contact persons and telephone numbers for the projected groups
21. Comparison of the HMO's benefits and premiums vs. its competitor(s) for account enrolled/reenrolled within the 90 days prior to the site visit and any accounts scheduled for enrollment/reenrollment subsequent to the sitevisit, where available.
22. 1310 activation package
23. Enrollment projections for the proposed service area for each component. Projections should begin with actual enrollment as of the date of the site visit or the start of operations (if preoperational) through one year beyondanticipated qualification.

HCFA is aware of the demands placed on managed care plans with dual Medicare/Medicaid contracts as well as commercial enrollment. A streamlining study is currently looking at the degree of agreement among public and private review entities. The project will access review processes, report of findings, use by review bodies and means of coordinating the public and private review processes in managed care. The Office of Managed Care, Healthcare Financing Administration contracted with the National Academy for State Health Policy in Portland Maine to access how HCFA standards compare to those of other federal agencies, states, and the private sector using the elements of quality improvement generally defined according to HCFA terminology. Ten programs/entities were selected for review: (1) Medicare risk contracting, (2) federal qualification, (3) federal Medicaid program, (4) Bureau of Primary Health Care, Public Health Service, (5) National Association of Insurance Commissioners, (6) Joint Commission for the Accreditation of Healthcare Organizations (Network component only), (7) National Committee of Quality Assurance, (8) Minnesota (Department of Commerce, Health, and Human Services), (9) Ohio (Departments of Health, Insurance and Human Services), and (10) the Pennsylvania (Department of Health, Insurance and Public Welfare) (Office of Managed Care, 1995).

ISO-9000

ISO (the International Organization for Standardization) is a world federation of national standards bodies based in Geneva, Switzerland, and founded in 1946 to develop a common set of trade, manufacturing, and communications standards. The ISO-9000 series of standards first were published in 1987. (*American National Standard*, 1987; Marquardt, 1987) It is the lineal descendant of the British Standards Institution (BSI) use of the 05 series of Ministry of Defense (MOD) quality standards and the Allied Quality Assurance Publication (AQAP) series of NATO standards from World War II. (Hakes, 1991) The organization is composed of approximately 92 member countries and has approximately 180 technical committees that draft standards. The standards have been adopted in the United States as the American National Standards Institute/American Society for Quality Control (ANSI/ASQC) Q9000 series. The United States Department of Defense has authorized the optional use of ISO 9000 standards in military contracts and the Food and Drug Administration (FDA) is incorporating the standards into its GMP regulations for medical devices. In the United Kingdom, the standards are found at the British Standards Institute (BSI) and are know as the British Standard 5750 (BS 5750). In some instances registration of compliance to ISO series standards is a legal requirement for entering the regulated European Community (now called the European union, EU). The Canadian government soon will demand ISO registration of most of its suppliers. (Harvy et al., 1995)

Preparation of International Standards are performed through ISO technical committees. Member bodies serve on technical committees (TC) of interest. International organizations, governmental and nongovernmental group take a liaison part in the work. Five International Standards form the ISO 9000 ("Quality 9000) series of quality assurance standards. The series contains concepts, guidance and several models for quality assurance. Standards are grouped into two categories, composed of two guidance standards and three conformance standards. ISO *9000-l: Quality Management and Quality Assurance Standards-Guidelines for Selection and Use* is the road map for the series. It defines key terms and provides guidance on selecting and tailoring ISO-9001, ISO 9002, and ISO 9003 to a company. ISO *9004-1 Quality Management and Quality Systems Elements* helps organizations determine the extent to which each series is applicable. It details the quality systems elements contained in the series and provides guidance for internal quality purposes. ISO *9001: Quality Systems-Model for Quality Assurance in Design/Development, Production, Installation and Servicing* is the most comprehensive of the conformance standards and most often applies to manufacturing and processing industries. ISO *9002: Quality Systems-Model for Quality Assurance in Production and Installation* is used when the product requirements are stated in terms of an already established design or specification. Blood banks with new areas of product development, such as bone, tissue and stem cell collection and processing, would be a potential fit. The Code of Federal Regulations (21 CFR Part 640) includes product specification. ISO *9003: Quality Systems-Model for Quality Assurance in Final Inspection and Test* is the least comprehensive standards. It addresses only requirements for the detection and control of problems during final inspection and testing.

A compendium published by the ISO Central Secretariat contains standards, draft standards, a list of other ISO publication, and a list of ISO members. The 1993 compendium also contains a paper entitled "Vision 2000 — A strategy for International Standards' Implementation in the Quality Arena During the 1990s," written by experts involved with ISO/TC 176, the quality management, and quality assurance technical committee. The paper is felt to be a valid indicator of future trends in quality standards. The compendium may be purchased from members bodies or directly from the ISO Central Secretariat:

ISO Central Secretariat
Case postale 56
CH-1211 Geneva, Switzerland
Telephone(O22) 749 01 11

The ISO 9000 series and related standards are intended for normal buyer–seller relationships. Quality system registration mandates the assessment and audit of an organization's quality system by an independent third part, called a Quality System Registrar. When the organization quality assurance system is in compliance with ISO 9001, ISO 9002, or ISO 9003, the registrar issues a certificate describing the scope of the system certified. The organization can then display the registrar's mark in its marketing efforts. The registration period is for three years, with audits approximately every six months. The registration process consists of six generic steps: application, document review, preassessment audit, assessment, registration, and surveillance. (Campbell, 1994)

Step 1　An organization, also known as a supplier, submits an application detailing its quality management system to an accredited registrar. A list of U.S.-accredited registrars can be obtained from the Registration Accreditation Board (RAB), an affiliate organization of ANSI.

Step 2　The registrar does a desk audit to detect potential problems with the reported quality system or application.

Step 3　A single auditor will then conduct a preassessment site visit to gather supplemental information.

Step 4　A team of auditors will confirm conformance with the respective ISO 9000 standard by reviewing documents and evaluating site operations during a three-to five-day audit.

Step 5　The final decision is made by the registrar's management, not the site audit team.

Step 6　The site is reaudited every six months, through announced and unannounced visits (Dyjack & Levine, 1995). More specific information on the registration process and registrar profiles are available. from the ASQC (telephone: 800/248-1946) or the Center for Energy and Environmental Management information services (telephone: 800/745-5565). Information for the United Kingdom is available from BSI Quality Assurance, PO Box 375, Milton Keynes, MK14 6LL, UK. (Nevelainen and Lloyd, 1995)

ISO has published a directory of quality system registration bodies — third-party bodies operating quality system registration programs. Countries submit entries through relevant ISO member bodies. The ISO Central Secretariat does not monitor these national activities, does not endorse the entries, and does not deliver ISO 9000 certificates on behalf of ISO.

VISION 2000

Vision 2000 was issued by The Ad Hoc Task Force of the International Organization for Standardization Technical Committee ISO/TC 176. The committee was composed of representatives from DuPont–USA (chairman), Conseil — France, Alkatel Kirk A/S — Denmark, DIN — Germany, British Telecom — United Kingdom, and Ontario Hydro — Canada. The article is part of a marketing strategy to gain acceptance for the principles and influence quality standardization activities globally. The Vision 2000 addresses global trends, critical issues, terminology distinction, an analysis of the marketplace for the ISO 9000 series standards, and recommendations on implementation.

Quality assurance remains a competitive weapon with increasing wide spread usage of third-party certification. Globalization now is a reality for all but the smallest of enterprises. The European Community use of the ISO/TC 176 standards will necessitate American and other non-European companies to use the ISO 9000 standards for European business ventures. Third-party certification will be most important in early purchaser/supplier partnerships. The competitive edge will necessitate both ISO 9000 certification and other supplemental audits. It also will result in the reduction of the costs of multiple assessments by multiple trading partners. Purchaser businesses often audit portions of the quality systems of their suppliers. Use of ISO-9000 would often mean the purchaser only would have to audit perhaps 20% of the seller service or product. The ISO 9000 contractual standards (ISO 9001, ISO 9002, ISO 9003) are being used is many business for many different kinds of services and products. It now is the quality assurance tool of choice for health care delivery systems in the United Kingdom, the Commonwealth countries, and most of Europe.

Under ISO 9000, products (services) are classified as to generic project category and the industry/economic sector of products. *Product* is defined as the result of activities or processes. The four generic product categories are: (1) hardware, (2) software, (3) processed materials, and (4) services. *Services* are intangible products relating to activities such as planning, selling, directing, delivering, improving, evaluating, training, operating or servicing a tangible product. This is the area most closely related to heath care delivery.

The industry/economic sector is defined as all sectors of the economy including service sectors. It is a grouping of suppliers meeting similar customer needs and/or whose customers are closely interrelated. Representative sectors and subsectors are extremely large. Health care, education, insurance, telecommunication, chemicals, banking, aerospace and tourism would be just a few. ISO 9000 strongly recommend precise use of the four generic product category terms in written documents and oral communications. The intermixing of categories and sectors terminology has lead to misunderstanding.

ISO 9000 plans to design usable standards in a timely fashion to prevent to proliferation of industry/economic standards based on supplemental documents. ISO believes a proliferation of supplementary service/industry specific documents can be prevented by segmenting the markets for standardization into quality management and external quality assurance. Segmentation criteria would be related to: generic project categories; complexity of purchaser need, product and process characteristics; contractual vs. noncontractual, and the combined use of the first three criteria.

Under the generic product categories, it is beleived that guidance standards written by ISO/TC 176 should deal with the special needs of each of the generic product categories. Neither ISO/TC committees nor other entities should write supplementary or derivative standards. Vision 2000 strongly discourages the production of industry/economic sector-specific generic quality standards supplemental to the ISO 9000 series. ISO 9000 does not discourage the development of product-specific standards relating to technical requirements for products or processes. It does not discourage defining specific product test methods.

The complexity of purchaser need, product, and process characteristics are dealt with by having three models for external quality assurance requirements (ISO 9001, ISO 9002, ISO 9003). Guidance is provided for selecting the appropriate model (ISO 9000, Clause 8.2) for a particular contract (ISO 9000, Clause 8.51). The contractual vs. noncontractual criteria is addressed by the existing ISO 9000 series architecture: ISO 9001, ISO 9002, ISO 9003 quality assurance contractual requirements. ISO 9004 addresses guidance to a producer for implementing and managing a quality system.

Current market place trends in all industry/economic sectors show rapid movement toward product offerings that are combinations of the generic product categories (software, hardware, services processed materials). Global competition will be the impetus for implementation of quality management and quality assurance terminology. Societal requirements including health and safety factors, environmental considerations, laws, statutes, codes and regulations will speed the movement. There is a perception that quality management and quality assurance for the four generic product categories are too different from each other for the ISO 9000 to adequately address all categories. It is believed that with ISO 9000 the underlying quality system elements and needs are the same.

The hardware products quality systems and quality technology are the most mature. However, the most rapid development will occur in the other three generic product categories. By 2000 it is envisioned that the need for separate documents for the four generic product categories will be minimal. Terminology and procedures for the generic product categories should be used and understood by all industry/economic sectors. ISO standards will be revised approximately every five years.

The recommendations on implementation contain many references to certification. Quality system certification schemes should register suppliers only to ISO 9001, ISO 9002, ISO 9003, and any future ISO 9000 documents. Industry/economic sector-specific external quality system standards should not be used as assessment documents for certification schemes. This admonition applies to both third-party and second-party assessment organizations. Auditor accreditation (certification) should be based on the ISO 10011 series audit standards. The accreditation and certification should be generic and not based on an industry/economic sector basis technical background. Each audit team should include at least one person knowledgeable in the industry/economic sector(s). This individual may be one of the accredited auditors or a technical expert on the audit team. It should be noted that the European Community has adopted a series of European Standards based on ISO/IEC Guides. The current guides deal with the general criteria for operation, assessment and accreditation of laboratories, quality systems and personnel, certification bodies relating to certification of products and supplier's declaration of conformity.

Four strategic goals have been set for the ISO 9000 series standards and the related ISO 10000 series developed by ISO/TC 176. The four goals are: (1) universal acceptance, (2) current compatibility, (3) forward compatibility, and (4) forward flexibility. Universal acceptance would be defined as worldwide use with few complaints and few supplementary standards. Current compatibility would mean supplements to existing parent documents would not conflict in requirements, numbering or clause structure. Supplements would not be stand-alone documents. Forward compatibility would mean a few minor revision would be needed for existing as well as new contracts. Forward flexibility would necessitate few supplements and the ability to combine to meet the needs of any industry/economic sector or generic category of products. Supplements should be easily consolidated into the parent document at the next revision if the supplement is found to have universal use.

The ISO 9000 was developed from existing quality standards and quality terms. The terms used in all ISO 9000 publications have specific meanings instead of the generic definitions found in dictionaries. In the ISO 9000 quality is defined as the totality of characteristics of an entity that bear on its ability to satisfy stated and implied needs. The specific and narrow definition are to be used to improve international communication and understanding. (*ISO 3534, Statistics — Vocabulary and Symbols ISO Guide 2*, general terms and their definitions concerning standardization and certification) Numerous other terms are defined. The term grade is emphasized and used to describe the sense of technical excellence of an entity. An entity could be a product, activity, process, organization, or person.

The terms quality control, quality assurance, quality management and total quality management means different things to different entities. Under ISO 9000 quality control deals with the operational means to fulfill the quality requirements. Quality assurance is defined as the process for providing confidence in this fulfillment of quality requirements within the organization and externally to customers and authorities. Quality management includes quality control, quality assurance, quality policy, quality planning, and quality improvement. Total quality management is defined as the global management strategy that uses all these concept for the benefit of the organization, its customers, and society.

Although the ISO 9000 as it applies to health care delivery is in its infancy in the United States, the standards are used widely in the business sector. The Cleveland Center for Joint Reconstruction at St. Vincent Charity Hospital in Cleveland, Ohio, and the American Legion Hospital in Crawley, Louisiana, are the U.S. pioneers in its initial application. The Cleveland Center's spokesman has noted lower cost, and more control. Dr. Bernand N. Stulberg one of the Center founders, believes the

ISO 9000 can demystify medicine for the consumer. ISO is perceived as a proactive approach that provides a systematic means of integration of measures from outcome evaluations, complications and mortality rates. (*Quality Systems Update*, 1995) Dr. Dennis Wilde, a partner of Dr. Stulberg, believes that ISO certification will be accepted as the buffer against third party payer questions concerning cost effectiveness in a health care setting. The director of Northeast Ohio operations for the Prudential Health Plan in the referring to the Center has noted the company will be more amenable to contracting with groups that have a standardization of procedures, goals and terms that are understandable in the business community (*Crain's Cleveland Business*, 1995). NASA, the Department of Defense, and many medical manufacturing companies are using ISO 9000. The number of ISO 9000 registrations is doubling every nine to 12 months in the United States. A total of 90 nations have adopted the ISO series for a variety of industries (*ADVANCE*, 1996).

ISO certification requires examination of the practice by an external body twice a year. In contrast, JCAHO has a three-year schedule and the Malcolm Baldridge National Quality Award has a five-year cycle. Although CCJR spent approximately $50,000 for consultation, certification, and registration, it was felt worthwhile. Wilde has noted that outcomes are better, surgeries go smoother, hospital stays are shorter, and complications are fewer. Stulberg believes that ISO closes the loop by tracking the whole process and empowering physicians.

One of the United Kingdom's health care applications experts is Pat Lampin at the British Standards Institute in London. According to a Mobile Europe Ltd. survey, more than 70,000 ISO 9000 registrations were issued in 76 countries by June 1994. The United Kingdom and Europe account for 78% of all certificates. The United States has approximately 4,700 registrations accounting for 6.9%, while Australia/New Zealand accounts for 6.6%. The Far East only accounts for 4.4%. It should be noted that the United Kingdom accounts for the largest foreign ownership of American businesses and resources.

The world is in the early stage of a major revolution in how work and quality are managed. Quality previously has had a narrow focus that was the responsibility of mid management. It is in the same boat as the understanding of basic requirements for competitiveness in the global market. To be successful in a world market, both ISO 9000 and a competitiveness registration or certification will be needed. The ISO 9000 and the Baldridge Award registration have a different focus and purpose. The focus of the Baldridge Award is to enhance competitiveness, while the focus of ISO 9000 registration is to ensure conformance quality. The Baldridge Award's purpose is education while the ISO 9000 purpose is to provide a common basis for an independent and transportable supplier qualification system in order to facilitate trade. The content of the Baldridge Award has two key components: (1) delivery of improving value to customers; and (2) systematic improvement of company operational performance. The content of the ISO 9000 requirements reflects consistent practice in specified operation, including documentation of the practice. Both systems need to be compared as to: customer focus, continuous improvement, sensitivity to the competitive world, integration via analysis, cycle-time reduction, public responsibility, human resource development and management, sharing of information, service quality, documentation, and self-assessment .

With the Baldridge Award, customer focus is the foundation of the category called customer focus and satisfaction. It is customer-driven quality directed toward customer retention and increased market share. Organizations are studied as to how they: address current and future customer requirements, customer-related information systems, relationship management and determination of satisfaction. Key requirement are explicit and detailed in the Baldridge Award approach, while ISO-9000 assumes customer requirements are known.

The definition of quality is different. The ISO 9000 registration defines quality as consistency in the production of a product or service. Differentiation from competitors based on overall value is not addressed. Also many of the registered organizations only involve their main production units. The Baldridge Award criteria catch phrase is continuous improvement embedment. Improvement embedment includes daily work improvement, elimination of problems at the source and improvements driven by the opportunity to do better. Sources for improvement include benchmarking, research and development, and other statistical information on processes and performance. With the Baldridge Award approach, improvements must be reflected in a composite competitiveness profile. (Reimann & Hertz 1996)

The competitiveness profile include customer indicators, market share profit rating by a third-party, product/service quality, productivity measures, human resource development, supplier performance and public responsibility. The profile also includes environmental health and safety. Trends and performance levels are to be reported for all seven areas. The analysis and result from the seven areas must be related back to the three areas of customer focus and satisfaction. The ISO 9000 does not use this results oriented approach. Peach wrote: "Notably absent in the ISO Standards are specific references to quality results and customer satisfaction. The ISO Standards specifies elements of a quality system, but does not discuss whether products resulting from that system actually meet customer requirements. (Peach, 1990)

There are three in-depth publications to assist in clarifying the different use of terminology in the ISO-9000. In a work by Beaumont (1995), practical advice is given on the applications of the standard. Each section is introduced with an illustration of its required elements. The explanation is in plain English, with notes, examples, and a checklist of the type of questions asked by an auditor. Keeney (1955) provides an ISO 9000 Auditor's Companion to assist in audit preparation or to research the changes between the ANSI/ASQC Standard Q91-1987 and the new ANSI/ASQC Q9001–1994 ((S)9001) standards. The 1994 revision is compared with the original, using strikeout text, shading, guidance notes, and related questions. Lamprecht (1994) provides a critical review of how the ISO 9000–9004 series relates to service organizations. A helpful tool is the ISO 9000 Bibliography website (htttp://www/exit109.com/~leebee/bibliog.htm).

IS IT WORTH IT?

By 2000, it is projected that at the current rate of growth, health maintenance organizations (HMOs) will cover close to 40% of insured employees. Such good prospects have resulted in shares of publicly traded HMOs growing by 35%. Most investors are ignorant of the quality debate and currently focus on costs, profit margins, and revenue growth. However, newspapers, magazines and big companies increasingly are accessing quality of care as well as the cost per employee. News media stories have turned from cheerful tales of cost containment to patient care horror stories. Big corporations want more than marketing strategies and anecdotal data. Gary Peters, manger of employee benefits at Rockwell International, says employers have the ability to direct the market. Companies are demanding audited data on the quality of care checked by third parties, such as the NCQA, JCAHO, AAAHC, HCFA and ISO 9000. Companies want valid statistical data on quality, not marketing propaganda. The health information manager at Massachusetts-based phone giant GTE notes that better quality health care will decrease lost time at work and lower productivity better than administrative reorganization.

IBM and Ameritech are dropping HMOs that don't earn NCQA accreditation. Xerox and other corporations have frozen enrollment on plans that don't make sufficient progress toward NCQA accreditation. As of 1997, the NCQA has reviewed many of the nation's HMOs. Only 36% have received full three-year accreditation, while 13% have flunked. Another 39% have received one-year accreditation and 12% received provisional accreditation. Other companies, such as Xerox and GTE, have provided financial incentives to employees who chose high rated HMOs. GTE using weighted quality criteria combining NCQA accreditation, and data from employee surveys. It then publishes a list of the best 15% of the 130 HMOs used. It is interesting to note that not one for-profit plan made the best 15% list. Fortune 100 companies are now beginning to use their clout to change the playing field in many different ways.

The argument by HMO companies that health care is not measurable illustrates a profound lack of knowledge of medical literature. Since 1989, the New York State Health Department has analyzed coronary bypass graft operation mortality rates by hospital and by physicians, using 17 variables to risk-adjust the cases. From 1991 to 1993, the risk adjusted mortality rate at Erie County Medical Center was 5.43%. while at New York University Medical Center it was 1.97%. The New York ratings of hospitals and physicians is available from Public Affairs, New York State Health Department, Corning Tower Building, Empire State Plaza, Albany, NY 12237.

Purchasers now are demanding documented improvements in preventive care from numbers audited by an outside firm that compare plans to a nationalized set of standards, HEDIS. The Pacific Business Group, an alliance providing performance and price data on 23 plans to employers, such as Bechtel, Chevron, BankAmerica, Safeway, Pacific Telesis, General Electric, and Hughes Aircraft, are leery of unaudited health plan data. Even the much touted consumer survey is loosing respectability.

The Oxford Plan in Connecticut is demanding a fixed price for the whole surgical procedure from the work-up through hospitalization and post-op. In addition it also wants mortality rates and reoccurrence rates on past operations, and the names of at least 25 clients who have had the operation. The results then are provided to any plan member needing that procedure. Another entity, the Foundation on Accountability, a Jackson, Wyoming, group sponsored by such employers as AT &T, Ameritech, GTE, and Electronic Data systems, will be providing a guide on assembling their own risk-adjusted data along with questions to ask health care providers in 13 disease areas. These developments constitute a new hard-edged phase.

The argument no longer centers around whether HMOs are good as traditional fee-for-service medical care, but which HMOs provide high quality at a good price. The period of grace for managed care is nearing its end. The consumers groping toward an intelligent choice of a health plan in the swamp of inconclusive information will soon be over. Over the next few years the health care world will be comprised of winners and losers, not big winners and small winners. Medical care is in a fairly pure phase of Adam Smith capitalism. It is the wild, wild west, but the sheriff is coming to town in the form of certification and standardized data collection sets. The providers, the HMOs, and the companies need to awaken from their sleep and watch how the patients vote with their feet. (Mahar, 1996) In the end, the plans people like the best are the ones with largest number of doctors and offer a familiar setting like the old doctor's office. After cost and quality comes concern over the extend of coverage offered by plans as it relates to childbirth and specialists. (Gottlieb, 1996)

Ethics and economics will continue their battle with the swords of accreditation and certification. The voluntary accreditation surveys conducted by impartial professional organizations, such as NCQA, AAAHC, JCAHO, HCFA, and ISO 9000 will continue to evolve, mutate and perhaps merge. Competition probably will decrease the cost of accreditation and increase the controversy.

Their emerging emphasis on quality will place the final nails in the coffin of low quality managed care. Unfortunately, it may be five–15 years until the final nails of sophisticated comparative data will be available. Until that time the distribution of scarce medical resources will be based as much or more on economics than ethics.

REFERENCES

Accreditation Handbook for Ambulatory Healthcare, 1996–1997 edition. Accreditation Association for Ambulatory Health Care, Skokie, IL, 1996.

A Healthcare Quality Improvement System for Medicaid Managed Care: A Guide for States. Medicaid Bureau, Healthcare Financing Administration, Element B, P. 9., July 6, 1993.

"ISO-9000 A State-of-the-Art Vehicle for Healthcare Quality." *ADVANCE for Physical Therapists*, Jan. 22, 1996.

American College of Obstetricians and Gynecologists. *Physician Responsibility Under Managed Care.* ACOG Committee Opinion 170, Washington, DC, ACOG, 1996.

American National Standard ANSI/ASQCQ90-1987. Quality management and quality assurance standards — guidelines for selection and use. American Society for Quality Control, Milwaukee, WI, 1987, and Marquardt, D. W. "Background and development of ISO 9000." *In The ISO handbook.* 2nd ed. R. W. Peach, ed. CEEM Information Services, Faifax, VA, 1994.

Beaumont, L. *ISO 9001, the standard interpretation: the international standard system for assuring product and service quality,* 2nd ed. ISO Easy, Middletown, NJ, 1993.

Burg, M. and Lane, D. "Mammography Referrals for Elderly Women: Is Medicare Reimbursement Likely to Made a Difference?" *Health Services Research,* 27: 505–515, 1992.

Campbell. M. K. *ISO-9000 registered company directory: North America.* CEEM Information Services, Fairfax, VA, 1994.

Chicago Tribune. "In Search of the Quality HMO," editorial, April 21, 1996.

Crain's Cleveland Business. 16 (39): Sept. 25–Oct. 1,. 1995.

Donahue, T. and Gilmore, C. "Joint Commission on Accreditation of Healthcare Organizations (JCAHO) and Quality Healthcare Resources, Inc. (QHR), USA: International Summary." *International Journal for Quality in Healthcare,* 6 (2): 1–3, June 1994.

Dyjack, D. and Levine, S. "Development of an ISO compatible occupational health standard: defining the issues." *American Industrial Hygiene Association Journal,* 56 (6): 599–609, June 1995.

Gardner, J. "Pilot NCQA report care rates managed-care plans." *Modern Healthcare,* pg. 2, Feb. 27, 1995.

Gottlieb, M. " Picking a Health Plan: A Shot in the Dark Who's Best? It can Be Hard to Tell." *New York Times,* Jan. 14, 1996.

Hakes, C. *Total Quality Management: A Key to Business Improvement,* Chapman & Hall, London,1991.

Harvy, E., Hewison, C., Nevalainen, D., and Lloyd, H. "Quality in blood banking." *Blood Rev.,* 9: 15–24, 1995.

JCI — Joint Commission International. *A Capabilities Statement.*

Keeney, K. *1947 — The ISO 9000 auditor's companion.* ASQC Quality Press, Milwaukee, WI, 1995.

Lamprecht, J. *1947-ISO 9000 and the service sector: a critical interpretation of the 1994 revisions.* ASQC Quality Press, Milwaukee, WI, 1994.

Laurie et al. "Preventive Care for Women: Does the Sex of the Physician Matter?" *The New England Journal of Medicine,* 329: 478–482, 1993.

Mahar, M. "Time for a Checkup: HMOs must now prove that they are providing quality care." *Barron's The Dow Jones Business and Financial Weekly,* pg. 31–35, March 4, 1996.

Medicare Contract Application for Federally Qualified Health Maintenance Organizations. Department of Health and Human Services, Healthcare Financing Administration, Office of Managed Care, 1993 final.

National Committee for Quality Assurance. *Health Plan Employer Data and Information Set and Users Manual: Version 2.* NCQA, Washington, DC, draft, 1993.

Network News from the Network Accreditation Program. Joint Commission on Accreditation of Healthcare Organizations, Issue One, 1996.

Nevelainen, D. and Lloyd, H. "ISO 9000 quality standards: a model for blood banking?" *Transfusion,* 6: 521–524, 1995.

Quality Systems Update. "A Global ISO 9000 and ISO 14000 Information Service." Vol. 5, No. 10, October 1995.

Network News News From the Network Accreditation Program. Joint Commission on Accreditation of Healthcare Organizations, Issue Two, 1996.

Office of Managed Care, Healthcare Financing Administration, Contract No. 5000-93-0018. *Quality Improvement Standards and Processes Used by Select Public and Private Entities to Monitor Performance of Managed Care Plans: A Summary.* National Academy for State Health Policy, Portland, ME, 1995.

Peach, R. "Creating a Pattern of Excellence." *Target,* 6 (4): 15,Winter 1990.

Qualification Application. Expansion and Medicare Contract, Department of Health and Human Services, Healthcare Financing Administration, Office of Managed Care, 1993 final.

Quality Systems Update A Global ISO-9000 & ISO 14000 Information Service. 5 (10), October 1995.

Reimann, C. and Hertz, H. "The Baldrige Award and ISO 9000 registration compared." *Journal for Quality and Participation,* National Institute of Standards and Technology, pp. 12–18, January/February 1996.

Survey Preparation Guide. Health care Network Accreditation. JCAHO, 1996.

Women's Health Issues, 6 (1), January/February 1996.

13 Alternative Quality Management Strategies in Managed Care

Anita Ghosh

CONTENTS

The dramatic growth of managed care has dominated the health care scene in recent years. The system of the future will emphasize cost-effective, high-quality care, and ultimately demonstrable improvements in the health status of entire communities. Health care executives face the challenges of managing health risks of enrolled populations, developing a customer service orientation, information management, clinical care standardization, aligning competing economic objectives of a diverse array of providers, and reengineering entire organizations. Visionary health care executives have already turned their attention to providing high-quality service. Many discriminating employers, such as Xerox and GTE, are dropping plans that do not meet stringent high quality care criteria because they believe that quality medicine can reduce their expenses in the long run. This chapter focuses on alternative quality management strategies with special emphasis on the managed care environment. Demand management, risk sharing, business coalitions, patient-focused management (PFC), report cards, and reengineering are some of the major topics discussed in the following sections.

DEMAND MANAGEMENT

The emerging science of "demand management" emphasizes the use of technology to reduce consumers' need for and use of the most expensive health care services,

1-57444-073-X/97/$0.00+$.50
© 1998 by CRC Press LLC

thereby controlling costs and even improving overall health status of a defined population. (Montrose, 1995) The managed care failure of "supply-side" efforts (precertification, peer review, etc.) to manage costs has resulted in innovative strategies to alter the demand-side of the health care equation. At the heart of the concept of demand management is a radical redistribution of information resources and decision making responsibility between providers and patients. Patients are empowered through timely information and training in making appropriate use of health care services, thereby reducing the need for, and use of, costly and/or unnecessary interventions.

Montrose gives several examples of emerging demand management strategies:

1. *Computerized health risk appraisals* A variety of databases have been utilized to compare the risk factors and health status of comparable population groups, in order to implement health interventions at the individual or group level. The Group Health Cooperative of Puget Sound has launched a health risk appraisal for its large subscriber pool, using computerized epidemiological screening to identify the high-risk individuals in their plan. (Goldsmith, Goran, and Nackel, 1995) Next, the plan engages in active disease management aimed at containing the risks associated with selected subscribers. Health Partners, a large Minneapolis HMO, has set ambitious health status improvement goals (e.g., a 25% reduction in heart attacks) for its subscribers by incorporating preventive care into the mainstream of its service.
2. *Patient education centers* Some plans are developing patient-education centers which provide a variety of reference materials (e.g., printed brochures, audiovisual presentations, online retrieval services) that provide information on common medical conditions and treatments, health promotion strategies and nontraditional approaches to health care.
3. *Telephonic nurse diagnosis and triage services* Many plans offer such systems where patients can call a nurse 24 hours a day who will follow a series of computer generated questions for common, as well as emergency conditions. Often an instantaneous telephone recommendation can be made as to the most appropriate care.
4. *Shared decision making with multimedia computer systems* Some plans are beginning to offer customized interactive information to guide patients' decision making. Sophisticated aids are available which enable providers to change presentation formats in order to accommodate different languages, learning styles, cultural differences, etc.
5. *Home health telemonitoring systems* Chronically ill patients or those convalescing at home, can report their health care status to a team of providers, with the help of a modem.

It is becoming increasingly more obvious that one of the biggest-culprits of rising health care costs and poor quality of care is inadequate information systems. Significant investment in developing information systems has become a priority with many plans, while smaller organizations are outsourcing information management in the short term or creating partnerships to jointly secure information management technology. (Fromberg, 1996) In addition, efforts to coordinate demand management strategies across communities should further reduce costs and improve quality of care.

RISK SHARING ARRANGEMENTS

While long-term cost control may be the main reason why employers are motivated to offer managed care plans, demonstration of short-term savings also is important. A risk sharing arrangement/contract between a managed care plan and an employer may be one method to ensure short term savings. (Leigh, 1995) Under such an arrangement, the managed care plan guarantees that its program will generate savings by managing the employer's medical claims. If not, the plan financially shares the employer's risk of adverse claims. Once the employer decides on a claims target, the managed care plan will project what it believes the employer's claims will be under its program. A "grace range" usually is set around the claims target, since it is very difficult to predict future medical expenses accurately. If the employer's actual claims exceed the upper boundary of the grace range, then the managed care plan will bear a portion of the cost of the excess claims. Sometimes (if defined in the contract), the managed care plan may share any cost savings realized with the employer.

Leigh (1995) lists several factors that influence target claims — a knowledge of these can assist employers in keeping track of where savings are expected to be generated and the size of the potential savings.

1. *Managed care discounts*   The managed care plan receives a discount on its in-network medical providers' fees. Since claims for in-network services will be lower than out-of-network services, savings will be realized only if employees have a high in-network utilization of services. Hence, it is important for the plan to ensure that there is an adequate number of accessible providers in order to guarantee high in-network utilization.
2. *Medical Trend*   It is critical to project accurately how much the average medical claim is going to increase in the future. In-network claims will usually increase at a lower rate than traditional indemnity claims because the rate of increase in the fees managed care plans pay in-network providers is lower than the general increase in medical providers' fees. Out-of-network claims usually increase at the same rate as traditional indemnity claims.
3. *Utilization management savings*   In-network claims will usually be lower since managed care plans generate savings by eliminating unnecessary medical treatments and by shifting care to lower cost settings (e.g., home care, free standing "surgicenters" and "emergicenters").
4. *In-network plan design*   In-network benefit plans offer attractive incentives to use in-network services over the traditional indemnity plan. Incentives could include more benefits, or reimbursements of a higher percentage of in-network claims by employers over traditional indemnity

plans. While this may result in increased claim costs for in-network services program savings may offset this cost.

5. *Out-of-network plan design*   Claim costs generally will decrease, since as a penalty for using out-of-network services, the out-of-network benefits are usually less generous than the traditional indemnity plan or the in-network services.

6. *Out-of-network adverse selection*   It is not uncommon to have employees who do not find the differences between in-network and out-of-network benefits significant, and who continue to use out-of-network services. Older employees who have long-standing relationships with specific providers, or employees with ongoing health problems, or wealthier employees sometimes are willing to pay for more expensive services.

7. *Managed care administrative fees*   While managed care administrative fees generally are not part of the claims target calculation, it is useful to realize that claims savings will be reduced by the amount of increase in administrative fees incurred by the managed care program.

It often is difficult to quantify the expected savings from managed care plans. In addition, calculating projected medical trends, determining the claims target and the grace range, defining the time period, and getting actual pricing concepts into a legal risk sharing contract can pose additional challenges to all parties involved. It is critical to recalculate the claims target using an actual trend in the second year of the risk sharing arrangements in order to calculate actual savings. If recalculation of the claims target is overlooked, the managed care plan may be erroneously rewarded or penalized because of errors in projecting trends rather than because of its performance. The managed care organization will attempt to limit their potential financial liability under the agreement by specifying a maximum amount they are willing to pay (e.g., a 50:50 risk sharing agreement with a grace range of plus/minus 10% of claims target but with a maximum ceiling of $150,000). In some arrangements managed care plans may be rewarded if the employer agrees to refund a percentage of the claims below the grace range boundary. Drafting a risk sharing contract should be undertaken after a thorough understanding of all of the aforementioned factors.

BUSINESS COALITIONS

Purchasers of health care today are more sophisticated and aggressive in seeking new and better ways to provide high quality affordable health care. A number of business coalitions of varied employers exist who share a common commitment to harness market forces in order to improve health care delivery. One such coalition is the Business Healthcare Action Group (BHCAG), with 20 employer members in June 1994 based in the greater Twin Cities community. (Kemnitz, 1994) Nationwide, the 20 BHCAG member employers cover in excess of 1.5 million lives and spend about $1.5 billion annually on health care. The members strongly believe that employers who purchase health care can use their combined power to improve the health care offered to employees and their families, as well as for the community as a whole. They are committed to improving quality of care, increasing provider competition and consumer knowledge (demand management), along with increased investment in continuous quality improvement.

Committees, subcommittees, and larger teams worked on choosing a model for group purchasing — Choice Plus was in operation by January 1993. The common plan design and administration is expected to reduce nonhealth care related expenses and is based on a point-of-service concept. When using preferred providers, participants receive comprehensive higher in-network benefits for a $10 copayment, whereas inpatient hospital coverage is 100% after meeting a $200 deductible. Out-of-network benefits are generally paid at 70% with an annual limit on expenses paid by the participant. All BHCAG members have contracted with the same network of hospitals, physicians, nurses, and allied health professionals called Health Partners. The health plan has agreed to a three-year guarantee on cost increases. Currently, contracted providers are held accountable for the cost of their care through negotiated fee schedules, but in future BHCAG hopes to negotiate an annual budget for that purpose.

Providers also are held accountable for their quality of care and for the medical necessity of care through the development of mutually agreed on guidelines and measures of patient outcomes. A joint physician purchaser organization called the Institute for Clinical Systems Integration, which was established for this purpose, is responsible for:

1. Developing all guidelines and measurement of all outcomes.
2. Designing an automated medical records system for use by in-network providers.
3. Using information systems in order to improve the quality and cost effectiveness of care by in-network providers (continuous quality improvement). The plan focuses on keeping its participants well, as opposed to a "cure" orientation by periodically measuring population health over time to facilitate development of guideline topics and through extensive investment in consumer education programs. Consumers also will be held accountable for services they utilize through reasonable copayments and efforts will be made to emphasize appropriate self care and preventive care. All of these measures are expected to yield first-year savings in the range of 5-10%, compared with other managed care options in the Twin Cities community.

The actual first-year financial results were encouraging — costs decreased by 11% compared to expected costs of previously available comparable managed care plans in the Minneapolis–St. Paul area. Sixteen guidelines were completed at pilot sites, e.g., cystitis, VBAC, pediatric asthma, depression, immunization, cervical cancer screening. Second-year guideline topics include colon cancer screening, cholesterol screening, anxiety, chest pain, and preventive service delivery, among others. BHCAG also started benchmarking quality across its provider network by identifying six clinical indicators, e.g., breast cancer, total hip replacement, childbirth, heart disease, childhood infectious disease, and childhood asthma. By emphasizing early detection/prevention/early treatment, BHCAG hopes to promote cost-effective care. Another key quality control initiative is joint provider/purchaser assessment of new technologies which precedes many benefits coverage decisions (e.g., cochlear implants, pancreas/lung transplants, PSA for prostrate cancer screening and excimer or laser use in opthalmology.

Development of a prototype automated medical record system is expected to provide substantial administrative savings and also significantly eliminate the potential for errors and delays in handling records. The BHCAG held a series of focus group meetings to assess current employee perceptions on the cost and quality of care as well as the consumer's role in the consumption of health care. Similarly network providers were also interviewed regarding the existing and ideal health care consumer. This feedback was utilized to develop consumer and provider education programs. Active demand management strategies are being planned in order to help consumers become active participants in health care decisions whereas provider education programs are aimed at assisting guideline implementation. By actively taking steps to provide cost-effective high quality health care for their employees, the coalition has spearheaded efforts to reform the health care system.

However, some employers continue to resist the dramatic changes sweeping the health care arena. Most employers have not acquired a sense of urgency for improved quality that matches their concern for costs, and some feel incapable of judging the quality of health care delivery alternatives. Along with this lack of awareness in purchasers is a concern among many benefits managers that they will not be rewarded for taking innovative approaches to improve health care delivery. Among the major obstacles thought to be impeding employers' progress in quality of care issues are:

1. Lack of top management support
2. Low cost alternatives are given preference over high quality.
3. Poor relationship with providers.
4. Inadequate knowledge about health care quality.
5. Inadequate standardized comparative information about competing health care plans.
6. General resistance to change.

PATIENT FOCUSED CARE

Health care managers are adopting a relatively new concept called Patient Focused care (PFC) in order to maximize use of resources, increase patient satisfaction, empower employees, and provide high-quality cost-effective care. The underlying theory behind PFC is that all of an organization's resources and activities should be organized around its patients as opposed to the organization's departmental units. (Sidky, Barrable, and Stewart, 1993) PFC, which has its origin in the continuous quality improvement (CQI) movement, emphasizes an "organizational focus" instead of the usual fragmented "departmental focus." Lathrop (1993) often considered to be the leading authority on PFC, explains that the main objectives of PFC are:

1. Improve continuity of care of patients.
2. Minimize the movement of patients through the hospital.
3. Improve continuity of professional relationships among providers as they collaborate on behalf of patients.
4. Increase the proportion of direct care activities as compared to other work.
5. Tailor operating environments to the specific needs of related groups of patients.
6. Empower employees to perform their duties in ways that are most responsive is patient needs.

Mang (1995) summarizes six different principles of PFC:

1. *Patient redeployment*   Patients with similar needs are grouped together so that providers can focus on the specific problems of those patients. By working with similar cases, instead of an array of different patients with different needs, the providers become familiar with and gain expertise in their work. By anticipating problems that could arise and dealing with them more effectively, providers are more successfully able to deliver high quality care.
2. *Services decentralization*   This principle emphasizes bringing the services closer to the patient so that each related needs patient care unit becomes self-sufficient and does not depend on the central laboratory or other departments. This would greatly reduce the paperwork, scheduling delays, and the movement of the patient through the hospital. Pharmacy, laboratory, registration, and some radiology services are some examples of services that best lend themselves to decentralization. (Moffitt et al., 1993)
3. *Cross-trained caregivers*   Continuity of care is expected to improve when caregivers are empowered through cross-training to perform additional tasks and take on more responsibility. Patient satisfaction is also expected to increase when cross-trained caregivers accomplish a major portion of care at the patient site.
4. *Enhanced patient autonomy and decision making*   Empowering the patient by providing him with all the relevant information and fully involving him in all care decisions will increase patient satisfaction. More and more organizations have instituted patient education programs which equip patients to have a greater say in what is to be done, how it is to be done, and when it is to be done.
5. *Task simplification*   Often it is necessary to completely reengineer systems in order to simplify old tasks and institute new more efficient ones. The investment in restructuring/redesigning tasks is more than offset by savings generated by more efficient processes that result in overall higher quality of care.

A survey of the implementation strategies of PFC across some hospitals reveals some interesting elements. (Mang, 1995) Generally outside consultants/experts were enlisted to assist in the implementation of PFC. However, a grass roots in-house redesign campaign also is popular. Danbury Hospital, a 450-bed acute care teaching hospital in southwestern Connecticut, initiated strategies to implement PFC in 1994. The hospital believed it could improve patient care by being more resource efficient and decided to adopt a grassroots up approach to PFC since management strongly believed that employees more readily would accept changes they designed themselves. Unlike other hospitals which are implementing PFC, Danbury Hospital is instituting changes slowly throughout the organization (subject to availability of resources) instead of fully renovating one wing as a PFC unit.

Danbury's highly customized approach to PFC includes satisfying specific criteria before it is approved. These criteria include six "success factors." Each new project must:

1. Be patient focused — the patient's needs must be considered before considering any potential benefits to the organization.
2. Be cost effective.
3. Be holistic — new positions/tasks must include rewarding elements so as to maintain employee morale and motivation.
4. Decrease delays in areas such as testing, pharmacy, deliveries, treatment, etc.
5. Decrease the number of "hands-off" because employees cannot/will not do some other person's job.
6. Decrease the number of steps necessary to perform any task.

Danbury Hospital already had established service lines before the implementation of PFC, which enabled patients with similar needs to be grouped together. The hospital also had established satellite pharmacies at key locations throughout the premises and planned to decentralize patient registration areas. In the area of cross training its service employees, Danbury formed a new position integrating the roles of the housekeeper dietary aide and patient transportation, which now is known as a guest service representative (GSR). In cross training, the hospital enlisted the help of those employees who knew the responsibilities involved in those tasks. Since it does not yet have a distinct PFC unit, patient needs teams are not being utilized at the hospital. Patient empowerment is currently being pursued through focus groups, discharge interviews, and written surveys to evaluate the care being given at the hospital. Task simplification efforts include installation of a new computer system which includes bedside monitors that are expected to reduce paperwork and errors in medication orders.

Health care managers must overcome several challenges in the implementation of PFC. Substantial up-front investment in decentralization, employee resistance to cross training efforts, and communication problems with caregivers (after implementing PFC) are some of the common problems. When the Medical Center (TMC) in Beaver, Pennsylvania, decided to eliminate a central nursing station and use nurse servers instead, they were faced with several difficulties in contacting caregivers by telephone. TMC leadership adopted several technologies, in addition to wireless phones that enable caregivers and patients stay to in touch with each other. These new solutions include a beeper system for nurses and caregivers, an electronic badge system for locating caregivers and keeping track of equipment, and a telemetry beeper system. Appropriate education and training of caregivers is undertaken to help them make the transition to the new systems.

REPORT CARDS

The managed care movement first gained prominence for its potential to contain health care costs. Currently, with premiums leveling off, purchasers as well as consumers are increasingly looking at "value," a concept which takes into account the quality of care as well as cost. Health care organizations are being pressured to measure and publish reports on the quality of their services. These report cards are used by consumers to make informed selections among various plans/providers and by employers/purchasers who want to make sure that they are getting their money's worth. Report cards also assist health care providers/plans in continually making improvements in their performance. Finally, report cards can assist in evaluating and revising public policy. The recent past has seen a dramatic increase in the area of measurement and reporting on the quality of care. The next few sections highlight some of the significant achievements in this area.

The National Committee for Quality Assurance (NCQA)   Historically, employees have asked health care plans to measure performance in terms of patient satisfaction, utilization, cost, quality, etc. However, no national standard for reporting quality measures existed. In 1991 a consortium of employers, such as Xerox, Digital Equipment, and Bull HN Information Systems, invited the NCQA to define a set of performance indicators for managed care organizations called the Health Plan Employer Data and Information Set (HEDIS). In November 1993, NCQA revised the HEDIS indicators into HEDIS 2.0, which represents a core set of performance measures and attempts to standardize definitions and specific methodologies for deriving these performance measures. (Ribnick, Carrano, 1995) The five major areas of performance which are reported by HEDIS 2.0 are:

1. Quality, which is classified into preventive care, maternal care, acute and chronic care, and mental health.
2. Membership and utilization
3. Member access and satisfaction
4. Financial measures
5. Descriptive information about health plan management.

In 1994, NCQA launched two initiatives to improve and refine HEDIS 2.0. First, it established a users' group dedicated to sharing issues and making recommendations about implementation. Second, NCQA created a one-year Report Card Pilot Project in collaboration with 21 health plans and key employer, consumer, health policy, and labor representatives. The project aimed at testing the feasibility of implementing a system of standardized performance measures that could provide timely information to interested users regarding the quality of care and service in managed care plans. Twenty-eight technical measures from HEDIS 2.0 were selected based on their relevance and value to users, the ability of health plans to supply the required data, and the appropriateness of the measures for across-plans comparisons. (Hiltunen, 1996) The total project resulted in the release of comparable data to the public.

HEDIS 2.5, a comprehensive technical update to HEDIS 2.0, released in 1995, did not contain any new measures, but replaced HEDIS 2.0 specifications with new ones. While improvement of measures and methodologies will enhance the utility of HEDIS to users, Hiltunen (1996) suggests that significant implementation issues exist. Many users believe that health plans may report inaccurate or misleading data, while others express concerns that some items that are feasible to measure may not be the best predictors of quality. Selecting the best data retrieval methods, (e.g., medical charts, administrative claims data, or a hybrid of the two), membership and enrollment complexities (e.g., identifying and counting members who are continuously enrolled), and case-mix adjustments are some other significant implementation issues. As NCQA refines its HEDIS criteria, users will be more effectively able to document the value of health care plans. Thus HEDIS 3.0 was released early in 1997 with a number of new changes and new guidelines for measurements and reporting. The major areas mentioned earlier however did not change, but the emphasis on some indicators vs. others did change as it was mainly based on plans experiences with the older versions of HEDIS.

The Joint Commission on Accreditation of Healthcare Organizations (JCAHO) JCAHO released the first mandatory report card from its current batch of accreditation inspections of hospitals in 1994. (HPR, 1995) The report card program which started with acute care hospital surveys, also will include home care facilities, mental hospitals, ambulatory hospitals, and long term-care facilities. Each report gives an overview of the organization surveyed, the date and final decision, areas with recommendations for improvement, and a comparison with other accreditation seeking organizations. The report also includes an evaluation of the performance areas reviewed during the review process, which for hospitals number 28 broad categories encompassing nearly 700 standards. Reports on all hospitals JCAHO accredits were to be available in 1998.

Healthcare Financing Administration (HCFA) This federal agency is developing two separate programs that will prepare report cards for health care organizations participating in Medicare and Medicaid. (HPR, 1995) The Delmarva Foundation for Medicaid Care, a peer review organization (PRO) covering the District of Columbia and Maryland, is developing performance measures for a Medicare pilot project based on the quality of care measures collected by peer review organizations. These reports are not intended for release to the public, but will be used by HCFA to rate the care provided by Medicare HMOs. While only a fraction of Medicare patients are enrolled in managed care organizations, most states are requiring their Medicaid populations to join managed care in order to save costs. The National Committee for Quality Assurance (NCQA) has agreed to work with the Medicaid program to develop quality measurements specific to that program. Report cards for Medicaid managed care organizations will be implemented after a testing phase is completed.

The Maryland Hospital Association's Quality Indicator Project (QI Project) The Maryland QI project was created to develop a "systematic and focused process for qualifying outcomes of care that could lead to performance assessment" and later was expanded to an ongoing study of appropriate and efficient care. (Kazandjian et al., 1993) By early 1993, the QI project covered 750 participants. A systematic review of the literature and expert panels help to develop indicator sets that describe specific events in individual processes of care. Each QI project hospital collects data elements for 21 indicators on a quarterly basis using data collection software. The indicators are adjusted for case complexity, risk of adverse outcomes, and patient group characteristics. Reports are developed which show the rate of indicator occurrence as well as a statistically determined position of a hospital's rates compared to the rates of all participants or to peer-hospital groups. Hospitals then use this information to determine if specific processes in the delivery of their care differ from those of other hospitals or preexisting practice parameters. Specific hospital initiatives that might benefit others are shared on a regional basis.

REENGINEERING

While a number of health care organizations have responded to the challenges of reform by adopting continuous quality improvement (CQI) strategies, survival may hinge on substantial improvement in productivity. As organizations struggle to satisfy the conflicting needs of major shareholders — patients, purchasers, governments, insurance companies, providers, and employees, many are turning to a radical change in philosophy, called "reengineering." Consultant and author Michael Hammer likens reengineering to wiping the slate clean and starting over. While CQI is considered a tool to make incremental improvements to existing processes, reengineering questions whether the processes are needed at all to achieve the organization's mission and seeks to fundamentally change processes. Deciding between CQI and reengineering should not simply be a matter of blindly following a current fad. Serious consideration should be given to specific needs of particular organizations and a realistic strategy should be undertaken to use resources more productively. Some processes may be basically sound and should be left alone while others may need to be completely overhauled.

In health care, organizations have been wary of embracing reengineering. However, interest has soared recently with several companies reporting millions in savings from reengineering efforts. Lee Memorial Hospital in Fort Myers, Florida, which is reengineering its orthopedic services by adopting patient-focused care (PFC), reported a significant improvement in quality indicators as a result of such changes, and is anticipating savings to the tune of $2.2 million. (Kennedy, 1994) A review of reengineering efforts in health care yields some interesting lessons. Most health care leaders warn of the substantial resources involved and caution that reengineering is not for the weak of spirit and can be traumatic for those organizations who are unprepared for dramatic change. Top management support, additional resources, retraining, and a lot of emotional support are necessary to make the transition easier.

The scope of reengineering projects varies widely across organizations. Some organizations are restructuring few processes, while others are reengineering the whole organization. However, many experts suggest that organizations focus their reengineering efforts in areas that promise high payoffs or core, or critical processes.

Patient-focused care seems to be a starting point for many organizations, who acknowledge that the patient is the central customer in health care. Memorial Hospital of South Bend, Indiana, is eliminating central nursing stations and decentralizing services such as pharmacy, pulmonary care, and laboratory. Patient care centers are organized around similar-needs patients such as orthopedics and neurology units. Everything that a patient commonly needs is located on the unit and all staff on the unit are cross-trained in certain universal skills as well as other services. In the first quarter since the surgery unit opened, patient satisfaction increased from the 68th percentile to the 99th, physician feedback was more positive, cost of medications fell by $400 per case (due to satellite pharmacy's location in the unit) and nurse overtime was reduced by 67 percent.

Nonpatient care processes also are being reengineered by organizations. Information management systems are the most common target for reengineering efforts, but other business processes also are receiving attention. Sentara (an insurance division) is restructuring itself according to customer segment (e.g., small employers, Medicaid) rather than by functional departments. Staff members were selected from different departments and organized into teams which service a single customer. With a new focus on customer service came more accuracy, quicker turnaround of claims, a sense of ownership by the team and an increase in productivity (e.g., a 35% increase in the small employer team's productivity). And finally, some organizations, such as two hospitals in the Sisters of Providence Healthcare system, have started the process of organizational reengineering. While Providence Hospital in Medford, Oregon, decided to redesign outpatient services, Providence Hospital in Anchorage, Alaska, is focusing on reorganizing itself around its inpatient population. Reengineering on a big scale inevitably involves redesigning related processes, hence experts urge organizations to maintain a systems focus.

Various models of reengineering work through some common stages (Kennedy, 1994):

1. A diagnostic stage — selecting a process or processes to reengineer, creating reengineering teams, understanding the current processes) and setting up measures to monitor key areas of performance are included in this stage.
2. Redesign stage — this stage includes stimulating innovative thinking.
3. Implementation Stage — a plan-do-check-act (PDCA) cycle is typically adopted at this phase of reengineering. At this point it is important to also implement strategies to reduce/eliminate conflicts which are generated by the dramatic changes involved. Kralovec (1994) states that one of the greatest threats to reengineering efforts is misconceptions about the role of information systems (IS) and information technology (IT). He cautions that unless organizations reengineer with the fundamental interdependence between operational processes and information in mind, they may not be able to successfully attain the goals of reduced cost, improved quality and access, and community accountability. If organizations accept the limitations of existing IS/IT and use reengineering for whatever improvements can be achieved, radical breakthroughs may not be achieved.

CONCLUSIONS

Managed care has emerged as a dominant force in United States health care financing. Purchasers of health care are shifting significant responsibility for managing future costs onto managed care plans. Health plans, in turn, shift responsibility for health care costs onto providers through predetermined fixed payments as well as onto patients through increased cost sharing. Risk management will be a critical function of health care executives. In addition to managing the health risks of enrolled populations, risks associated with utilization patterns, efficiency of services delivery, information management, effectiveness of cost management controls, monitoring appropriateness of care, customer satisfaction, credentialing provider networks, competing objectives of providers, and malpractice will steer decision making. (Coile, 1996) In order to succeed in today's competitive marketplace, health care executives must find innovative ways to set themselves apart from their competitors. Earlier strategies including increasing premiums, discontinuing coverage of high risk individuals, and tightened underwriting are being sharply restricted by changes in federal and/or state policy. Once managed care penetration reaches saturation point, future earnings will increasingly depend on demonstrable improvements in quality of care and ultimately on improvements in health status.

Currently health care organizations are focusing on improving quality of care in order to strengthen their position in the marketplace. The near future may well be the era of outcomes management, which in turn will pave the way for improvements in the health of the population. The ultimate justification for adopting a managed care approach to health care delivery will be improvements in public health.

REFERENCES

Coile, R. C., Jr., "Management Teams for the 21st Century," *Healthcare Executive*, 10–13, January/February 1996.

Fromberg, R.,"Capitation is Coming," *Healthcare Executive*, 4–9, January/February 1996.

Goldsmith, J. C., Goran, M. J., andNackel, J.G. "Managed Care Comes of Age," *Healthcare Forum Journal*, 14–24, September/October 1995.

"Healthcare Performance Reporting," *The Report on Report Cards*, 1–12, January 1995.

Hiltunen, K. "HEDIS: Implementation Issues," *Journal for Healthcare Quality*, 18 (1): 32–35, January/February 1996.

Kazandjian, V. A., Lawthers, J., Cernak, C. M., and Pipesh, F. C. "Relating Outcomes to Processes of Care: The Maryland Hospital Association's Quality Indicator Project (QI Project)," *Journal on Quality Improvement*, 19 (11): 530-538, November 1993,

Kemnitz, D. M. "An Employer Model for Reform," *Journal of Healthcare Benefits*, 12–17, May/June 1994.

Kennedy, M. "Reengineering: A Radical Approach to Process Improvement," *The Quality Letter for Healthcare Leaders*, 1–10, September 1994.

Lathrop, P. J. *Restructuring Health Care: The Patient Focused Paradigm*, Jossey Bass, San Francisco, 1993.

Leigh, J. R. "Understanding Managed care Risk Sharing Arrangements," *Benefits Quarterly*, 11 (1): 33–37, 1st Quarter 1995.

Mang, A. L. "Implementation Strategies of Patient-Focused Care," *Hospital and Health Services Administration*, 40 (3): 426–435, Fall 1995.

Moffit, K. G., Daly, P. B., Tracery, L., and Galloway, M. "Patient Focused Care: Key Principles to Restructuring," *Hospital & Health Services Administration*, 38 (4): 509–521, 1993.

Montrose, G. "Demand Management May Help Stem Costs," *Health Management Technology*, 16 (2): 18, 21, February 1995.

Ribinick, P. G. and Carrano, V. A. "Understanding the New Era in Healthcare Accountability: Report Cards," *Journal of Nursing Care Quality*, October 1995: 1–8.

Sidky, M., Barrable, B., and Stewart, H. "Patients First: Small Hospitals in Ontario Favor Patient-Focused Care," *Leadership*, 2 (6): 8–11, 40, 1993.

ADDITIONAL READING

Gramling, A. "What's So New About Demand Management?" *Managed Care*, 4 (4): 33–37, April 1995.

Fries, J. F. "Healthcare Demand Management," *Medical Interface*, 7 (3): 55–58, March 1994.

D'Andrea, B. G. "Advantages of Risking Sharing," *Health Affairs*, 13 (4): 236, Fall 1994.

Danner, C. D. "Aligning Incentives: The Key to Risk Sharing." *California Hospitals*, 9 (2): 16, 18, Summer 1995.

McQueen, J. and Marwick, P. "Introduction: Evolution of Patient-Focused Care Within the Contextual Framework of an Integrated Delivery System (IDS)," *Journal of the Society for Health Systems*, 5 (1): 5–9, 1995.

14 Quality Prizes

Tammy Brown and Sabra Hopkins

CONTENTS

INTRODUCTION

Quality prizes and awards began as early as the 1950s. Since that time the focus has evolved from one of the ability to perform according to contract specifications, to statistical process control, and, finally, to one of customer satisfaction. Each award, ISO 9000, Deming, and Baldrige, has its own relative strengths and weaknesses.

To develop an international perspective on quality improvement it is necessary to include an evaluation of each set of criteria. The ISO Standards are utilized extensively by the European Community. The Pacific Rim, specifically Japan, focuses on Deming's concepts. In the United States, the development of the Malcolm Baldrige National Quality Award in 1987 has been avowed to be all you need for an excellent quality management system.

The following will review the history and current criteria of each set of quality standards. A comparison and contrast of the standards is presented. Some standards

0-8493-????-?/97/$0.00+$.50
© 1997 by CRC Press LLC

monitor the same elements and some have advantages over the others. However, the benefits of an improved quality system are many and will be explored in the conclusion.

THE INTERNATIONAL ORGANIZATION FOR STANDARDIZATION (ISO) QUALITY PRIZE

HISTORY

The objective of the ISO (International Organization for Standardization), headquartered in Geneva, Switzerland, is to encourage the trade of goods and services through the promotion and development of standards, testing and certification. The organization is comprised of representatives from 91 different countries.

The U.S. is represented by the American National Standards Institute (ANSI), which was founded in 1918 to clarify the process and get rid of the duplication and conflict that existed with the voluntary standards. (Mahoney, 1994) ANSI participates in writing the ISO 9000 standards through the U.S. Technical Advisory Group (TAG). The ISO 9000 standards are administered in the U.S. through the American Society for Quality Control (ASQC). (Process Innovation, 1994)

Even though based in the European community, the award is not limited to the European organizations. Originally there were 12 nations in the European community that were involved in the award, but, as the award increased in importance and credibility, more organizations are interested in joining the effort.

ISO 9000 is a series of five international standards for quality management and quality assurance. The ISO 9000 standard provides concepts and definitions; ISO 9001, 9002, and 9003 cover specific aspects of quality assurance programs, and ISO 9004 gives advice on creating and sustaining a quality management system. ISO 9000 certification is becoming a prerequisite for participating in international trade. At the time this was written, registration in the ISO series was not mandatory. However, in the future, nearly all manufacturing organizations will be expected to be registered under ISO 9001, 9002, or 9003 standard. (Process Innovation, 1994) Effective in 1992, the European block decided that the ISO concept would be a basis for all future contracting.

CRITERIA/CATEGORIES

The ISO 9000 standard covers multiple categories, which are: (Process Innovation, 1994)

- management responsibility
- quality system
- product identification and traceability
- inspection status
- inspection and testing
- inspection, measuring and test equipment
- control of non-conforming product

- handling, storage, packaging and delivery
- document control
- training
- statistical techniques
- internal auditing
- contract review
- purchasing
- process control
- purchaser supplier product
- corrective action
- design control
- servicing

Each ISO standard increases in complexity and detail. Details of the standards are: (Mahoney, 1994)

ISO 9000

- good starting point to create a top management system
- road map to the other quality standards in the series
- provides key definitions and principal concepts
- provides for the use of quality standards for contractual purposes
- provides assistance in selecting the appropriate standard
- helps to achieve standards that are negotiated in a contract ISO 9001
- best choice for a full management system
- this is a quality system model for a contract requiring supplier capability to design, produce, inspect, test, train, install, and service

ISO 9002

- less comprehensive and easier to achieve than ISO 9001
- this is a quality system model for a contract requiring supplier capability to produce, inspect, test, train and install

ISO 9003

- fits the needs of many small, basic organizations
- starting point for the development of a quality system
- this is a quality system model for a contract requiring supplier capability to inspect, test, and train

ISO 9004

- gives advice on developing and maintaining a quality management system.
- this standard has two parts:

- Part 1 — This is a quality system and quality management guideline to develop and implement an effective system
- Part 2 — Services organization standard, including policy and objectives, system management, human resources, and documentation

APPLICATION PROCESS

There are two different phases to the registration process. The first involves choosing the appropriate standard to use, creating a quality system as evidenced by a quality manual, and installing the system as evidenced by achievement of relative objectives. The second involves third-party certification that acknowledges the organization's registered status under ISO 9000. The frequency of the renewal of the registration process and site visits depends on the registering body, however the recommended time frame is between two and three years. (Mahoney, 1994)

Before going through the application process, an organization needs to determine if the ISO process is right for it to pursue. The following are a few basic questions to consider: (Mahoney, 1994)

1. Why consider registration under the ISO 9000 series?
2. What ISO standard makes sense at your location?
3. Do all elements of the selected standard seem to fit?
4. What steps must you take to achieve registration?
5. What can you do with a registration? What are the pluses for our organization?
6. Are there some registration negatives to consider? If so, what? Why?
7. What level of training investment will be needed?
8. How will a program leader be identified and selected?
9. How will you staff for process installation and the assembling of the Master manual?
10. What budgeting actions do you need to get started?

Once an organization has asked themselves the above questions and decided the ISO 9000 series is what they want to obtain, the following steps need to be taken: (Mahoney, 1994)

1. Set up a steering group or task force, initiate a communication effort to create awareness of the quality initiative and the need for it.
2. Select an appropriate standard and review existing procedures against the standard requirement in detail.
3. Identify tasks to be accomplished
4. Launch your quality program/process
5. Define, document, and implement new or revised operating procedures, using charts when appropriate

6. Compile a master manual for management processes and quality initiatives
7. Develop documentation, tracking, and evaluation procedures
8. Initiate basic quality training
9. Monitor implementation, check use of procedures, and develop results data
10. Meet with the assessment organization or agency for a preregistation audit, obtain feedback and make needed adjustments
11. Develop your final version of the master manual and secure needed approvals
12. host compliance audit site visits, and clear discrepancies
13. Achieve certification/registration

As with any award, the ISO has many advantages and potential problems with the system. The advantages to the registration process are: (Mahoney, 1994)

- builds a quality system and provides a foundation for a management system
- facilitates trade through assurances of contract performance
- provides international recognition and engenders global uniformity
- meets European Community business requirements
- eliminates customer audits or surveys
- enhances credibility and improves documentation and traceability activities
- leads to an organized, written collection of fundamental practices

The potential problems with the registration process are: (Mahoney, 1994)

- proper accreditation of auditors and registrars
- consistent administration by registers
- consistent interpretation of criteria among registrars
- possible conflicts of interest among those who provide registration and also consult
- universal acceptance across all industries
- significant direct and overhead costs for the implementation and certification process, including staffing and training
- minimal attention to statistical quality or process control
- no attention to broad-gauge deployment of quality processes throughout the organization, continuous process improvement, or the ensuring of system longevity

The central contact point for information about registration sources in the U.S. is the ASQC. This organization is a not-for-profit subsidiary, the Registrar Accreditation Board (RAB) accredits agencies who can conduct independent, third-party, onsite audits and provide registration for the ISO 9000 series. (Mahoney, 1994)

256 Managed Care Quality: A Practical Guide

THE DEMING PRIZE FOR INDIVIDUALS AND THE DEMING APPLICATION PRIZE

HISTORY

The Deming Prize was established in 1950 by JUSE (Union of Japanese Scientists and Engineers) in recognition and appreciation of Dr. W. Edward Deming, his friendship, and achievements in the cause of industrial quality control. (Walton, 1986) It originally was funded by proceeds from Deming's lectures in Japan. Deming originally was invited to Japan in 1950 to present a series of lectures that were part of the quality seminars organized and presented by JUSE. As a result of his teachings, the Deming philosophy was adopted in almost all areas of the Japanese industry. It also has become a standard for Japanese companies who are looking to improve their performance. Participants in the award not only benefit from the honor of being involved with the Deming Prize process, but also from the improvements that result from the implementation of Total Quality Control.

The Deming Prize itself is made up of two broad categories: the Deming Prize for Individuals and the Application Prize. The Application Prize has four subcategories: (1) overall organization, (2) overseas company, (3) division, and (4) small enterprise. The Deming Prize first awarded was in 1950 to companies who showed competence in Statistical Quality Control (SQC). By the 1970s, the concept of quality became widespread within the Japanese organizational culture and companies began encompassing all of Deming's Fourteen points and moving toward Total Quality Control (TQC). (Walton, 1986)

CRITERIA/CATEGORIES

The Deming Prize criteria is designed to be used as guide for individuals and organizations who are trying to obtain organizational excellence. The award criteria is based on 10 different main points and multiple subpoints, they are: (Process Innovation, 1994)

1. Policy
   1.1. Policies pursued for management, quality, and control
   1.2. Method of establishing policies
   1.3. Justifiability and constancy of policies
   1.4. Utilization of statistical methods
   1.5. Transmission and diffusion of policies
   1.6. Review of policies and the results achieved
   1.7. Relationship between policies and long and short planning
2. Organization and its management
   2.1. Explicitness of the scope of authority and responsibility
   2.2. Appropriateness of delegations of authority
   2.3. Interdivisional cooperation
   2.4. Committees and their activities
   2.5. Utilization of staff

2.6. Utilization of quality control circles

2.7. Quality control diagnosis

3. Education and dissemination

    3.1. Education programs and results

    3.2. Quality and control consciousness, degrees of understanding of quality control

    3.3. Teaching and extent of dissemination of statistical concepts and methods

    3.4. Grasp of the effectiveness of quality control

    3.5. Education of related entities: contractors and vendors

    3.6. Quality control circle activities

    3.7. System of suggesting ways of improvements and its actual conditions

4. Collection, dissemination and use of information on quality

    4.1. Collection of external information

    4.2. Transmission of informational between divisions

    4.3. Speed of information transmissions

    4.4. Data processing, statistical analysis of information, and use of results

5. Analysis

    5.1. Selection of key problems and themes

    5.2. Propriety of the analytical approach

    5.3. Utilization of statistical methods

    5.4. Linkage with proper technology

    5.5. Quality analysis, process analysis

    5.6. Utilization of analytical results

    5.7. Assertiveness of improvement suggestions

6. Standardization

    6.1. Systemization of standards

    6.2. Methods of establishing, revising, and abolishing standards

    6.3. Outcome of the establishment, revision or abolition of standards

    6.4. Contents of the standards

    6.5. Utilization of statistical methods

    6.6. Accumulation of technology

    6.7. Utilization of standards

7. Control

    7.1. Systems for the control of quality and related costs

    7.2. Control items and control points

    7.3. Utilization of such statistical control methods as control charts

    7.4. Contribution to performance of quality control circle activities

    7.5. Actual conditions of control activities

    7.6. State of matters under control

8. Quality assurance

    8.1. Procedure for the development of new products and services

    8.2. Safety and immunity from product liability

    8.3. Process design, process analysis and process improvement

    8.4. Process capability

8.5. Instrumentation
8.6. Equipment maintenance and control of purchases
8.7. Quality assurance system and its audits
8.8. Utilization of statistical methods
8.9. Evaluation and audit of quality
8.10. Actual state of quality assurance

9. Results
9.1. Measurement of results
9.2. Substantive results on quality, services, delivery time, cost
9.3. Intangible results
9.4. Measures for overcoming defects

10. Planning for the review
10.1. Grasp of the present state of affairs
10.2. Measures for overcoming defects
10.3. Plans for future advances
10.4. Linkage with the long-term plans

WINNERS

In the first 36 years of the Deming Prize, there have been a total of 138 Japanese winners and one U.S. winner (Florida Power & Light). Two U.S. companies (Texas Instruments and Xerox) were part owners of Japanese companies which have won the Deming Prize. A break down of the winners follows: (Mahoney, 1994)

Prize	Number
Application Prize (overall)	88
Application Prize for Small Enterprise	32
Application Prize for Division	5
Application Prize for Overseas Company	1
Quality Control for Factory	13

APPLICATION PROCESS

Preparation for the formal application process usually takes an organization three to five years. The general thought is that it will take any organization this amount of time to obtain a TQC process that is worthy of the Deming Prize. The norm is for an organization to go through at least one "quality diagnosis" by JUSE prior to the formal application. This allows an organization to discover its inefficiencies and get a chance to improve upon them so they can qualify for the Deming Prize. Unless an organization can demonstrate a firm management commitment to quality, a large system of QC circles, an employee suggestion process, use of statistical methods, a continuous improvement plan, an education process for employees, and strong customer commitment, an organization cannot be considered for the application process. Japanese organizations take the qualifying and application process very seriously, because failure is believed to be a dishonor. (Walton, 1986)

The application process for the Deming prize is composed of many steps, which are: (Mahoney, 1994)

1. JUSE consultants work with companies to prepare them for a quality control diagnosis. The actual prize application process does not begin until the year after JUSE consultants finish their work with the company.
2. All applications are to be completed by Nov. 20.
3. A decision is made by Dec. 20 as to if the company has met the technical eligibility requirements for its prize category.
4. Once a company is notified its application has been accepted, the applicant must submit the following by Jan. 20:
   • A description of its quality control practices, written in Japanese. This description should contain a maximum number of pages, depending on the number of employees in the organization.
      • Under 100 employees: 50 pages
      • Under 2,000 employees: 75 pages
      • For each additional 500 employees over 2,000:   5 pages
   • a company business prospectus, written in Japanese
5. If the description is approved, the applicant's onsite examination will be scheduled between March 20 and Sept. 30. Each onsite inspection team will contains two to six examiners. The onsite inspection itself will last from 1–2 or 2–3 days depending on the level of the organization. A passing grade of the inspection at all levels is 70%. A score of 505 or below will fail any organization immediately. If an unsatisfactory grade is received at the first onsite visit, provisions are made for a follow-up inspection.
6. Prize winners are selected between Oct. 10 and 20 by the Deming Prize Committee.
7. A prize ceremony is held in November

The Deming Prize Committee is composed of the chairman of the board of directors of JUSE, or another person recommended by the board. The body of the prize committee is made up of members who are officers of organizations related to quality and those with knowledge and experience of the quality process. The Application Prize Subcommittee is composed of university professors and quality control experts in government and other non-profit organizations. (Mahoney, 1994)

The application cost includes the following:

   • current per diem for each examiner of $810 to $1,215 per day
   • first class air fare
   • first class hotel accommodations (single room with bath)
   • three meals a day
   • miscellaneous expenses
   • cost of preparing a written opinion
   • interpreter or translator fees

THE MALCOLM BALDRIDGE NATIONAL QUALITY AWARD

HISTORY

The history of the MBNQA began in the 1980s when United States business and government leaders became concerned about the nation's ability to compete. Numerous councils, conferences, and committees were formed to determine ways to compete with the Japanese and others.

In 1983, a final report from seven computer networking conferences sponsored by the American Productivity and Quality Center was released recommending a national quality award. These conferences were attended by 175 corporate executives, business leaders, and academicians. Later in the year, the National Productivity Advisory Committee recommended a national medal for productivity achievement. In April 1984, a White House Conference on Productivity called for a national medal as well.

In September 1985, the Committee to Establish a National Quality Award began a series of meetings. Over the next year it developed a structure for administering and funding it. During this time parallel efforts to legislate a national award were spearheaded by Florida Power & Light. At the same time FPL worked with the Union of Japanese Scientists and Engineers to apply for the Deming Prize.

During the next two years, two congressmen and one senator sponsored versions of a bill to establish a National Quality Improvement Award. It passed the House of Representatives in June 1987 and went to the Senate where no action was taken on it for six weeks.

Part of the problem was President Ronald Reagan's "hands-off" philosophy of government since the bill called for government intervention in administering the award program. Secretary of Commerce Malcolm Baldrige adhered to Reagan's philosophy. Ironically he ended up providing the final push to create the award program. Baldrige, a professional horse rider who won many awards on the rodeo circuit and He was inducted into the National Cowboy Hall of Fame in 1984, he was killed in a riding accident on July 25, 1987. Shortly after his death, the idea to name the national quality award after Baldrige surfaced at a dinner attended by a small group of staffers for Senators and Representatives. The idea appealed to the president, who wanted to honor the friend he had lost. Three days after Baldrige's death, the bill was passed and on Aug. 20, 1987, Reagan signed the Malcolm Baldrige National Quality Improvement Act of 1987 into law. Responsibility for the award was assigned to the Department of Commerce, which, in turn, gave it to one of its agencies the National Institute of Standards and Technology (NIST).

The Baldrige program relied on new and existing business and government organizations: American Society for Quality Control (ASQC), Board of Overseers, Foundation for the MBNQA, Board of Examiners, and National Institute of Standards and Technology (NIST). Applications are submitted to the ASQC, which administers the award under NIST's management. They also create promotional materials, write the winners' briefs, work with NIST to organize the awards ceremony, and produce the award ceremony videotape. The Board of Overseers provide broad direction for the program. By legislation, the Board must consist of at least five people selected by the Secretary of Commerce, in consultation with the director of NIST, for their success in the field of quality management.

Since the beginning of the Baldrige Award, health care professionals have been involved with the Board of Examiners, award recipients, and some state and local programs have included health care categories. In 1993, a decision was made to launch a pilot for health care criteria. During 1994, health care professionals were involved in testing and training programs, developing case study materials, and submitting comments on criteria. In 1995, the Health care Pilot Program and an Education Pilot Program were conducted parallel to the Baldrige Award for businesses. The criteria and evaluation process are quite similar. However, neither health care nor educational organizations will be eligible for awards during the pilot period.

CRITERIA/CATEGORIES

The purposes of the Healthcare Pilot Criteria are:

- to provide a basis for evaluating the improvement practices of health care organizations and for giving feedback to Healthcare Pilot Program applicants;
- to help improve organizational performance by making available an integrated, results-oriented set of key performance requirements;
- to facilitate communications and sharing of best practices information within and among health care organizations of all types based upon a common understanding of key performance requirements;
- to foster the development of partnerships involving health care organizations, businesses, schools, human service agencies, and other organizations; and
- to serve as a working tool for improving organizational planning, training, and assessment." (*Malcolm Baldridge National Quality Award/Healthcare Pilot Criteria*, 1995)

The focus is on two, results-oriented goals:

- "delivery of ever-improving value to patients and other stakeholders, contributing to improved health care quality; and
- improvement of overall organizational effectiveness, use of resources, and capabilities" (*Malcolm Baldridge National Quality Award/Healthcare Pilot Criteria*, 1995).

There are seven Categories in the Healthcare Pilot Criteria:

1. Leadership
2. Information and analysis
3. Strategic planning

4. Human resource development and management
5. Process management
6. Organizational performance results
7. Focus on and satisfaction of patients and other stakeholders

There is a framework that connects and integrates the categories with four basic elements:

The Driver   "Senior leadership sets directions, creates values, goals and systems, and guides the pursuit of health care value and organizational performance improvement.

The system comprises the set of well-defined and well-designed processes for meeting the organization's patient and performance requirements.

Measures of Progress provide a results-oriented basis for channeling actions to delivering ever-improving health care value and organizational performance.

The goal of the system is the delivery of ever-improving health care value to patients and success in the health care marketplace" (*Malcolm Baldridge National Quality Award/Healthcare Pilot Criteria*, 1995).

The first category is *leadership*, which has an assigned value of 90 points. It examines senior executives' and health care staff leaders' personal leadership and their involvement in promotion of patient care and organizational mission, clear values and expectations, and a leadership system that promote quality services and performance excellence. The integration of the mission, values, and expectations into the management system is examined. Also included are public responsibilities and citizenship.

The *information and analysis* category, worth 75 points, looks at the management and effective use of data and information to support organizational performance in both health care and business.

For 55 points, the *strategic planning* category examines how the organization develops strategic direction and key strategic plan requirements. Included is the translation of these plan requirements into an effective system.

The *human resource development and management* category evaluates how the organization's entire staff is enabled to develop and utilize its full potential, while in alignment with the strategic and performance objectives. It also evaluates how the organization establishes an environment that promotes performance excellence and full participation by all employees for personal and organizational growth. This category is assigned 140 points. It includes HR planning and evaluation, work systems, education, training, development, staff well-being, and staff satisfaction.

For 140 points, *process management* examines the key aspects of process management. Examined are design and introduction of patient health care services, delivery of health care, patient care support services, community health services, administrative and business operations management, and supplier performance management.

The sixth category, *organization performance results*, is worth 250 points and examines performance and improvement in key patient health care areas, in business/administrative areas, and performance levels in relation to competitors. Included are: patient health care results, patient care support services results, community health services results, administrative, business, and supplier results, and accreditation and assessment results.

The final category, *focus on and satisfaction of patient and other stakeholders*, is worth 250 points. This includes learning about patients and stakeholders, building and maintaining relationships with them, and measures of success in delivering patient care services. Patient satisfaction, loyalty, and referrals are very important. Examination of satisfaction and retention of stakeholders is also evaluated. Satisfaction relative to competitors is included as well.

SCORING SYSTEM

Three evaluation dimensions are utilized for the scoring system: (1) approach; (2) deployment; and (3) results. Applicants are required to furnish information relating to these dimensions. "Approach refers to how the applicant addresses the criteria requirements — the *method(s)* used. Deployment refers to the *extent* to which the applicant's approach is applied to all requirements of the criteria. Results refers to outcomes in *achieving* the purposes given in the criteria" (" (*Malcolm Baldridge National Quality Award/Healthcare Pilot Criteria*, 1995).

APPLICATIONS

Information and data must be collected, organized and distilled into a concise written response. Those who have gone through this process talk about it, taking from 10,000 to 50,000 hours. This is the cost of applying for the award. However, the benefits to them outweigh the costs. The time was well spent because they ended up with a complete picture of the strengths of their quality systems and the areas they needed to improve.

The application process involves several major tasks: assessment, organization, interpretation, collection, and application.

During the *assessment* period senior management and other key decision makers become familiar with the Baldrige criteria, the benefits and costs of applying are identified, and a preliminary assessment of what the examination requests and what the company does is conducted.

Organization involves training key participants in interpreting the criteria, identifying tasks involved in completing the application, and assigning responsibility for pieces of the application. Top management's support and participation is secured, the application process is scheduled, and the use of outside assistance is evaluated. During this phase methods of communication among teams, leaders, etc. is developed.

During the *interpretation* phase consensus is reached on what the criteria are asking for and obtaining clarification on criteria in question from NIST. A core group is assigned to keep the application process on track. Also involved is creating and updating a list of areas for quality improvement, as identified through the application process.

Collection involves creating and implementing a data collection system, organizing a file system, and securing the types of documentation required. Also expert sources of information and data are identified and interviews with these sources are conducted.

Finally, the work of organizing to write the *application* and assigning responsibility for writing each category is completed. A schedule and format for the completion of each draft is developed. After each draft is written a system must be in place to give approval. Next comes the actual writing of the application and evaluation/scoring of the application, both internally and externally. The completion of the final draft is coordinated as well as printing and delivering the document.

EVALUATION

The entire evaluation process takes about six months. The Board of Examiners report raw scores to the Panel of Judges, which eliminates the lowest scoring companies from the list of manufacturing, services, and small business applicants. The team of judges select the companies to receive site visits.

Following the site visits, the examiner teams forward their scorebooks and site visit documentation to the judges, who spend three days reviewing the feedback before making any recommendations for award winners.

Examiners typically get three or four applications to score. They utilize a scoring system in increments of 10%. The scoring guidelines included in the Baldrige criteria outline what these percentages mean.

WINNERS

The companies that have won the Baldrige Award agree to spread the quality message. In agreeing to spread the message, winners of the award fulfill the main reason for which the award was established. The Purposes Section of The Malcolm Baldrige National Quality Improvement Act of 1987 Public Law 100–107 states, "providing specific guidance for other American organizations that wish to lean how to manage for high quality by making available detailed information on how winning organizations were able to change their cultures and achieve eminence" (*Malcolm Baldridge National Quality Award/Healthcare Pilot Criteria*, 1995).

QUALITY AWARDS COMARISON

Table 1 is a comparison of the ISO Quality Prize, Deming Prize, and the Malcolm Baldridge National Quality Award (Mahoney, 1994)

TABLE 1
Quality Awards Comparison

	ISO 9000	Deming	Baldridge
Purpose	To effectively document that the quality system elements which are to be implemented, or which are currently in place, have the ability to perform; voluntary registration by an accredited third party	Award prizes to those companies recognized as having applied Company wide quality control based on statistical quality control (SQC). The prize emphasizes word-class accomplishments	Promote quality awareness, recognize quality achievements of U.S. companies, and publicize successful quality strategies
Emphasis	The validation of the ability to perform according to contract	The statistical process control	Customer satisfaction, prevention of quality problems
Eligibility	Companies, divisions, locations in countries signatory to the ISO protocol (includes U.S. and Canada)	Individuals, factories, and companies — global since 1984	Limited to U.S. companies
Participants	Organizations involved in international trade that wish to be acceptable as vendors	Any number of companies that meet the standard established by the JUSE	Maximum of two manufacturing companies (plus their divisions), two small companies, (less than 500 employees), and two service companies
Evaluation Criteria	ISO 9001/Q91 Definitions ISO 9001-3/Q91-93 Standards at three levels of depth and breadth ISO 9004/Q94	One page of guidelines that are very brief and include some objective interpretation	Twenty-five pages of guidelines
Orientation	Process (80%) at the 9001 level, heavy on QA initiatives Management and administration (20%)	Process (60%) plus results (40%) heavy on statistical process control	Results (60%) plus process (40%), heavy quality results, customer satisfaction, human resources orientation
Mechanics	Select registration agency, preassessment choice of standard, submission of quality Master Manual, site assessment visit, onsite assessment of three to five days	Qualification based on review off-/on-site by JUSE	Qualification for site visit, competition

TABLE 1
Quality Awards Comparison (continued)

	ISO 9000	Deming	Baldridge
Examiners	Select staff or registration agency, ASQC maintains a list of recommended registrars, some companies prefer to use an EC '92 source	Select panel of senior members of JUSE	Open examiner system, annual application and selection, assignment avoids conflict of interest
Cost	Low to moderate dollars with sound quality assurance program in place, some consulting on system may be useful	High dollar and effort, consulting fees from JUSE are a major component	Low to high dollars, high effort if excellent quality system(s) not in place
Time Frame	Registration takes six to twelve months depending on starting point and urgency	Two to five years	One year cycle, renew after five years
Common Emphases	Administration, procedures, controls and training	Administration, procedures, controls and training	Administration, procedures, controls and training

CONCLUSION

Companies have found that they can lower costs, retain customers and employees, and improve profitability by dramatically improving their quality systems. Japan has been awarding the Deming Prize for quality since 1951. The elements measured by the Deming Prize and Baldrige Award overlap in the criteria of process management. The Deming Prize criteria dig deeply into the quality assurance of products and services, whereas the Baldrige criteria have a broader scope and less depth. Deming Prize subcategories define major areas of emphasis, in more general terms than the Baldrige items.

The ISO 9000, established in 1988, ties closely with the Process Management category of the Baldrige criteria. Any relationship with the other Baldrige categories is minimal.

The Baldrige Award program is a leader in defining the elements of a complete quality system. It is the most visible sign of a national quality movement. It is a superb profile of what American industry should aspire to. The Baldrige criteria are the only set that, just recently, target health care. The criteria are not perfect, but they are the best description of a total quality system on the market.

A winning quality organization takes what they need from the quality smorgasbord, keeps some and declines others, always with their own tastes, their own sense of themselves, in mind. These tools can be used by organizations to diagnose the condition of their quality systems, identify their strengths and weaknesses, and plan their improvements.

REFERENCES

Appel, F. *Improving Organizational Performance Using the Malcolm Baldrige National Quality Award Health care Criteria.* National Association for Healthcare Quality, Minneapolis Convention Center, Minneapolis, MN, Oct. 10, 1995.

George, S. *The Baldrige Quality System.* Wiley, New York, 1992.

Mahoney, F, X. and Thor, C, G. *The TQM Trilogy.* AMACOM, New York, 1994.

Malcolm Baldrige National Quality Award/Healthcare Pilot Criteria 1995. American Society for Quality Control, Milwaukee, WI, 1995.

Process Improvement and Quality Criteria. The Electronic College of Process Innovation. Department of Defense, 1994.

Walton, M. *The Deming Management Method.* Dodd, Mead, New York, 1986.

Index

definition of quality costs, 185–186
direct and indirect, 188–189
effectiveness and efficiency, 186–187
expectation and non-achievement costs, 191
immediate versus subsequent, 187–188
internal and external failure costs, 190–191
opportunity costs, 189
prevention costs, 189
of measuring quality, 191–195
performance measurement, 94–95
of poor quality, 183, 186, 188, 196
and quality, 33
quality improvements and, 56
standard setting considerations, 73, 88
Credentialing, 13
Criteria, *see also* Indicators of quality;
Measurement; Performance measures
decision/priority matrix, 141
defined, 98
measures of success or failure of improvement
programs, 137–138
standard setting, 80
Critical paths, 77
Cultural variables, 113
Culture, organizational, 67
Curative medicine, 163–164
Customer service department, 12
Customer of quality process, 176–177

D

Data
analysis and display, 141–158
bar charts, 148–150
cause-effect diagram, 144–146
data collection tool, 146–147
decision/priority matrix, 141
flow charts, 143–145
flow charts, opportunity analysis with, 132
histograms, 151–153
Pareto charts, 153–156
pie charts, 146, 148
run charts, 150–151
scatter diagrams, 156–158
voting, 142
clinical information, 165
collection, 146–147
implementation of quality improvement
program, 66
medical record review, 103
management information systems, 11, 96–97
managing processes of care, 166–168
medical outcomes, motivation of physicians
with, 48

performance, baseline, 131
quality assurance program, 71
quality improvement
determination of information needs, 134
display and analysis of, 134–135
quality monitoring
data time frame, 100
indicators, 100–101, 103
reliability of, 105
statistics and demographics, 15–18
Data entry accuracy, 198
Decentralization of services, 243–244
Decision making
computer systems, 238
patient focused care, 243
Decision/priority matrix, 141
Decision-support tools, preventive medicine
guidelines, 160–163
Decision trees, 76
Defensive medicine, 14
Definition of quality, 43–52
clinical guidelines, 47–48
data, 48
employers, 51
medical director, 46–47
medical services director, 47
operational, 44–46
patients, 50
plan, 46–49
provider communication, 48–49
providers, 49–50
Definitions, 3–5
guidelines, 72
improvement activities, 118, 127–129
operational planning, 56
of quality, 35–38, 48–49, 51,
75–76
medical definition, 44
patient definitions, 36, 45, 50
social definition, 44–45
of quality cost, 185–186
quality monitoring, 97, 98
standard setting, 72–73
Delivery system integration of, 8
Demand management, 9, 12–13, 238
Deming prizes, 256–259, 265–266
Demographics, 15–18, 167
Diagnosis Related Groupings
(DRGs), 26
Direct costs, 188–189
Dissemination
communicating standards, 84
implementation stages, 67–68
Double-peaked distribution, 153–154